Princeton Theological Monograph Series

D0851306

Dikran Y. Hadidian

General Editor

49

ON THE CHRISTIANITY OF THEOLOGY

Franz Overbeck

FRANZ OVERBECK

ON THE CHRISTIANITY OF THEOLOGY

Translated with an Introduction
and Notes

By

JOHN ELBERT WILSON

Pickwick Publications
San Jose, California

Published by

Pickwick Publications
215 Incline Way
San Jose, CA 95139-1526

Printed in the United States of America

Library of Congress Cataloging-in-Publication Data

Overbeck, Franz, 1837-1905
    [Uber die Christlichkeit unserer heutigen Theologie. English]
    On the Christianity of theology / translated with an introduction
and notes by John Elbert Wilson.
       p.   cm. -- (Princeton theological monograph series ; 49)
    Includes bibliographical references (p.).
    ISBN 1-55635-040-6
      1. Theology, Doctrinal--History. I. Wilson, John Elbert, 1942-
    II. Title. III. Series.

    BT21.3 .O9413 2002
    230'.044--dc21

                       2002026945

Printed in the United States by Morris Publishing
3212 East Highway 30
Kearney, NE 68847
1-800-650-7888

CONTENTS

Contents v

Preface vii

Notes xii

INTRODUCTION

Introduction by John E. Wilson 1

Criticism and Faith, Theology and Church 1

The Religious-Political Situation..15

"Fides Humana," "Fides Divina." Overbeck at the Time of the "Christianity of Theology" 18

The Late Overbeck and the Problem of Overbeck-Interpretation ...27

Concealment in the "Christianity of Theology" 34

Notes 39

THE "CHRISTIANITY OF THEOLOGY"

The "Christianity of Theology" of 1903 53

Preface of the 1st Edition 55

Preface of the 2nd Edition 56

Introduction 57

Chapter:

    1. The Relationship of Theology to Christianity Generally 65

    2. The Apologetic Theology of the Present 75

3. The Liberal Theology of the Present 89

4. Critical Theology and Its Positive Relationship to
   Christianity in the Present. Strauss' Confession 107

5. The Possibility of a Critical Theology in Our Protestant
   Churches 113

Afterword: What I Have Experienced with My Book 127

The Public Criticism of My Book 127

The Consequences of My Book for Me 134

The Modern Theology of Contemporary Protestantism and
   What Has Resulted from It for Me as the Author of My
   Book 146

Notes 153

PREFACE

Franz Camille Overbeck (1837-1905) was professor of New Testament and early church history at the University of Basel, Switzerland, from 1870 until his retirement in 1897. His parents belonged to the German middle class, the father being involved in banking. At the time of Franz Overbeck's birth the family lived in St. Petersburg, Russia. His mother was French and Roman Catholic; he was reared Lutheran. He took his university degree from the University of Leipzig in 1860 and habilitated in 1864 at the University of Jena.[1] In 1876 he married Ida Rothpletz, who died in 1933; the marriage remained childless. Overbeck is known in two contexts: among historians of theology as a church historian and sharp critic of theology, and among historians of philosophy as the loyal friend of the German philosopher Friedrich Nietzsche.

The work that is here translated is the second edition of *Über die Christlichkeit unserer heutigen Theologie* (*On the Christianity of Our Today's Theology*) (Leipzig: C.G. Naumann, 1903). The first edition was published in 1873 (Leipzig: E.W. Fritsch). I shall refer to the work as the *Christianity of Theology*. Its significance lies first of all in its critical assessment of the theology of its period and in its hermeneutical statements on the relationship of historical criticism and Christian faith. It reflects a period of great ferment, when theology was intensely involved in trying to comprehend the meaning of recent progress in the historical criticism of the Bible. In the forty years prior to the publication of the *Christianity of Theology*, criticism had shaken the Christian tradition about the authorship, dates and purpose of several New Testament writings, including the Gospels, especially John, and the Acts of the Apostles, and it had also given serious attention to assessment of the difference between Paul and the synoptic Gospels. The book was written at the time of the consolidation of Germany, when laws regulating the study of theology in the universities were being formulated. The Afterword of the second edition of 1903 discusses the reception of the work and the development of theology since the first edition, a development that came to be known as "modern theology," the age of Adolf Harnack.

Together with the posthumous publication of late notes by Overbeck under the title, *Christentum und Kultur*, edited by C.A. Bernoulli (Basel, Benno Schwabe, 1919), the *Christianity of Theology* was a major source of inspiration for the "dialectical theology" of the 1920's, especially that of Karl Barth. The English-speaking world has known about this influence since Barth's works were first published; wherever Barth's origins have been discussed, Ovebeck has been mentioned. Yet not only has Overbeck not been translated, but also, especially since the 1960's, a growing body of German literature has supported the view that Barth was seriously mistaken about Overbeck. The problem was not just that Barth wrongly thought Overbeck was a Christian in the guise of a critic of Christianity, but more importantly that he had made such emphatic use of Overbeck in what he and his comrades "between the times"—Rudolf Bultmann, Friedrich Gogarten, and Eduard Thurneysen—understood as a radical new beginning in theology. In the 1920's Barth had had a "witness" for his interpretation, namely Franz Overbeck's wife, Ida; I give the evidence for their conversation in my introduction. As is well known, Barth's theology took a decisive new turn in the 1930's, namely to the *Church Dogmatics*, which were to occupy him for the rest of his life. For whatever reason, Overbeck belonged to an increasingly distant past.

Intermittently Overbeck has occupied my attention for over thirty years, beginning with my Ph.D. dissertation (Claremont, 1975)—in which I too thought Barth was mistaken—and I have worked from time to time on the translation of the *Christianity of Theology* for almost as long. In the 1970's I was able to work for a considerable period of time in the Overbeck manuscripts in Basel, from which a large part of the material in my introduction is drawn. With time I became convinced that in the 1920's Barth was essentially right about Overbeck. The key, as I came to think, was Overbeck's method, which he developed through his extensive interaction with the patristic writer, Clement of Alexandria.[2] Contemporary interpreters of Overbeck generally support the view that Barth was mistaken. In my introduction I present arguments for my position, but the main argument is the work here translated. Originally published in 1873 and published again in 1903, two years before Overbeck's death, it both represents the continuity of his thought and is the most definitive public statement of his "theology."

My work in the Overbeck manuscripts was made possible by a publication that catalogued the manuscripts: *Overbeckiana. Übersicht über den Franz-Overbeck-Nachlass der Universitätsbibliothek Basel. II. Teil. Der wissenschaftliche Nachlass Franz Overbecks*, described by Martin Tetz (Basel: Helbing & Lichtenhahn, 1962). The first volume of this two-volume series, published in the same year and edited by Ernst Staehelin, *Die Korrespondenz Franz Overbeck*, was also a significant help. Almost all of Overbeck's works published during his lifetime were reprinted by offset process in the 1950's and 1960's by the Wissenschaftliche Buchgesellschaft in Darmstadt, and these publications received wide distribution in libraries in the United States as well as Europe. I have used them for this work, including the Darmstadt reprint (1963) for my translation of the second edition of the *Christianity of Theology*.[3]

In 1994 an editorial commission in Basel began the publication of several volumes of Overbeck's published and unpublished works: *Franz Overbeck Werke und Nachlass* (Stuttgart: Verlag J.B. Metzler). Volume One contains the first edition of *Über die Christlichkeit unserer heutigen Theologie.* It also contains an important work not reprinted by the Wissenschaftliche Buchgesellschaft, namely Overbeck's inaugural lecture at Basel in 1870, *Über Entstehung und Recht einer rein historischen Betrachtung der Neutestamentlichen Schriften,* which was published in a limited edition in Basel in 1871. In this case my references are to the publication of the work in the *Werke und Nachlass.* This edition of Overbeck's works, Volume 6/1-2, also contains an important critical edition of Overbeck's *Christentum und Kultur,* a work based on excerps from a part of his manuscripts he called the "Kirchenlexikon" (Church Lexicon, also called the "Collectaneen") and published in 1919. The critical edition, edited by Barbara von Reibnitz, is a highly valuable demonstration of the procedure followed by the editor of the work and includes many corrections of the 1919 text in favor of Overbeck's original words. My limited references however are to the 1919 edition, for the reason that they do not have to do with problematic wordings in this edition, and that this edition has been a very widely used text since its publication and has its own important history.

Volumes 4 and 5 of the *Franz Overbeck Werke und Nachlass* publish largely unpublished material from the Kirchenlexikon that I had read earlier and from which I had made handwritten copies of my own. The German titles from the Kirchenlexikon in my text and footnotes correspond to the titles in these published volumes, so that the original German of many if not all notes can be found there. Giving the original German in every case where I have translated from what are, in some instances, still unpublished manuscripts, would have encumbered and lengthened the work to a very great degree. The same is true of untranslated German books I have used.

The Kirchenlexikon is an alphabetically arranged compilation of notes on historical and theological subjects. Overbeck began it as a collection of references to and quotations from different sources, but very soon it served for personal comments, which are in some cases rather lengthy. The individual pages have a uniform size, approximately 7 1/4 inches by 4 1/2 inches. In Martin Tetz's catalogue, all the manuscripts, including those in the Kirchenlexikon, are identified by a number beginning with the letter "A." Where I have quoted from the Kirchenlexikon, I omit the catalogue number but give the title of the note in the Kirchenlexikon. In the case of other manuscripts I give the catalogue number. Where a date is not given in a note, Overbeck's handwriting usually makes it possible to differentiate between earlier and later notes. It is notable that research in the manuscripts, which has concentrated on the Kirchenlexikon and other personal notes on theology, has left Overbeck's lectures virtually untouched. I have read several of the lectures, but not all.

Works in English on Overbeck are very limited.[4] Recently Martin Henry, who has also worked in the Overbeck archives, published his book on Overbeck, *Franz Overbeck, Theologian?* (Frankfurt a.M.: Peter Lang, 1995), which in spite of an occasional harsh judgment gives a good introduction to the interpretation and reception of Overbeck while leaving its wealth of quotations untranslated.[5] Henry has also recently published a translation of the first chapter of the work I translate here, in the *Irish Theological Quarterly*, Vol. 66/1, 2001. Recent works in German on Overbeck have been written mainly by young scholars who have done at least some manuscript research, above all in the Kirchenlexikon.[6]

As has already been said, the dominant view in today's theological scholarship is that Barth misunderstood Overbeck, that Overbeck was an unbelieving theologian who lost his faith (at some undetermined point) but continued to serve on the theological faculty at Basel. This view is represented, for example, by both Martin Henry and a recently published dissertation on the history and interpretation of the *Christianity of Theology*: Nikalus Peter, *Im Schatten der Modernität, Franz Overbecks Weg zur Christlichkeit der heutigen Theologie* (Stuttgart: J.B. Metzler, 1992). The book contains valuable unpublished material and well represents its point of view. But it omits important information promised in the second line of the title—"Overbeck's way to the *Christianity of Theology*," and it illustrates that Overbeck interpretation is strongly influenced by how the interpreter responds to Nietzsche, whose shadow still falls on the understanding of modernity.

As Overbeck states in his introduction to the second, 1903 edition of the *Christianity of Theology*, his relationship to Nietzsche was quite important for him personally.[7] But Nietzsche was not Overbeck's teacher in religion, nor was Overbeck ever anti-Semitic. The relationship is well documented by their exchange of letters: *Friedrich Nietzsches Briefwechsel mit Franz Overbeck*, edited by Richard Oehler and C.A. Bernoulli (Leipzig, 1916). Among these [p. 134] one finds Nietzsche writing to his friend in the year 1880, "I have read your 'Christianity' [of Theology] once more and rejoiced a great deal in its astonishingly rich content and excellent disposition ... As I now to my shame realize, when you wrote it I only believed I understood nine tenths of it."[8] This is an important commentary on the book, for it contains many twists and turns to be recognized and to be reflected on.

While it would be a mistake to interpret Overbeck without knowing Nietzsche's works, any attempt here to enter into an interpretation of the enigmatic Nietzsche, about whom there is significant disagreement among his interpreters, would burst the limits of both this preface and the introduction, although I do speak of him briefly in the fourth part of my introduction. I can say that I am well acquainted with Nietzsche's works and have published an interpretation of them, and I am comfortable with omitting consideration of him here.[9]

My introduction focuses on the central interest of Overbeck's book, the nature of theology. Many aspects of the book not mentioned in the introduction receive comment in the endnotes; others remain unmentioned and are left to the reader's own reflection.

Finally, I express my thanks to the Basel University Library, especially Dr. Martin Steinmann and the manuscript division for their gracious assistance. Thanks are also due to my colleagues at Pittsburgh Theological Seminary, Professors Dale Allison and John Burgess, for their reading of the manuscript, corrections and suggestions, and to Dikran Hadidian for the acceptance of this work in the Princeton Theological Monograph Series.

On the Translation of the "Christianity of Theology"

Among the most frequently occurring terms in the book are "Wissen" and "Wissenschaft." "Wissen" is a verbal noun based on the verb "wissen," to know. "Wissenschaft" means science in the broad sense of both natural sciences and the humanities. "Wissen" and "Wissenschaft" mean all knowledge developed by autonomous human thought. Overbeck can substitute for "Wissen" the word "Denken," thinking or thought. Insofar as Overbeck makes a definite point in consistently using these words as inclusive of philosophy and history, and insofar as English has no equivalent other than "science" to the broad German meaning of "Wissenschaft," both in Overbeck's text and in my introduction I have adopted his usage and normally translated "Wissenschaft" as "science." Only where the word specifically means philosophy or history have a I used these words instead.

The closely related words "Kultur," culture and "Bildung," formation or education, define the integrated ideas and institutions that characterize an historical period, above all its science (in the broad sense). In Overbeck's usage "Kultur" is very nearly synonymous with "Welt," world.

I have translated Overbeck's word "Urchristentum," meaning the New Testament period, as "original Christianity," and "die alte Kirche" (the post-New Testament period) as "the ancient church."

In important contexts Overbeck uses words of viewing and vision that usually have to do with a certain view of the world of life: "Betrachtung," "Ansicht," "Anschauung," and also "Ideal." They are related to the common 19th century expression, "Weltanschauung," worldview. Another frequent word is "Empfinden," a verbal form meaning a perception in which the emphasis lies in the sensing or feeling of what is perceived, something religious for example. Overbeck only rarely uses the word "Gefühl," a word meaning "feeling" that is entirely subjective.

The book is marked by an unusual and difficult style, especially in the Afterword. Perhaps this was intentional and an aspect of his method. Other publications, especially *Über die Anfänge der patristischen Literatur*, are written in a lucid style. I have tried to make the work as clear as possible. Unusually long sentences have been made into more than one sentence, and in the Afterword repetitive words and phrases have been omitted. Paragraph breaks have been added that are not in the original text. In some instances a new thought is introduced at the end of a paragraph rather than at the beginning of a new paragraph; in these instances I let the paragraph begin with the new thought.

In the text and footnotes of the *Christianity of Theology* my additions are in [brackets]. Overbeck's few additions to the text in the second edition of 1903 are in {curved brackets}.

NOTES

1. The history of the family and Overbeck's early years is given in an autobiographical essay by the late Overbeck and published by Eberhard Vischer under the title, *Selbstbekenntnisse* (Basel: Benno Schwabe, 1941). The main part of the book was later reprinted with an introductory essay by Jacob Taubes (Frankfurt a.M.: Insel Verlag, 1966).

2. I am indebted to Martin Tetz's article, "Über Formengeschichte in der Kirchengeschichte," *Theologische Zeitschrift*, 1961, 413-431, especially the discussion of Overbeck's interpretation of Clement.

3. *Studien zur Geschichte der alten Kirche* (Schloss-Chemnitz, 1875); *Über die Auffassung des Streits des Paulus mit Petrus in Antiochien (Gal. 2,11 ff) bei den Kirchenvätern* (Basel, 1877); *Zur Geschichte des Kanons* (Chemnitz, 1880); *Über die Anfänge der patristischen Literatur*, separate reprint from: *Historische Zeitschrift*, 1882; *Über die Anfänge der Kirchengeschichtsschreibung* (Basel, 1892). Not published in later Darmstadt editions: "Aus dem Briefwechsel des Augustin mit Hieronymus," *Historische Zeitschrift*, 1879; *Die Bischofslisten und die apostolische Nachfolge in der Kirchengeschichte des Eusebius* (Basel, 1898); and *Christentum und Kultur* (Basel, 1919). Besides this last book, Bernoulli edited and published three other books from the Overbeck manuscripts, one of which was reprinted by the Wissenschaftliche Buchgesellschaft: *Vorgeschichte und Jugend der mittelalterlichen Scholastik* (Basel, 1917). The other two are: *Das Johannesevangelium. Studien zur Kritik seiner Erforschung* (Tübingen, 1911), and *Titus Flavius Klemens von Alexandria, Die Teppiche (Stromateis)*. Deutscher Text nach der Übersetzung von Franz Overbeck. Im Auftrage der Franz-Overbeck Stiftung in Basel herausgegeben und eingeleitet von C.A. Bernoulli und L. Früchtel (Basel: Benno Schwabe & Co. Verlag, 1936). An article written by Overbeck that was not reprinted is: "Aus dem Briefwechsel des Augustin mit Hieronymus," *Historische Zeitschrift*, Vol. 42, 1879, 222-259. Overbeck's numerous reviews and short dictionary articles are listed in *Overbeckiana*, Vol. l.

4. Notable is Karl Löwith's brief treatment in: *From Hegel to Nietzsche. The Revolution in 19th Century Thought*. Translated from the German by David Greene (NY: Holt, Reinhart & Winston, 1964), pp. 377-388.

5. See also Robert Luehrs, "F. Overbeck and the Theologian as Antichrist," *Katallagete*, 1973, IV, 16-20; "Christianity against History: F. Over-

beck's Concept of the Finis Christianismi," *Katallagete*, 1975, V, 16-20. Luers wrote his Stanford University Ph.D. dissertation on Overbeck: *Franz Overbeck* (1968). Another dissertation, by James Overbeck, *History against Theology, an Analysis of the Life and Thought of Franz Overbeck*, was accepted at the University of Chicago Divinity School in 1975.

6. The most important general introduction in German and the work most cited in recent scholarship is Arnold Pfeiffer, *Franz Overbecks Kritik des Christentums* (Göttingen: 1975). The following are some of the most recent works: Rudolf Brändle and Ekkhard Stegemann, eds., *Franz Overbecks unerledigte Anfragen an das Christentum* (Munich: Kaiser, 1988); Hermann-Peter Eberlein, *Theologie als Scheitern? Franz Overbecks Geschichte mit der Geschichte* (Essen: Blaue Eule, 1989); Eberlein, *Flamme bin ich sicherlich! F. Nietzsche, F. Overbeck und ihre Freunde* (Cologne: Schmidt von Schwind, 1999); Johann-Christoph Emmelius, *Tendenzkritik und Formengeschichte. F. Overbecks Beitrag zur Auslegung der Apostelgeschichte im 19. Jahrhundert* (Göttingen: 1975); Ulrich Körtner, *Theologie in dürftiger Zeit* (Munich: Kaiser, 1990); Andreas Urs Sommer, *Der Geist der Historie und das Ende des Christentums* (Berlin: Akademie Verlag, 1997); Rudolf Wehrli, *Alter und Tod des Christentums bei F. Overbeck* (Zürich: Theologischer Verlag, 1977).

7. The major work is still C.A. Bernoulli's two-volume *Franz Overbeck und Friedrich Nietzsche. Eine Freundschaft* (Jena: E. Diedrichs, 1908), which contains many quotations from Overbeck's manuscripts. It also tells the story of Overbeck's struggles with Nietzsche's sister concerning her manipulation of information after Nietzsche became insane and after his death in 1900.

8. These letters have recently been newly edited by Katrin Meyer and Barabara von Reibniz, *Briefwechsel F. Nietzsche, Franz and Ida Overbeck* (Stuttgart: Metzler, 2000). Other important letters of Overbeck have been published: *Franz Overbeck, Erwin Rhode, Briefwechsel*, edited by Andreas Patzer (Berlin, NY: W. de Gruyter, 1990). *Briefwechsel Franz Overbeck, Heinrich Köselitz [Peter Gast]*, edited by David Marc Hoffmann, Niklaus Peter and Theo Salfinger (Berlin, NY: W. de Gruyter, 1998). Another, much earlier publication of letters is also notable, namely Nietzsche's mother's letters to Overbeck during the period of Nietzsche's insanity: *Der kranke Nietzsche, Briefe seiner Mutter an Franz Overbeck*, edited by Erich Podach (Vienna, 1937).

9. J. E. Wilson, *Schelling und Nietzsche. Zur Auslegung der frühen Werke Friedrich Nietzsches*. Manuskripte und Texte zur Nietzsche-Forschung, Bd. 33 (Berlin and NY: Walter de Gruyter, 1995). I agree with the view that at the time of the writing of the *Christianity of Theology* there is no evident hostility in Nietzsche toward Christianity.

INTRODUCTION

Criticism and Faith, Theology and Church

"Your theological personality is for me a psychological problem. Its still unfound solution intrigues me, and indeed in the same measure that I have every reason greatly to appreciate so many sides of it, yet find others foreign to me. Each line is in itself intelligible but not the center, where they must come together in the unity of your person and as unity go out again: the positive point where your positive and negative relationship to Christianity are truly inwardly united. ... But where is it?"[1] As Overbeck indicates in the "Afterword" to the *Christianity of Theology*, questions such as this one from the liberal Zürich theologian, A.E. Biedermann (1819-1885), were hardly unusual. Biedermann writes in response to Overbeck's gift to him of another book, *Studien zur Geschichte der alten Kirche* [Studies in the History of the Ancient Church].[2] As also stated in the "Afterword," the book was published as a continuation of the earlier book, the *Christianity of Theology*, and "with the most definite advocacy of its essential ideas." In a previous letter, dated Oct. 30, 1873, Overbeck had replied to questions from Biedermann about the *Christianity of Theology*, specifically about Overbeck's understanding of faith (Glaube) and science (Wissen). Overbeck's answers basically repeat arguments in the book: "... science, or, if you wish, thought [Denken, autonomous thought] can have only a critical relationship to faith. Faith will call on thought only out of necessity or weakness, but thought will not remain with the task of freeing faith, for example, from a burdensome superstition, but will go on to demonstrate that all the forms of faith it can take in its grasp are themselves essentially superstition.... You ask further, what value I place on instruction about the 'essence of religion,' and I answer: little, if it is a matter of an abstract instruction that goes beyond the limits of experience. I really am of the opinion that every living religion has something incomprehensible for science, and I see no value in an alleged comprehension of religion in purely abstract concepts."[3] In Overbeck's understanding, an abstract comprehension or definition in abstract concepts would already be a form of science, and therefore a first step in the process of science's dissolution of faith. Biedermann responded to this letter on Nov. 6, 1873: "I see that in the scientifically [wissenschaftlich] fundamental question about what scientific thought can and cannot do—the answer to which determines the method and

aim of our efforts—you are in agreement with the contemporary return
to Kant's determination of 'limit.' " Biedermann, an Hegelian, goes on
to say that such a return is understandable, given the excesses of post-
Kantian speculation, but he deplores the rejection of speculation he
finds implicit in Overbeck's answers.[4] Yet neither these answers nor
Overbeck's *Studien zur Geschichte der alten Kirche* were able to clarify the "psychological problem" of Overbeck's "theological personality"
for Biedermann.

That Overbeck sees "no value" in a "comprehension of religion in
purely abstract concepts" is highly unusual for 19th century German
theology and philosophy. The century begins with Schleiermacher's famous definition of religion as "the feeling of absolute dependence" and
ends with Adolt Harnack's definition, derived trom the Schleiermacher
tradition, of "religion itself" as "God the Father and the human soul so
ennobled that it can and does unite with Him."[5] Biedermann relates
Overbeck's statement to a return to the Kantian "limit." Certainly there
was such a turn at this time. Along with the strong growth in the empirical sciences and a corresponding emphasis on scientific demonstration
in the historical sciences, philosophy and theology had begun to turn
away from the predominantly Hegelian speculation of the earlier part of
the century to restate in one form or another Kant's theory of the limits
of human perception. Kant had said perception is limited to experience
and to pure and practical reason; metaphysics that went beyond these
was unrealistic. But Kant's own effort in defining and comprehending
the practical significance of religion—for example in *Religion within
the Limits of Reason Alone*—is a work in purely abstract concepts. For
Kant himself, religion falls within the limits of practical reason.

Looking to Overbeck's own time for expressions of a limit between faith and science, the theology of Albrecht Ritschl (1822-1889)
should be noted. The first volume of his major work appeared in 1870,
the second and (most important) third, in 1874: *The Christian Doctrine
of Justification and Reconciliation*.[6] He adopts Kant's understanding of
the limit between experience and metaphysical speculation, and Kant's
practical reason becomes for him the philosophical ground of his conception of the Kingdom of God. Theology is the Christian science of
moral or spiritual value in the service of the Kingdom of God, which is
defined as spiritual dominion over the world. Abstract definitions of religion are at the core of Ritschl's work: "Religious knowledge moves in
independent value judgments, which relate to man's attitude to the
world, and call forth feelings of pleasure or pain, in which man either
enjoys the dominion over the world vouchsafed him by God, or feels
grievously the lack of God's help to that end" [III, §28, cf. §27]. Christ
and Christianity guarantee for Ritschl the dominion over the world,
which extends into state and culture [III, §48, §68].

Ritschl and Overbeck could hardly be further apart on the theological spectrum. As we shall see in the *Christianity of Theology*, for

Overbeck all science and all autonomous thought, from which science originates, is "worldly." He would agree with Ritschl that science is practically directed to serve humanity's dominion over its environment, but religion is something else entirely. In fact one may say that for Overbeck it is based on the failure of humanity's dominion over the world. Reflecting the failure, instead of teaching how to succeed in dominating the world, it teaches "world denial," as expressed in original Christian eschatology. Ritschl addresses Overbeck's *Christianity of Theology* in Vol. III, §62, where he calls Overbeck's understanding of Christianity "Buddhist." He reiterates that in his view early Christianity's expectation of the end of the world is "the shell and not the kernel" of Christianity.[7] Here also he expresses his conviction that an understanding such as Overbeck's is a form of "barbarism": it contradicts the continuity of civilization, culture and religion. Both Overbeck's *Christianity of Theology* and Ritschl's *Justification and Reconciliation* appeared at a decisive moment for the church in Germany, namely at the time when the newly unified nation was consciously attempting to clarify its religious identity. The most influential answer was to be given by Ritschl and his school, and for the rest of Overbeck's life Ritschlianism was the dominant theology in the universities.

Two other prominent figures in the Kantian revival of the time were the philosophers Arthur Schopenhauer (1788-1860) and Frederick Albert Lange (1828-1875). In Overbeck's Kirchenlexikon one finds scattered references to Schopenhauer that mainly have to do with the chapter "On Man's Need for Metaphysics" in *The World as Will and as Representation*. The references to this chapter focus on its concluding words: "For the rest, philosophy is essentially world-wisdom; its problem is the world. With this alone it has to do, and it leaves the gods in peace; but in return for this, it expects them to leave it in peace also." Overbeck once quotes this passage as support of his own view of the "limits" between philosophy and religion, between "Wissen" and "Glauben."[8] But Overbeck is more consistent with this distinction than Schopenhauer, for whom religion is metaphysics in popular allegorical form. The philosopher translates this form, much as in Hegelianism, into philosophical concepts.[9] Schopenhauer's work is based on pessimism about life in the world and advocates world denial, and for this reason Overbeck's work has been associated with it; but the form of denial is philosophical and hence, in terms of Overbeck's *Christianity of Theology*, a form of science (Wissen).

The "limit" has clearer definition in F.A. Lange's *History of Materialism*—its first edition was published in 1866—which is generally credited with beginning the neo-Kantian movement in late 19th century German philosophy. Lange distinguishes between the "thing in itself" that is absolute reality and the limited perception of this reality in science. Religion is grounded in ideas innate in the mind and relates in intuitive feeling to the "thing in itself," but it can express this relationship

only in poetic expression or other forms of art. Because of the limit between scientific perception and absolute reality, scientific metaphysics
is impossible. Science can only focus its efforts on empirical reality.
Religion can transcend the limit, but only in poetic feeling and vision.
Both science and religion have partial aspects of truth, attained by different methods—Lange speaks of a "double sense of the word truth"—
and both are needed in human life. Both are also in process of development. Scientific progress usually contradicts the mythical forms of religion, provoking their reaction into rigid dogmatism. While many out-
moded expressions retain their poetic power even after falling to
criticism, religion undergoes reformulations that correspond to the
progress of scientific knowledge. For Lange it retains its value as a psy-
chic or "spiritual" process in human life that responds to the human
need for a vision of higher reality.[10]

In Overbeck's Kirchenlexikon there are only a few references to
Lange, all of which are later than the publication of the Christianity of
Theology. The most important is under the title "Wahrheit (zweifache)"
[Truth (twofold)]: "How one can speak of twofold truth, religious and
philosophical, without having to admit to the common reproach of a
'double entry in the account book,' see Lange, Geschichte des Materia-
lismus." Page citations follow.[11] In the first place cited by Overbeck,
Lange writes: "In the relations of science we have fragments of truth,
which are continually multiplying, but continually remain fragments; in
the ideas of [metaphysical] philosophy and religion we have a figure
[Bild] of the truth, which presents it to us as a whole, but still always
remains a figure, varying in its form with the standpoint of our appre-
hension." In the other place cited by Overbeck, Lange faults a theologian, who had criticized his theory of twofold truth, with having fused
the two truths into one dogmatic statement, thus producing a hybrid
that satisfies neither science nor religion.

The concept of a twofold truth has a certain parallel in Overbeck's
division of science and faith, yet there are also significant differences
between Lange and Overbeck's Christianity of Theology. For Lange, all
metaphysics falls with religion in the area of poetic instead of scientific
truth. In Overbeck's analysis of theology, philosophical metaphysics is
science. Furthermore on the basis of his psychological analytic, Lange
is able to give an abstract definition of religion, which Overbeck refuses to do because it would be scientific. It may be asked whether Lange
remains with any real religion at all, insofar as his vision of a future religion is essentially philosophical. The "core of religion," he writes, is
found in the "elevation of our souls above the real and in the creation of
a home of the spirit," where the "purest forms may produce essentially
the same psychical processes" as the "creed of the uncultured masses."
In another place Lange speaks of helping the common folk of the
church religiously advance, through "an art of translating religious
forms into philosophical ideas" already prepared by Kant and Hegel.

These ideas must correspond to current culture: "Not any given poetical idea [of religion] can serve our purpose, but only that which is adapted to our time and to the character of our culture."[12] According to the *Christianity of Theology*, such adaptation would in fact be the end of religion, its disappearance into culture.

Lange's concept of religion in relationship to scientific thought was hardly new, as was not the Kantian "limit" in application to religion: they had long since been given classical expression by Friedrich Schleiermacher (1768-1834). In his famous work *On Religion, Speeches to Its Cultured Despisers*, first published in 1799, Schleiermacher posits that science and religion are two different aspects of mind, the one being objective and analytic, the other, the subjective feeling (Gefühl) of the unity of the All and one's dependence on it. Religious expressions are originally expressions of particular inner feelings. Dogmatic thought focus on the "outward," the concept, and where dogmatics becomes dominant, the original source in inner feeling, above all the feeling of love and dependence on God as exemplified by Christ, must be rediscovered.[13] While this bears a certain similarity to Overbeck's distinction between science and religion, Schleiermacher's central effort in the *Speeches* is something Overbeck criticizes in the *Christianity of Theology*, namely apologetic theology. It is addressed to nonbelievers and defines religion—"the sense and taste for the infinite," "the feeling of absolute dependence"—as an experience common to all persons who do not close themselves to it.

In spite of Schleiermacher's attempt to exclude science from the area of religion, Hegelian theologians recognized that his definition of religion was accessible to science, to both psychology and metaphysics. By the mid-19th century it was almost a commonplace in liberal theology that, given an Hegelian scientific comprehension of Schleiermacher's concept of religion as subjective existential experience, science and religion could be reconciled.[14] How this was to happen was more difficult. Science could claim anything in the religious tradition it thought it could explain, but the essential subjective experience would remain. The problem was the definition of the essential experience. In any case Schleiermacher's definition of religion was "graspable" by science, so that it could be explained and categorized in ways Schleiermacher never intended.

Schleiermacher himself was aware of the problematic relationship in his theology between autonomous or scientific thought and religion. In a famous letter from the year 1818, he states: "With the understanding (Verstande) I am a philosopher; for this is the original and autonomous activity of the understanding; and with the feeling (Gefühle) I am completely a person of piety, and indeed as such a Christian…" Trying to maintain an equilibrium of understanding and feeling "is certainly nothing other than an alternate lifting of one and sinking of the other. But, my friend, why should we not accept this? The oscillation is the

general form of all finite existence.... So my philosophy and my dogmatics are decided not to contradict one another, but hence they are
also never finished, and for as long as I can remember they have mutually influenced one another and come ever nearer to one another." "Understanding and feeling remain apart for me too, but they make contact
and spark an electrical current. The inmost life of the [human] spirit is
only in this electrical operation, in the feeling of understanding and the
understanding of feeling, whereby however both poles always remain
turned away from each other."[15] Schleiermacher's central interest was
not reflection on the separation, but the unending work of mediating the
opposing poles. One example is his historical work in the New Testament, where he tries to reconcile objective critical method and religion.
Toward the end of his life he had an ominous awareness of a nearing
time of criticism that would intensify the separation: orthodox piety on
the one side and unbelieving criticism on the other. He resists the
thought: "Shall the knot of history be untied and go apart like this?—in
one direction Christianity with barbarism, in the other science with unbelief?"[16]

Making sure that the "knot" stayed tied became the business of
the "Vermittlungstheologie," the "theology of mediation."[17] D.F.
Strauss (1808-1874) was to untie it in his critical assessment, published
in 1865, of Schleiermacher's history of the life of Jesus and with ex-
plicit reference to the letter from the year 1818 quoted above. In that
letter, said Strauss, Schleiermacher had announced a "treaty" between
faith and science, but it is an impossible treaty that only functions because Schleiermacher is biased for the Christ of faith. In truth his Christ
"is only a reminiscence of days long past, as it were the light of a distant star that we still see, while the star itself has long since extin-
guished."[18] Here and in earlier writings Strauss, a "left-wing" Hegelian,
denies the premise of any theology that tries to "mediate" between traditional Christian faith and science. Science must make its claim to the
whole of Christianity. It explains Christian faith's historical origins,
eliminates its out-dated aspects and lifts its true elements into philosophical knowledge. Historical criticism and philosophy are two parts
of the same science.

For the Hegelians the mediating factor between faith and knowledge or science was the verbal term "Vorstellung," which literally
means "place (something) before (the mind)," in the sense of thinking
about something. For the Hegelians it means the level of perception
prior to philosophical knowledge; philosophical knowing lifts any giv-
en thing (Vorstellung) to its inherent concept or idea. According to the
Hegelian interpretation, "Vorstellung" in Christianity is equated with
the entire content of the New Testament and all traditional derivative
dogmas.[19] Hence for these theologians Christianity had two levels:
"Vorstellung," as the way of thought and belief (Glaube) for traditional
Christians, and "Wissen," as philosophical knowledge. Because a "Vor-

stellung" inherently contains the possibility of being lifted into philosophical knowledge, by definition "Vorstellung" and "Wissen" cannot contradict one another.

This two-level conception of Christianity is well illustrated in the 1840's and 1850's in the *Theologische Jahrbücher*, the journal of the "Tübingen School" of historical critics gathered around Ferdinand Christian Baur (1792-1860).[20] Understanding the relationship between faith or religion and science in this, the most progressive school of historical criticism of its time, is especially important because Overbeck, in the introduction to the 2nd edition of the *Christianity of Theology*, associates himself with it, albeit not with its Hegelianism. The spokesman of the Tübingen School, in the sense of stating what it thought about current issues, was the editor of the journal and Baur's son-in-law, Edward Zeller (1814-1908). An example of the two levels is found in Zeller's article in the journal of the year 1845 entitled, "On the Essence [Wesen] of Religion." He discusses a growing problem, namely the gap between the Christianity of the "masses" and the "scientific views" of the educated theologian (427-430), a problem that had become acute especially since the publication of Strauss' *Life of Jesus* in 1835. Zeller admonishes theology never to halt its progress in science. In order to overcome the gap, he suggests that it lead the masses "with a sparing hand into general education." It should not do this through an "untrue accommodation," but "in the form of Vorstellung," the "popular form." In other words, the masses need greater sophistication in matters of religion.

Zeller makes these comments in a discussion of a recently published book by A.E. Biedermann, who argued for a free scientific theology and (at the level of Vorstellung) for the compatibility of this theology with the popular [volkstümliche] Christianity of the church. Biedermann's work also illustrates another point: the way the Hegelian theologians appropriated Schleiermacher's concept of religion: "The inmost essence of Schleiermacher's theology of feeling is speculative," for example, when Schleiermacher speaks of an "absolute."[21] Such appropriation was common in the Tübingen School. Indeed according to another article by Zeller, Schleiermacher's concept of religion counterbalances Hegel's "all too abstract objectivity." Criticism, he writes, has shown that a supernatural revelation is impossible because it "contradicts the general laws of all known events." But this does not mean that religion is an illusion. The mythical explanation of the evangelical history (given by Strauss) does not deny the historical Christ, and criticism merely asks how Christianity and its founder originated on the ground of historical reality, that is, how they are to be scientifically explained.[22] In an article from the year 1858 another prominent member of the Tübingen School, Adolf Hilgenfeld (1823-1907), referred to Schleiermacher's theology of feeling as having correctly understood "the root of all religion" and indeed in a way compatible with Hegel's science, while Ludwig Feuerbach's atheism "contradicts both the basic laws of reason and the needs of the human spirit."[23] Hence Schleiermacher has served a new midcentury theological synthesis in opposition to radicalism.

Zeller returned again to the same problem in 1850 in an article entitled "On the Relationship of Theology to Science and Church." He notes that objections to scientific theology continue. The charge is made that it is undercutting the foundations of the church, that the poison of unbelief is being sowed in the parishes. "Should the church entrust the education of its pastors to open atheists, notorious pantheists, deniers of the evangelical history, doubters of God and immortality?" Such objections are used to justify a politics of censorship. A "change of form" from religious feeling or belief to the idea or concept does change the content, but, he says, one should not fear this, because it serves to separate what is merely accidental from the "essence of religion." He advises those who think the apparent contradiction between the belief of the church and science is irreconcilable not to become either a teacher of religion in the school or a professor of theology in the university. Finally, the theological faculties of the universities must maintain their scientific freedom, for the future of the church depends on it.[24]

F.C. Baur's *Kirchengeschichte des Neunzehnten Jahrhunderts*—lectures on the history of the church in the 19th century edited and published by Zeller after Baur's death in 1860—reflects essentially the same view of theology and church, but Baur addresses the problem of "church" theology directly. He characterizes it as either, on the one hand, strictly confessional theology, which Baur dismisses as unscientific, or, on the other hand, "consensus-dogmatics," by which he means the confessional agreement of the relatively individualistic theologies of mediation. Speaking of this last group, he writes: "One no longer has the right mind for the old system and yet one also does not have the strength and courage to lift oneself to a new system. One knows that inwardly one is no longer one with the church [sc. the advocacy of its confessions], and yet one will not risk breaking with it outwardly." In a previous place Baur had written: "The character of the most recent time lies in working out the opposing points of view [science and church] in their principal significance, which since [D.F.] Strauss has been the clear tendency of the period. The false mediations, which rest on no more than appearance and illusion, should cease ... Those elements must separate that can no longer remain together. If the church cannot tolerate scientific criticism, it must throw it out; if criticism can see in the church only unhistorical presuppositions, there remains nothing for it to do but to break with the church."[25] Baur does not predict a successful mediation of criticism and church. Rather he says: "The principle of [our] time is the self-consciousness of humanity as the absolute power over everything, as the most immediate thing on which humanity has to hold itself; but if one does not set the truth of self-consciousness in the universal [Allgemeinheit], which has all subjective thought and will as its necessary presupposition—this is for Hegel the chief point—if one does not do this, then all that gives life its unity and connection is dissolved into the crude rule of egoism."[26] Baur understood this "universal" in connection with the moral teaching of Jesus. In one of his most important late works, the *Vorlesungen über die Theologie des neuen Testaments*, the moral teaching of Jesus, above all in the Sermon on the Mount, is Christianity's most universal and therefore most enduring or timeless statement: "If the Father is the moral idea in itself,... so the Son is only to be conceived as the self-realizing idea, and the more perfectly the idea realizes itself, all the more perfectly the unity of Father and Son is presented."[27] The truth of the idea of the Son is God, the reality of the idea of God is the Son. "Sonship" is an abstract universal that all humans in some degree make concrete or real in their own lives. In the *Kirchengeschichte des Neunzehnten Jahrhunderts*, Baur agrees with D. F. Strauss: Because it is a universal concept, the unity of God and humanity cannot be perfectly fulfilled in Jesus, but only in the human race through its universal history; yet Jesus is unique in one sense: as a religious genius he is "relatively" evaluated as the "highest" humanity has known.[28]

As has already been seen, Schleiermacher anticipated the alienation of church and scientific theology with concern. In 1829, in the "Second Public Letter to Lücke," he faulted the Hegelians for creating, with their distinction between the religious "Vorstellung" of common Christians and the higher conceptual knowledge of the philosopher-theologian, a distinction between hierarchic "esoteric" (philosophical) and common "exoteric" (traditional) doctrine, whereas the will of Christ is that "all be taught by God."[29] And yet Schleiermacher himself contributed significantly to the problem, namely as the historical critic who tried to reconcile science and faith, admittedly without success. According to Baur's analysis, Schleiermacher had done the same thing he accused the Hegelians of doing, if in a different form.[30] The Hegelians were simply more honest.

Remarkably almost all of the above statements of Zeller and Baur —which represent the essential elements of the discussion on faith and science in the Tübingen School from the 1830's practically to the time of the *Christianity of Theology*—are anticipated in the concluding section of D. F. Strauss' *Life of Jesus* (in the 4th edition of 1840). For Strauss, the idea of Christ (the Son) applies only to the totality of individuals, and the critical thinker understands the evangelical narratives "for the most part as myth." He cites Schleiermacher's charge that the speculative or Hegelian theology in effect introduces a distinction between an "esoteric" and an "exoteric" doctrine. The problem Strauss addresses in the concluding section is precisely that of the clergyman who is enlightened by critical and philosophical science in his relationship to the "popular conception" (Vorstellung) of the common people in the church. While the cleric risks being called a hypocrite, it cannot be good for the church, Strauss argues, that science be excluded and the scientifically educated theologians "depart from their position as teachers" in church-related positions. "Where truth is concerned, the possible consequences have no weight." Moreover, more and more of the laity are achieving high levels of education. Strauss suggests "a mode of reconciling the two extremes": "In [the cleric's] discourses to the church, he will indeed adhere to the forms of popular conception, but at every opportunity he will exhibit their spiritual [geistige, sc. philosophical] significance, which for him constitutes their sole truth, and thus prepare —though such a result is only to be thought of as an unending progress —the resolution of those forms into their original ideas also in the consciousness of the church." Strauss offers the example of Easter and its interpretation. "[The cleric] will indeed set out from the sensible fact of the resurrection of Christ, but he will dwell chiefly on the being buried and rising again with Christ, which the Apostle himself has strenuously inculcated...." This, as Strauss points out, is also what the orthodox clergy do, although they hold to the historical foundation of the resurrection, while the critical and philosophical theologian, for himself, abandons it. In any case the theologian cannot avoid the collision of science and the church's faith. "Our age has not arrived at a certain decision on this subject"; the collision "is necessarily introduced by the progress of the time and the development of Christian theology."[31]

Strauss published another important work in 1840-1841, the two volumes of the *Christliche Glaubenslehre* (Doctrine of the Christian Faith), which treats the traditional doctrines of the church. The word that repeatedly occurs in the chapter titles is not, as one would expect from an Hegelian theologian, "Aufhebung," the lifting of a doctrinal "Vorstellung" into a philosophical concept, but "Auflösung," the "dissolution" of the doctrine. Strauss' thesis is that since the New Testament period a gradual but definite historical development of autonomous, scientific thought has taken place within Christianity that has led to the freedom of modern humanity from faith. The pre-Strauss period of modernity was that of mediation between faith and science, but now one must demonstrate the "deception and lie" in so-called "Christian philosophy" and in any and all attempts to mediate between faith and science. Religion, however, survives. Schleiermacher was right in understanding religion as a unique activity of mind in relationship to the absolute, but not in understanding it philosophically. Agreeing with Ludwig Feuerbach, Strauss writes that religion is essentially fantasy based on "practical" subjective need. Those who do not lift themselves to science and philosophy find these needs expressed, and to some degree met, by the forms of religious faith, while the enlightened philosopher comprehends the need, understands its deceptive religious productions (the forms of faith), and is able to re-focus the need on truer personal fulfillment. There is, says Strauss, no direct relationship between the Christian church's beliefs and the philosophical truth that the Hegelian theologians derive from them. The Hegelian theologians, and in important instances Hegel himself, were wrong in thinking that the content of faith and the content of speculative Hegelian philosophy are essentially the same, that only the form changes in the move from one to the other. According to Strauss, in the shift from faith to philosophy the content changes with the form. Neither the form and the content of faith nor the form and content of science can be separated. Hence faith and science (Glaube und Wissen) can only be distinctly different. Faith can exist without science, and science can exist without faith, but they cannot be mixed or mediated. The problem is theology, which is in an impossible situation, insofar as it tries to mediate what cannot be mediated.[32]—Strauss is famous for his criticism of theology as "half" faith and "half" science, for which the mediating theologies of his time offered ample evidence.[33]

In Strauss' modern world, freedom of thought can find a home only in science. He agrees with Feuerbach in contrasting the "Christian world view," as a metaphysics of the other world [Jenseits], with the modern philosophical worldview, in which the finite and infinite are reconciled in this world [Diesseits]. The Christian worldview dualistically sets this world and the other world in opposition, whereby only the other world has true reality.[34] In anticipation of his later work on Jesus, he states that Jesus is irrelevant for the modern world and can be given over to historical criticism.[35] The modern mind is free from the constraints that bind faith to its deceptive perceptions, and the expression of this freedom is historical criticism.

Strauss' later, so-called "second life of Jesus," *Das Leben Jesu für das deutsche Volk bearbeitet* [The Life of Jesus presented for the German People], published in 1864, attempts to explain, for the educated person, not only the concept of myth and its presence in the Gospel history but also Jesus' religious mind. According to Strauss, the core of Jesus' message is the "inner" truth of conscience as expressed in the Sermon on the Mount, although Jesus mistakenly projects the fulfillment of the Sermon's ethical requirements into a vision of the coming Kingdom of God. For Strauss, the "inwardness" preached by Jesus contrasts with Jewish "outwardness," the fulfillment of the extensive commandments of Jewish law. Indeed, Jesus' religious mind is essentially Hellenic. Instead of the absolute difference between the transcendent God and humanity that Judaism teaches, Jesus experiences a happy unity with God more characteristic of Greek than Jewish thought.[36] When the ancient world's concept of God, whether Hellenic or Jewish, is critically evaluated, what remains of Jesus' religious mind is the happy inwardness, as the unity of finite and infinite, of his moral conscience. This is the core thought that Strauss also finds in a modern "religion of humanity," after the empty shell of the historical aspects of Christianity

and its myths have been discarded. In a famous metaphor Strauss compares the New Testament myths that obscure the actual life of Jesus to a
parasitic vine that grows up around a tree, sapping its life, so that the
tree's own leaves fall away, its limbs decay and all that is visible is the
vine, as if it itself were the tree.[37] If Strauss nevertheless finds sufficient traces of Jesus' religion in the Gospels for his characterization of
it, the overriding point is that Christianity is based on the myths and
dogmas (the vine). The "religion of humanity" does not need Jesus any-
way.

Since the myths and dogmas are what is Christian, and since the
extracted essence of Jesus' thought is recognized in the modern scientific mind as a universal truth, it was only natural that Strauss, in his
last work, *The Old Faith and the New*, rejected the "old faith" and
found the universal truth as the fruit of historical development in the
modern scientific worldview, if mixed with other modern fruit, such as
nationalism.

In looking back on the discussion about historical criticism and
theology from the perspective of Overbeck's *Christianity of Theology*,
it is Strauss that emerges as the most noticeable point of reference, especially Strauss' criticism of theology as "half" science (Wissen) and
"half" faith (Glaube). How much of one or the other might be involved
in the mediating attempts of theology was never a matter of only a half.
In *The Old Faith and the New*, Strauss speaks of the "religious domain"
in the modern human soul as comparable to the constantly shrinking
lands of the Native Americans in the United States.[38] If the term "Vermittlungstheologie" applied in first half of the 19th century to theologies that sought scientific support for a more or less orthodox Protestantism, in the second half, when criticism made such startling and
rapid gains, it could apply to almost any theology that tried to come to
terms with criticism.[39] In fact it seemed to characterize all theology, especially to Overbeck, who called it not theology of mediation but, using
a more traditional term, apologetic theology.

Overbeck habilitated in 1864 as a "Privatdozent" at the University
of Jena in the area of early church history. His mentor, the famous
church historian, Karl Hase (1800-1890), was one who had come under
Strauss' attack for being a "half and half" theologian. His *Life of Jesus*,
first published in 1829 (the 4th edition of 1856 was translated into English) is guided by the attempt to understand the connection between the
divine and the human. He is generally identified with the liberal wing
of the Schleiermacher tradition, and in a way similar to Schleiermacher
he tries to make certain key miracles, and the greater miracle of Christ
himself, comprehensible to the scientific mind: "the mysterious" must
be "thinkable" [denkbar], although some miracles are unthinkable and
hence impossible, such as the feeding of the multitude. The means of
comprehension is a "higher law of nature" manifested in these miracles; the pure rationalist who accepts no miracles must be driven to

Strauss. Hase reacted strongly to Strauss: "If it is not possible to overcome Strauss' *Life of Jesus* by means of science, historical and popular
Christianity would receive as violent and far-reaching a blow as can be
given by a mere book." And yet "our time" has overcome the naive
childlike faith in the letter of the Gospel, the faith that risked no doubt
in believing the factuality of a legion of devils going into a herd of
swine.[40]

Baur had included an evaluation of Hase, the truly "modern historian of the church," in his *Epochen der kirchlichen Geschichtschrei-
bung* (Tübingen, 1852). According to Baur, it is the "tragic" ambiguity,
at once melancholic and joyful, of the division between traditional faith
and science that characterizes Hase's history. He lifts up Hase's interpretation of modernity as the time in the life of the church when the
church takes second place, as the mover of history, to things "worldly"
[das Weltliche], especially to science and the political development of
the state. Baur finds in Hase no core idea or principle to keep the
church from "dissolving" into these historical elements [242f]. Hase's
response acknowledges that he has wrestled with the division, and indeed with mixed feelings historically described the "revolution" of the
[scientific] undermining of the old faith [des altväterlichen Glaubens]
and the corresponding rise of modern autonomous self-consciousness.
"It would not be contrary to my intention, if some readers, alongside
their insight into the matter and its necessity, also experienced such a
mixture of melancholy and joyful participation; yet finally every true
and great history ends tragically."[41]

The *Christianity of Theology* also discusses the division between
traditional faith and modern science, Glauben und Wissen, but without
Hase's attempt to mediate them. How does Overbeck understand their
relationship? As seen in Biedermann's letters to Overbeck quoted at the
beginning of this section, "Wissen" and "Glaube," the central subjects
in the *Christianity of Theology*, are not related in such a way that they
are easily comprehended. Overbeck does exclude two previously unmentioned ways of relating them. One is a theology that makes an arbitrary use of science; this Overbeck deals with in the second chapter of
the *Christianity of Theology*. The other is far more important: the negation of faith by science. The exchange of letters between Overbeck and
Biedermann includes Biedermann's comment: "You nicely repaid Hartmann for his agreement with you, such as it is—in every sense a sign
that you cannot be bribed."[42] Biedermann's remark refers to several
lines at the end of the preface to Overbecks *Studien zur Geschichte der
alten Kirche*, published in 1875. Referring to the important work of scientific enlightenment, he writes: "We will hardly be able soon to do
without a discipline that calls us to sober reflection in the religious confusions of the present, when presently the spirit of giddiness [Schwin-
del] seems to overcome even this discipline itself, so that from this spirit laughable births spring forth. An example is the attempt that has

recently come to us from Berlin under the misleading title 'Religion of the Future.' For this unknown future religion it already wants to find the proper philosophy, a scholasticism before its time and without necessity."

The reference was to a recent publication by Edward von Hartmann (1842-1906), *Die Selbstzersetzang des Christentums und die Religion der Zukunft* [The Self-Dissolution of Christianity and the Religion of the Future] (Berlin, 1874). With his previous work, *Philosophie des Unbewussten* [Philosophy of the Unconscious] (Berlin, 1869), Hartmann had quickly achieved fame in the German cultural world. The work is largely dependent on the philosophy of Schopenhauer, whose fame had recently risen in a remarkable way. In the "Self-Dissolution of Christianity," Hartmann uses Overbeck's *Christianity of Theology* as a statement of such dissolution. He also uses Paul de Lagarde's religious-political tract of 1873, which we will discuss below. According to Hartmann, Christianity has an antiquated, other-worldly view of the world that in modern theology clashes with the modern immanentist worldview and its science, and Christianity in all its forms finds itself in a necessary process of dissolution. He agrees with Overbeck (and Nietzsche) that Strauss' optimistic picture of modern culture in the *Old Faith and the New* is unconvincing. But he adopts essential points from Strauss' critical assessment of Christianity and its history, and, also like Strauss, his metaphysics is a theory of the impersonal "One" behind all appearances. Hartmann's "religion of the future" is a religion of the One, a new world religion uniting east and west. Science (Wissenschaft) can prepare the way for it, but not create it.[43] Religion is distinct from philosophy in that it is essentially feeling, not thought, but the new religion must have a suitable metaphysics for its expression that will be acceptable both to science and to the common people. This will happen through religious genius that gives "the power of vivid and graphic depiction to timely [zeitgemässer] religious ideas." These will be derived from both popular belief and science [93f]. Pantheistic philosophy will open the way for the new religion by channeling its superior ideas about reality into the pool of ideas that the future creator of the world religion will use.

Nothing in Hartmann's theory is innovative, it is rather a common piece of late 19th century religious philosophy and hermeneutics, even as it also represents, as does the *Old Faith and the New*, the intellectual secularism of the time. Overbeck's comment on Hartmann's work addresses primarily the "religion of the future," but this religion is the product of the "spirit of dizziness"—Overbeck's word "Schwindel" has a double meaning: not only dizziness but also deceit. Like Strauss, Hartmann dissolves religion into philosophical theory, into "Wissen" and "Wissenschaft." Hartmann's misuse of Overbeck is a notable testimony to the ease with which the *Christianity of Theology* can be misunderstood.

The Religious-Political Situation

The "spirit of dizziness" with which Overbeck characterizes this particular period of time is very probably a reference to the post-war situation in Germany. The Franco-Prussian War had ended in 1871 with a Prussian victory and the unification of the German states under the king of Prussia. The task of writing a constitution for the new Germany included writing laws on church and state. All the German states had religious establishments, and theological faculties were located in the universities. Very many books and pamphlets were written at this time on this situation. What was the cultural identity of the new nation, and what role should religion play in it? "Cultural" identity meant most importantly what should be taught in the schools and how religion was to be supported. Strauss' *Old Faith and the New* was an appeal for his point of view. He includes long discussions on the incompatibility of antiquated Christianity with contemporary education: in natural science, Darwin, in philosophy, Feuerbach. Hartmann's book on the "Self-Dissolution of Christianity" was also part of this broad discussion. Both he and Strauss appeal for religious liberty, insisting that the freedom of science and philosophy, the historical product of German culture, demands it. Hartmann, who was not a theologian, makes use of a religious-political tract, F.A. Müller's *Briefe über das Christentum* [Letters on Christianity] (Stuttgart, 1870). Speaking from his knowledge of theology and in advocacy of disestablishment and the relegation of religion to the privacy of each individual, Müller asks, "what is the Christian religion? Perhaps the Jewish teaching of Jesus, or the teaching of Paul, which contradicts it, or the mystical fantasies of John, or the contradictory mixture of all of them?" He adds that none of these corresponds to the beliefs of either Catholicism or Protestantism [276]. Thus Müller, in his appeal to the politicians, assesses the results of historical criticism and applies them to the definition of Christianity. "Over ninety percent of all educated men in Europe are at bottom thoroughly unchristian, and yet with only few exceptions they give themselves to the tactful lie of seeming to be what they are not" [280].

In the preface to the first edition of the *Christianity of Theology* Overbeck writes that two previous publications had given the immediate occasion to write the book, Strauss' *Old Faith and the New*, and a recent work by Paul de Lagarde (1827-1891), *Über das Verhältnis des deutschen Staats zu Theologie, Kirche und Religion. Ein Versuch Nicht-Theologen zu Orientieren* [On the Relationship of the German State to Theology, Church and Religion. An Attempt to Orientate Non-Theologians] (Göttingen, 1873). Lagarde was a professor of oriental languages and history of religions at the University of Göttingen. Overbeck's interest in his publication has to do with its proposal for a new arrangement of the study of theology in the universities. Before turning to Lagarde's work—it is of special importance for the last chapter of the *Christianity of Theology*—the situation in Germany as it relates to this discussion needs brief clarification.

Prussia was Protestant, and the result of the Franco-Prussian War was seen not only as a victory of Germany but also of Protestantism. Nationalist feelings were high. The immediate task of the new nation was formulating its constitution and laws. Chancellor Bismarck's religious program favored the mediation of Christianity and "culture," meaning essentially modern liberal education, under strong state leadership. Catholic influence had been sharply reduced by Prussia's earlier military defeat of Austria. In 1870 the anti-modernist First Vatican Council had declared the dogma of papal infallibility, which led in Germany to conflicts over church authority. "Kulturkampf" (fight for culture) was the word for the state's opposition to conservative Catholicism. A first group of laws governing religious institutions came into effect early in 1872. They provided for state control of the church at all levels, with clergy and high lay officials appointed to state posts and subject finally to the leadership of the Minister of Culture. The laity had little to say in the appointment of clergy. With regard to the government's religious program, there was no clear idea of what a union or mediation or cooperation of religion and culture actually meant. Theologians and clergy representing different conceptions formed into a variety of parties that sought influence on the government. Further laws came into effect in January, 1873, that provided for the education of clergy. The theological faculties had been located in the universities since their founding and, as part of the universities, were financially supported by the state. The main change effected by the new laws in Protestant theological education was state control of examinations, which were now to include "Culturexamen," exams in culture, which meant exams in liberal education.[44] "Culture" generally meant education in the natural sciences and humanities.

We turn now to Lagarde's publication, "On the Relationship of the German State to Theology, Church and Religion," which was also an attempt to influence the policies of the new nation. Taking his point of departure from a positivist understanding of science that requires objective proofs, Lagarde's argument is for a university theology that will prepare the way for a "new religion" by means of a scientific understanding of the nature of all religion. The two current religious forms in Germany, Protestantism and Catholicism, are dead or dying because they are identified with time-conditioned elements that necessarily fall into the past. Protestantism has been in dissolution since the peace concluded with Catholicism at the end of the Thirty Years War, which effectively ended its development. The Enlightenment or "classical" period of German culture (Lessing, Goethe, Kant) was a major shift to a new historical development. While it resulted in the inclusion of many enlightened cultural elements in Protestantism, it also led to the general alienation of the educated from traditional church belief [16ff]. True re-

ligion is made up of timeless elements, the laws of spiritual life, and
these are as scientifically demonstrable or subject to proof as Newton's
law of gravity. Such proofs are historical, derived from the observation
of all existing religions, but they have to do with truths that are ascer-
tainable by personal experience. True religion is "gospel," which includes the doctrine of sin and how it is overcome (repentance and for-
giveness), and "kingdom of God" as the following of the dictates of
religion in life [36, 60f]. Hence true religion is not faith but life [41].
Religion "binds together, educates, leads, comforts" [49]. Gospel includes relationship to the God who is eternally present [39], and true religion dominates all life: "all is duty or sin." Following God means "renouncing the world," that is, sin [60]. While Jesus demonstrates gospel,
through the subsequent mixing in of historically limited Jewish, Greek,
and Roman ideas, he was made into the Christ of Christianity [28ff].
The essential religious task in modernity is to reformulate gospel with
living ideas of the culture, specifically of German culture. The religion
of the nation is its "soul" [62]. It is therefore in the vital interest of the
state to draw religion into its sphere of work. The state can only prepare
the way for the new religion, which must be created by religious genius
combining the elements of true religion with viable popular ideas. To
create the right conditions for the birth of the new religion, the state
must reduce the current established churches to sects that teach their
theology in private seminaries; their use of science is compromised by
antiquated traditions. The state should allow a place in the university
only to purely scientific theology, which studies religion historically
and demonstrates its essential laws. This theology will be the "pathfinder" of the coming religion. Lagarde thinks that one can already "calculate the curve" of the new religion based on what purely scientific theology already knows about both the elements of true religion and the
culture of modernity [48ff].

　　　Largarde's program is obviously an attempt to persuade the government to take a further step in its liberal program, namely to a "purely scientific" definition of university theology. In fact its thoughts are a
further development of the historical critical theology traced above.
Both his perception of the situation in theology and church and his reform proposals are not only compatible with the direction of the
Tübingen School's discussion of theology and church, but also may be
taken as a consistent extension of that direction in the new situation of
the development of laws governing theological education. Lagarde's
"gospel" is essentially the concept of universal moral values, with God
as its transcendent point of reference. One is reminded of F.C. Baur's
recognition of the universal [Allgemeine] in Christianity in distinction
from its historically limited forms represented by the churches. Furthermore Baur's history of the church in the 19th century, like Lagarde's
historical analysis, ends with the opposition of purely scientific theology and the theology of the churches. Neither Lagarde's analysis nor his

essentials of religion nor his idea of a new religion is innovative. What is new is the proposal for a radical restructuring of the theological faculties, which Overbeck discusses in the last chapter of the *Christianity of Theology*.

The political strength of the conservative and liberal parties in the church and in theological education was, at the time the *Christianity of Theology* was written, so widely spread that no single party could claim dominance. Each had its newspaper or journal (or both) and sought to extend its influence as well as it could. The once powerful conservative newspaper, *Evangelische Kirchenzeitung*, infamous for its vilification of anyone threatening the conservative-orthodox system, including its synthesis of faith and science, lost influence steadily in the 1860's. Its founder and editor, and professor of theology in Berlin, Ernst Wilhelm Hengstenberg, died in 1869. It was continued as the *Neue Evangelische Kirchenzeitung*. The theological middle was represented most prominently by a "theologian of mediation," Isaac August Dorner in Berlin and, beginning in the 1870's, Albrecht Ritschl.[45]

Fides Humana, Fides Divina. Overbeck at the Time of the "Christianity of Theology"

In the introduction to the *Christianity of Theology* (as elsewhere) Overbeck makes it clear that he was never an Hegelian, that his association with the Tübingen School had only to do with historical criticism, which meant principally the reconstruction of the history of New Testament literature (authorship, date, context and original meaning). He generally accepted mythical interpretation, with the important correction in "source criticism" given by F.C. Baur, namely that the context, the "tendency" (formative interest) and intent of the authors of the Gospels were more determinative of the form of the Gospels than Strauss' concept of early Christian "unintentional poeticizing" about Jesus. With source criticism of the Gospels, Baur had applied the earlier discovery of his School, the "tendency" of the Book of Acts, to Gospel criticism.[46] Overbeck's only major publication prior to the *Christianity of Theology* was his historical-critical interpretation of Acts, which identified him with the Tübingen School, or what remained of it ten years after Baur's death.[47] Generally speaking Overbeck's critical work acknowledged no limits not inherent in the method or object of criticism itself. What scientific or historical criticism can explore, it must explore, and it must be forthright with its results.

Overbeck's inaugural lecture, on coming to Basel from Jena in 1870, has the title *Über Entstehung und Recht einer rein historischen Betrachtung der Neutestamentlichen Schriften in der Theologie*, "On the Origin and Right of a Purely Historical Consideration of the New Testament Writings in Theology."[48] The way the title is printed on the title page of the publication is noteworthy: the words "einer rein historischen Betrachtung" are set in very small type, type one would ordinarily use for footnotes, so that at first glance the title reads, "On the Origin and Right of the New Testament Writings in Theology." Overbeck begins his discussion [83ff] by stating that, through the dominance of historical-critical questions, theology is unavoidably placed in a new situation—a "new house" that it must adjust to, as he later says [104]. The critical questions have caused great conflicts and theologians represent many different conclusions. Overbeck's intent is to ask about the origins of the conflicts, which leads him back to the patristic period and to the subsequent history of the question about the historical sense of Scripture. While no age of the church has been without a sense of the need for an understanding of the original sense of the canonical writings, in the past the dogmatic interests of each age (whether allegorical or orthodox) pushed the historical sense into the background, which generally resulted in an increasing inability of the church to distinguish between its contemporary theological interests and original Christianity. This was especially true in the Middle Ages [91f]. The Reformation and its concentration on Scripture, together with the historical period's general rebirth of the sciences, was a major turning point, although the Reformation's interest in Scripture was mainly religious, not historical-critical. Luther's Commentary on Galatians "is one of the most powerful books ever written," but it is hardly an historical commentary. "Luther writes his explanation of Galatians as a poet, full of One Perception [Einer Empfindung voll]," namely justification by faith, the core doctrine of Protestantism. It is for him an "inexhaustible and deep content that extends into the unmeasured [das Ungemessene, sc. the infinite]" [93]. The following periods of Orthodoxy, with its theory of the divine authorship of the canon, and Rationalism, with its imposition of its own rational concepts on the biblical writers, have now been superceded [94-97]. "A more inner perception [Empfindung] in things of pious faith, an enormously widened knowledge of the world and of history, the powerful general progress of the historical sciences have certainly furthered historical theology. They have finally placed it on the ground of the question about the origin of Christianity and its oldest documents." And they have made it possible to give "purely historical" explanations of them. The most prominent name in this development is Ferdinand Christian Baur, even if a number of his chief results are questionable. The point is that the "face" of theology has now changed, it must deal with the historical-critical questions. For contemporary theology, the focal question is not whether or not the history is miraculous, as it had been for Rationalism and as important as this question generally is, but "how it was [wie sie gewesen ist]" [97-99]. The focus of criticism today is not the "negative" question about the biblical writings' historical credibility, but the "positive" question about "what they are credible for [wofür sie glaubwürdig sind]" [99f].

As it confronts the problems it faces, Overbeck continues, theology cannot return to an earlier period, such as the Reformation or the following period of Protestant Orthodoxy. No theologian can legitimately preclude critical work or its results by making use of Orthodoxy's theory of divine authorship of the biblical writings. But criticism can make the opposite mistake of committing itself to the rationalism of the Socinians and Arminians. "The Socinians and Arminians openly said that they wanted to found the religious value (fides divina) of the biblical books on their historical credibility (fides humana). Precisely this the Orthodox dogmaticians did not want to do, and entirely correctly. And the theologians who contest the so-called negative criticism of the canon do not want to do it either" [102f]. Criticism is not the only component of Protestantism. Protestant theologians are united by common problems, problems that remind it that it is not a pure science. "Serving neither purely religious nor purely scientific interests, theology works on the moral task of establishing the inner harmony between our faith and our scientific mind. It lies in the nature of this constantly moving task—which is affected in the most manifold way by the richness of life—that theologians will oppose one another over results, and that such opposition, where it is serious, will amount to the concession that theology has failed its task" [105]. Today theology must face the complexity of the task. To close itself to historical criticism would be to welcome ossification, as seen in the tridentine Catholic Church, which has erected a wall between itself and the "unending task of encompassing all earthly life" that it says it owns. Such issue must be prevented in Protestantism. Finally, the Protestant theologian will least be led astray "as long as he has within him a yet living memory of the inestimable goods of purer faith and deeper perception [Erkenntnis] that we owe to its [sc. Protestantism's] first confessors" [105f.] With these words Overbeck ends the lecture.

Two points need clarification: the "more inner perception in things of pious faith" that characterizes the theology of Overbeck's time, and the expressions "fides divina" and "fides humana." A favorite word, so to speak, of 19th century German theology is "inner," which stems from early Romanticism, Schleiermacher and Kant. The point is that not the "outward" or objective observance of laws and dogmas is the core of religion or faith, but subjective feeling, conscience or perception [Gefühl, Gesinnung, Empfindung]. Typical references were to the Sermon on the Mount, where Jesus appeals to the conscience, not the letter of the law, and to Paul's understanding of faith as trust in God's actions, not as objective dogmas. When Overbeck speaks of "a more inner perception in things of pious faith," he is contrasting the theology of his time in general with the dominance of objectivity in Protestant Orthodox dogmatics and in the reasoning of Rationalism.

"Fides divina" and "fides humana" are doctrines of Protestant Orthodoxy and have to do with certainty in the doctrine of Scripture: fides divina is belief in the content of Scripture worked by the Holy Spirit;

fides humana is any kind of proof or reasoned argument that can be made for this content. Karl Hase was especially responsible for bringing these terms into use in 19th century theology. His popular *Hutterus Redivivus*, which first appeared in 1828 and later went through many new publications, was based on the work of the orthodox Lutheran theologian Leonard Hutter (1563-1616). Hase's method in the book is to give a synopsis of Hutter's position on a doctrine together with brief statements of other positions from the history of Lutheran theology, often followed by a brief review of recent positions and his own commentary. In the 11th edition (Leipzig, 1868), fides humana and fides divina are discussed in §37, §42-§43, where Hase points out that they were developed doctrinally in opposition to Arminianism and Socinianism. In 19th century theology there was considerable discussion about fides divina and the credibility of New Testament writings, above all in the "theology of mediation."[49] In the *Christliche Glaubenslehre* Strauss rejects any legitimacy of the fides divina.[50] The Hegelians generally had difficulty with the concepts because in the Hegelian scheme faith as "Vorstellung" was lifted into philosophical knowledge (Wissen), whereby the difference between fides divina and fides humana disappeared.[51] In his *Evangelisch-Protestantische Dogmatik* (5th ed. Leipzig, 1860), Karl Hase points out that in Protestant Orthodoxy the significance of the distinction between fides divina and humana lay in the fact that fides humana was recognized as producing only probability [381]. Hase takes up the distinction in his own argument for the authority of Scripture, but he does not apply the fides divina to the whole of Scripture. The Spirit witnesses to the core truths of the Gospel, as originally preached. Its witness extends only secondarily and derivatively to the New Testament writings, which contain much human weakness and error.[52] In the same way texts in the Old Testament contain revelatory content, especially the prophets, but also much that is not revelatory. It belongs to the revelatory event that Spirit in us today witnesses to the Spirit speaking through the authors of the Bible. Hase divides theology into two parts, one serving the church, in which historical criticism plays no part ("it makes little difference [to the church] who wrote a Gospel"). The other part is historical criticism, which alone "decides about the dogmatic-historical use [Gebrauch] of every biblical book, as it does in the case of any other document." "Given the difficulty of these investigations, in times of conflict opposing viewpoints will seldom be lacking. But according to the previous results [of criticism]—and since in any case a core of [genuine] Pauline letters has withstood the most wanton criticism—it is not to be feared that the basic thoughts of original Christianity could ever be in doubt" [392f].—One easily recognizes Hase's mediation of science and faith.

Overbeck, in the *Christianity of Theology* (Chapter 3), speaks of the difference between the "spirit of the individual books" of the Bible—these are subject to historical criticism—and the "Spirit of the

Bible," which cannot be grasped by scientific means. This has an obvious connection with the mentioning of fides divina and fides humana in the inaugural lecture discussed above. Moreover, the distinction in the *Christianity of Theology* is clearly reminiscent of Hase's distinction between Spirit witnessing to the truth in the text (fides divina) and criticism of individual texts (fides humana). For Hase, fides divina and humana are not incompatible, in spite of problems in biblical criticism; they are the subjects of his mediating intent.

In the *Christianity of Theology* faith and science, or fides divina and humana, are not compatible "sisters" (to use a metaphor Overbeck once uses), but are naturally opposed to one another. For Hase, theology succeeds at its task, which is essentially mediation; for Overbeck, it fails. As seen above, Overbeck's inaugural lecture states that "harmony" (mediation) of faith and science is indeed the task of theology. The failure is demonstrated most obviously by the many conflicting results of the theologians in their new "house," historical criticism. It is significant that in the realization or awareness of this failure, Overbeck refers the theologian to "the inestimable goods of purer faith and deeper perception that we owe" to the Reformers, above all Luther, whose Commentary on Galatians is given prominent mention.[53] We now move to Overbeck's understanding of the origin of theology.

The Tübingen School's view of the canonization of the scriptures of the New Testament, as expressed by F.C. Baur, was that it came about in defense against Gnosticism and in effect established the Catholic doctrine of the authority of tradition. Insofar as the Tübinger saw their work as superceding such doctrine, the canon was of relatively minor importance in the world-historical development of the ideas that shaped Christian history.[54]

In the third of Overbeck's best known works—the other two being the *Christianity of Theology* and *Christentum und Kultur*—namely *Über die Anfänge der patristischen Literatur* [On the Beginnings of Patristic Literature], published in 1882,[55] canonization occurs in the church's transition from an existence that had little or nothing to do with the world of culture (Wissenschaft) and that was little or not at all recognized by it, into an existence that took culture into itself and came to be recognized as a factor in the culture. The canon is an "Urliteratur" [original literature] "that Christianity created so to speak by its own means, insofar as this literature grew exclusively on the basis of and within the particular interests of the Christian community prior to its mixture with the surrounding world."[56] An important feature of the canon is that, with the exception of the authentic letters of Paul, which contain their own witness to Paul's authorship and personal history, these writings are not accompanied by traditions about authorship, date of composition and historical situation. Furthermore, with the exception of letters (which have a personal address), the canon sets an end to the forms of literature it contains (as well as to the remaining noncanonical instances of these forms), insofar as the following patristic literature neither repeats nor imitates the forms, but bases its own forms of exegesis and theology on them. The forms of patristic exegesis are forms adopted from the culture or world which the canon has now entered and are forms of "Wissenschaft." The first Christian apologetic literature shows the beginning of the transition to the world of culture and marks the beginning of patristic literature. But patristic literature is first actually established when Christians use the adopted cultural ("profane") forms to communicate not with non-Christians, but with Christians [47ff]. It is this transition that is the focus of Overbeck's interest: he finds it in the literature of Clement of Alexandria, whose three-part chief work, *Protrepticus* [Admonishment of the Heathen], *Pedagogus* [The Teacher], and the lengthy *Stromata* [Colorful Tapestry], was begun prior to the beginning of the third century, approximately at the time or perhaps somewhat after the canon was first established. The chief feature of this transition is that the church finds itself in the situation of teaching heathen peoples Christianity in a way that had not occurred before. Irenaeus' apologetics against the heretics already addresses a problem within the church itself [48f]. Clement takes the further step of teaching Christianity to an increasingly large heathen public within the church, which he does on the presupposition of the canon of New Testament literature. This marks the transition not only to patristic literature but in a broader sense to all post-canonical Christian literature.

Clement wrestles with the problem of the inadequacy of his form of expression, including his theology of the universal Logos, which was derived mainly from Greek philosophy. He is profoundly aware of the hermeneutical problem of discussing the Christian faith in forms derived from Greco-Roman culture [66]. His purpose in his three-part chief work is to lead the new Christian through an initiation into Christianity, beginning with his conversion from paganism. The final and by far longest part of this literary initiation is the *Stromata*, in which Clement's intent is to make the educated Christian who seeks understanding "ripe" for the highest truths of Christianity. The form Clement chooses is paradoxical: while it has the practical purpose of instruction, it conceals rather than reveals its content. As Clement says, it is like the shell of a nut that has to be broken to reveal its fruit. The casual reader will be turned away, but the reader who has achieved "ripeness" will find the fruit.[57] The plan of the work is intentionally "formless." This not only serves Clement's pedagogical purpose but also expresses a genuine dilemma, for there is an unbridgeable gab between Clement's presentation and highest truth: it cannot be communicated in the "profane" forms of Clement's theology. The canonical expression of Christianity is the New Testament, which contains highest truth, yet this truth lies beyond the initial understanding of Clement's educated new Christian.[58] Therein lies the practical need—the "passion" [Leidenschaft], as Overbeck writes—that drives Clement to write the book in spite of his serious reservations [62]. According to Overbeck Clement's plan is not only formless but also endless. Clement launches the attempt without knowing how it will end, and the work has no real conclusion, but arbitrarily stops [51f, 56f].

The content of Overbeck's work on Clement, published in 1882, is already present in a lecture of Overbeck's from the year 1870, *Christliche Literaturgeschichte bis Eusebius von Caesarea* [A103]. Moreover between 1868 and 1870 Overbeck translated into German Clement's entire *Stromata*.[59] His understanding of Clement was therefore developed prior to and is a presupposition for both the *Christianity of Theology* (1873) and the inaugural lecture, *Entstehung und Recht* (1870), considered above.[60] In this lecture the task of establishing harmony between faith and "our scientific mind" is the 19th century expression of Clement's "practical" problem of teaching the Christian faith to the educated Greek. Both are part of the "unending task of encompassing all earthly life," the task of the church in general. Both look back to the "purer faith" of a religiously purer period—in Clement's case, the New Testament period, in the case of contemporary theology, the Reformation. And if Clement found no conclusion to his work, neither does Protestant theology, which obviously fails its task of harmonizing faith and science, which is to say its task has no end. According to the *Christianity of Theology* [Chap. 1], Christian theology—as a post-canonical historical form of literature—originates with Clement and his student Origen. It is not purely science or purely a form of cultural knowledge (Wissen, Wissenschaft), insofar as it is also determined by its "practical" interest of teaching Christian faith. The subject of Clement's theological reflection is the hermeneutical character or structure of every theology. Patristic literature is specifically "the Greco-Roman literature of Christian confession."[61] But structurally the definition can be used for any historical period.

In his work on the beginnings of patristic literature [62f], the feature of world or cultural literature that Overbeck mentions most prominently is that it is written for an "ideal public," that is, a public the author does not know and that does not know him, as for example in a work of philosophy or history. It is as history or philosophy that the work gains the attention of the reader. This is the basic form, "literature" itself, that Clement and all later theology assumes. Overbeck's occupation with the features of world literature is illustrated in a lecture from the year 1879, *Geschichte der christlichen Literatur bis Eusebius* [A104]. In the literature of a culture the writer is an individual who, precisely as an individual, writes for a public to whom he has no personal relationship. "In this sense there could be no Christian literature in the original Christian community. Here no one had the right to teach the community as such in his own name.... It is a matter of religious revelations that no individual in his own name can communicate." [64f]

A few pages later Overbeck writes [72-74]:

> According to the original Christian view, no one in the Christian community had the right to become a teacher in this community who was not in possession of the Spirit. Only the writing that could assert that it was written out of this Spirit could claim universal significance in the community. No human individual as such could assert himself as a preacher of truth. For the truth had already revealed itself, and no human individual as such could expand it. Such a subjective expansion of the truth does, however, take place in every work of real literature and especially in the work of Clement. It is very interesting to observe ... how deeply Clement feels the responsibility of what he does, how great his reluctance is, when he, from his own means and in his own name, undertakes the task of presenting the Christian truth. Is this truth not endangered by such a presentation? Is it not disfigured by such arbitrariness of the individual who places himself fully on himself [sich auf sich selbst gestellt]? Moreover does not a purely literary treatment draw into the light and profane what previously showed itself only in the mysterious, all conflict overcoming [allen Streit niederschalgenden] form of divine revelation? These are the questions that occupied and distressed the oldest Christian Alexandrians, the first real theologians and literary authors of the church.... Only with the canon is the possibility given in the Christian community of a free literature that stands only on the talent of the individual author and that is separated from the special source of Christian life.

In an earlier lecture, on the Gospel of John from the year 1877 [A92, 191f], he had written: "The author [of John], instead of lifting up himself with his work, which is certainly the usual way of literature, brings his product as it were as a sacrifice to the divine, the higher being that he worships. So the individuality of the writer disappears fully behind the subject he represents." The author of John knows the synoptic history of Jesus, but "knowledge" hardly expresses his relationship to it. He is "wholly filled" by it and "hangs on it with his whole faith"; he lifts it in holy poetry above all reality and is himself "transported" [entrückt] beyond it [184]. Nothing motivates him to write but his faith, no "talent for writing" [185]. Perhaps most remarkable is Overbeck's description of John's experience: "Subjectively, personally, with his own will and feeling [Empfindung], he is to the least possible degree involved in [what he writes] ... For only such silence of his own will and feeling permit perception [Erkenntnis], the quiet and clear view [Blick] that indeed sees the things [Dinge] as they are ..." [181]. Overbeck generalizes beyond the limits of the canon: "In every century, where Christian faith has been a living faith, church history is full of holy poetry" [187]. Poetic vision of truth is a subject of German Romanticism. In his work on the life of Jesus, Christian Herrmann Weisse, who taught Overbeck at Leipzig, writes that poetic vision is the core of Christian myth. Mundane reason cannot contain the fullness of revelation; myth is "spirit-filled vision that penetrates through the veil of outer historical facts to their inner essence and connection." [62]

The New Testament period is for Overbeck the eminently spiritual period of the church, when faith is expressed as a vision of Christ that is so strong that the church lives in it. In the *Studien zur Geschichte der alten Kirche* from the year 1875, Overbeck had written that Christian teachers of the New Testament period comforted Christian slaves "by holding before them no other worldview [Weltbild] than their Lord" [225]. This "worldview," the Lord Christ, is a wholly other world than "this world" and its sinful reality, and no compromise between them is possible. Only for a "worldly" culture, in whatever form and in whatever time, Christ is real only as mediated with, as taken into culture as an element within it. In his work on Clement, Overbeck reflected on the task of theology as mediator between worldviews that, for original Christianity and for Clement himself, cannot be mediated. This is also the theme of the *Christianity of Theology*.

Overbeck's "Lectures on the Doctrine of the Trinity and Christology," held in Jena in 1865/1866 [A108], is the only lecture Overbeck gave on doctrine. Not only the subject but also the method distinguishes it from his other works. This lengthy lecture, based on the concept of a development of doctrine from Genesis to Nicea, has as its center a very brief statement on the religious life of Jesus. In Jesus, God and humanity are one in the "unbroken simplicity" of his person and teaching, as illustrated in his saying, "you should become as children." Jesus knows that such unity is possible only by "breaking with the world." Overbeck remarks that this is only apparently similar to the asceticism of the philosophy of the time, insofar as Jesus' break with the world occurs at a far deeper level.[63] "This philosophy was not able to renounce the world, no matter how hard it tried; it had gone out from the world and returned ever again to the world ...." So also there is little evidence of "becoming as children" in later (patristic) theology's doctrinal wars about Jesus' divinity [200-202]. This theology "did not mediate," but "forced together" the original teaching of Christianity and pre-Christian philosophy [204].

Overbeck's presentation of Jesus is not remarkable; it corresponds to expressions in the tradition of Schleiermacher. The "break with the world," however, is not a part of this tradition, as was not the failed attempt of ascetic philosophy. Overbeck dealt with essentially the same theme in special lectures at Jena in 1864 and 1867, on the origins of Christian monasticism: In a time when the church had rapidly become all too worldly, monastic renunciation of world originated as an attempt to gain or regain the purer faith of the apostolic period of the church; it expanded dramatically in the Constantinian era, when an unholy mass swarmed into the church. But its attempt to live in renunciation of the world failed; indeed with time it became a worldly tool in the hands of the medieval church.[64] Similar to Clement of Alexandria's high regard

for the New Testament canon and church, in its origin monasticism ele-
vates the purer faith of the New Testament period. And its tragic fall
into wordliness prefigures Overbeck's understanding of the fate of theology in modern Protestantism.

The Late Overbeck and the Problem of Overbeck-Interpretation

Overbeck's late work is chiefly criticism of Christian theology.
The Kirchenlexikon swells with ever new expositions of its problematic
methods and assumptions, its triumphalism and hidden egoism—in
brief its accommodation to the "modern world." The church itself is
"modern." In a late manscript Overbeck writes that he withdrew from
public worship services after the publication of the *Christianity of Theology* [A272c]. Perhaps he was motivated by something like what motivated those early monks to withdraw from the world.[65]
Most interpreters have drawn the conclusion from the late notes
that Overbeck lost whatever Christian faith he had earlier. Yet it is possible that the "formless" method of Overbeck's late notes is, in a certain
way, learned from Clement of Alexandria's method, in the *Stromata*, of
teaching the educated heathen in the church.[66] Overbeck's situation is,
however, in an important sense the reverse of Clement's, insofar as in
the modern period the world's scientific understanding has taken possession of Christianity, explaining faith in its terms. But theology continues to work as if science were in its service, naively betraying its
own worldliness. The late 19th century is the period when "modern"
German theology was most confident of its union of science or "Wissenschaft" and faith, the age of Adolf Harnack—the "gilded age" of
theology, so to speak.
The interpretation of Overbeck as, in a certain sense, a student of
Clement of Alexandria's method must withstand the serious doubt
raised by radical late statements of Overbeck concerning his personal
relationship to Christianity, which are found mainly in a manuscript
dated in January, 1898 [A267c "Tagebuchartiges"]. Overbeck writes
that out of regard for the city of Basel he does not reveal its content
publically; he left it together with the rest of his late manuscripts, such
as the Kirchelexikon, for later discovery. His comments have to do with
his position as professor of theology: "I was indeed professor of theology but as such [dabei] neither theologian nor Christian." "Since my
Christianity of Theology, no serious person may consider me a Christian. In the book I explained the reservation with which I wanted to remain a theologian, namely my personal unbelief...."[67] That is a serious
invitation to read the book, and his comments in its second edition of
1903 clearly say that the *Christianity of Theology* states what he thinks
late in life as much as it did when he wrote it. The expressions of unbelief may be ironic, which is a literary device he employs elsewhere. The
sentence beginning, "I was indeed professor of theology," may be re-

formulated: "Indeed I professed theology, but in doing so was neither theologian nor Christian." Certainly one wonders how a person such as Overbeck, whose integrity is so broadly acclaimed, as a non-Christian could have remained a (prominent) member of a theological faculty, who by virtue of this office also served as Rector of the University of Basel, especially if the problem arose already with the publication of the *Christianity of Theology* in 1873 (cf. the discussion of Lagarde's proposal in Chapter 5 of the *Christianity of Theology*.)

If his radical late notes are nothing more than statements of unbelief, then obviously the Christian religion dissolved for him into scientific knowing or "Wissenschaft," as it had for Strauss some forty years previously. According to Strauss original Christianity was fantastically eschatological, and no one more than Strauss advised theology to get on with being truly modern by ridding itself of its outdated "half-and-half" nonsense. If the late Overbeck is nothing more than a skeptic, then he has hardly progressed beyond Strauss, unless a pessimistic worldview were considered progress. But in this case one would have to compare him with Eduard von Hartmann in *Die Selbstzersetzung des Christentums*, which, however, Overbeck rejected. Moreover, since nothing resembling a new religion had appeared to take Christianity's place for him, Overbeck would seem to be nothing more than a skeptic, that is, a person without benefit of even a philosophical belief system (which Strauss certainly had), a person who found no greater meaning in life than endlessly and perhaps pathologically filling manuscripts with skeptical arguments about theology and modern Christianity. But this would be to ignore all that speaks against such an interpretation.[68] According to a note in the Kirchenlexikon entitled "Religion und Offenbarung [Revelation]," science has to conclude that revelation is of human origin; "in science man is the measure of all things." This is his perspective in the late notes: "profane" science, man as the measure: fides humana.

Assuming that both his profane method and his comments about his unbelief in Christianity contain an element of concealment—that here one may have to do with a method learned from Clement of Alexandria—what purpose might such a method have served? Overbeck is famous for the statement, made in these late notes, that he demonstrates "finis christianismi am modernen Christentum" [the end of Christianity in modern Christianity].[69] "Modern" Christianity is dying of old age, as evidenced by its being indistinguishable from culture and world; its theologians are but rouge on its pale cheeks.[70] Overbeck's message is radical: "modern" theology cannot work in support of faith; its only possible service to faith would be to give up being "modern" and recognize the difference between "world" and faith, which effectively means its own dissolution. Quite obviously Overbeck means to be a scandal for theology, and he could give no greater offense than by saying that for some thirty years he had been a professor of theology, but "as such" not a Christian. Hypothetically speaking, had he in some way or other confessed faith in these notes, there would have been no offense; he would have been "theologically" dealt with and relegated to a paragraph in a theological dictionary.[71] Instead he ironically mirrors the reality he criticizes. In *Christentum und Kultur* [292] one finds the words, addressed to "modern theology": "you are modern, but I even more!" "Modern" theology is theology that is "conscious of its timeliness [Zeitgemassheit]."[72]

In a rather famous note, dated May 7, 1905, approximately two months before his death on June 26, entitled "Letzte Theologie" [Last Theology], Overbeck writes that what he has experienced, especially from his studies, in the continuing "earthly world" has taken away his childlike belief [Kinderglauben] in God, but not such belief in humanity [den Menschen]. He expresses his thankfulness for his medical doctor and for the humanity the doctor represents in overcoming his sense of resignation in the face of death. On the reverse side of the page he writes: "Religion has no other foundation than myth and legend, that is, insofar as one can at all think of its scientific foundation, it is only to be taken from myth and legend. But therefore religion is useless for the salvation of humanity ... For legend is itself human work and only this and therefore in its effects cannot go beyond the limits of humanity..." But there is, he continues, a covenant among persons [Menschenbund] that we humans need to lift us out of the confusion of world [Weltgedränge], a covenant that must have its ground in us. "If we cannot expect salvation from ourselves, the individual from himself or from his kind, then it is for us generally unforeseeable [unabsehbar]."[73]

The presupposition is the "scientific foundation," from which follows salvation within the limits of human covenant and work. Religion or religious faith, or the limit between science and religion, has disappeared altogether. And yet in the late notes Overbeck writes about this limit. For example, in the Kirchenlexikon under the title "Philosophie und Leben" [Philosophy and Life] one finds a discussion of Schopenhauer, written with reference to Johannes Volkelt's book, *Arthur Schopenhauer* (Stuttgart, 1900), in which Overbeck speaks of the "eternal barriers [Schranken] between religion and philosophy." "In the human world religion and philosophy exist side by side ..."—Why has the "limit" disappeared in the note on "last theology"? Is the title an ironic commentary on theology's "last" consequence, its disappearance into the secular world? There is a note with a theme similar to "last theology" and with a later date, May 17, 1905, under the title "Markus 1,12. 13" [A207 Exegetika]. Here Overbeck writes, "if one cannot imagine another proof for religion than myth and legend, there should be no objection to obtaining a proof for religion from a poet rather than a dry and barren demonstrator such as a theologian ..." Such proof occurs "within the unclear limits or outlines in which human poetry can let truth shine forth" [Wahrheit hervorleuchten lassen kann].[74] What "truth" can he mean? This is clearly reminiscent of what Overbeck wrote earlier [25] and of F.A. Lange's theory of the "twofold truth," that of science and that of poetic religion, and of the limit that separates them.

The late notes contain not only criticism of theology and "modern" Christianity but also comments on the Gospel and Christianity that illustrate original Christianity's "break with the world." For example, under the title "Matthew 7,1" [A207 Exegetica] he writes that the verse "judge not that you be not judged" (Matth. 7:1) is "one of the greatest in the Gospel" and can only be unusable for and stand outside any moral philosophy [i.e., science]. The note lists a cross-reference to a note in the Kirchenleikon, "Religion und Moral. Vermischtes," which contains a longer discussion on Matth. 7:1. Here the verse is called one of the "deepest" in the Gospel. The discussion links Matth. 7:1 with Matth. 19:19, "love your neighbor as yourself." Another note, "Matthew 18,3" [A207], "become as children," names this verse a "foundational law" of the Gospel. Jesus knows he cannot ask this of his disciples in "this world": he means it only in the context of his second coming and the near end of the world.[75] In a late note in the Kirchen-lexikon, "Theologie (moderne) Urchristentum," Overbeck writes: "Genuine Christianity is never anything other than the perception [Empfindung] of the nearness of eternal life and the forgetting of the fact that the duration of world history shoves itself between this eternal life and the life in the temporal world."

Other late notes have to do with the knowledge of God. "In every assertion, at least in every such religious confession, of a human knowledge [Kunde] of God, it can only be a matter of whether or not God knows us, not whether or not we know him. For we know [wissen] that the latter is not the case." This note in the Kirchenlexikon under the title, "Gott bekannt" [God known], is cross-referenced by another note under the title "Gottesglauben," which was published in *Christentum und Kultur*, 266: "Religion gives us less knowledge [Kunde] of God ... than it wants to assure us that God knows us. In itself, knowing God on our part could help nothing, insofar as we feel in need of help. Rather, everything would depend on God knowing us ...." These statements seem and indeed must be pointless, unless one remembers texts in Paul that have to do with God knowing us, for example 1 Corinthians 13:12. A lecture of Overbeck's from 1868/69 on 1 Corinthians [A114; it ends at 1 Cor. 8:6] gives a commentary on 1 Cor. 8:1-3, which reads (I translate from Overbeck's German): "Knowledge [Erkenntnis] inflates, love upbuilds. If anyone thinks he has perceived [erkannt] something, he has perceived nothing at all as one must perceive. If one loves God, such a one is known [erkannt] by him." Overbeck's commentary on these verses is as follows: "Because common gnosis is not at all the right knowledge, Paul designates it as an imagined knowledge.... To perceive as one must—to this belongs necessarily love. In verse three Paul

names the highest in relation to agape, which is also the highest in relation to gnosis: whoever loves God has the right love, and the consequence is that he is known by God. Here it is self-evident that he also
has the right gnosis. That he is known by God means that God has entered into a direct relationship with him, that an activity goes from God
to and in him, a relationship that must have effect and so brings true
gnosis." —Such knowledge is not "worldy," that is, not a form of science, but religious and entirely dependent on revelation. In a late note
in the Kirchenlexikon, "Christentum (modernes) Charakteristik Allgemeines," Overbeck writes, in obvious contradistinction to fides humana: "In Christianity the name of Christ proves all or nothing.... That is
the divinity of this name, that it proves itself or is not to be proven...."
Here too the proof is religious, not scientific, and the knowledge that
comes from it is derived purely from the religious proof. In Paul the
perception of Christ is also the perception of the sinfulness of
"world"—a "higher criticism" of another kind.

   After *Christentum und Kultur* was published in 1919, Karl Barth
discussed it in a long article published in English under the title, "Unsettled Questions for Theology Today," in *Theology and Church,
Shorter Writings 1920-1928*, edited by T.F. Torrance (New York:
Harper & Row, 1962). Barth's evaluation was highly positive: Overbeck's criticisms of theology and church were prophetically accurate,
and as a critical and skeptical theologian he was "a witness to the mission" of the Christ-proclamation of (the practical theologian) Johann
Christoph Blumhardt. He "was not without holy fire," and "presumably
there is great appreciation in heaven" for his work. What Barth also
highly valued in Overbeck was the recognition that for Jesus and original Christianity the near end of the world was an indelible part of the
Gospel, and that there was a clear difference between theology's worldliness and original Christianity's proclamation of the Kingdom of God.
Overbeck became a major inspiration for a new beginning in theology,
a theology "between the times," as the new group of "dialectical theologians" called it.[76] The second edition of Barth's commentary on Romans, published in 1921, which gave prominent mention to Overbeck,
became the marker of this new beginning.[77]

   Wherever Overbeck was read with appreciation in the 1920's, the
old liberals of Adolf Harnack's time were targets of criticism. Barth
said they as a generation had failed to hear what Overbeck was saying.
The response was soon heard, primarily in the writing of a friend of
Harnack and colleague of Overbeck at Basel, Eberhard Vischer, who
published a sharp three-part criticism of Overbeck in the leading theological journal of the time, a publication with the portentous title
"Christian World": *Die Christliche Welt* [1922, 108-112; 125-130; 142-
148], to which Barth replied with a short article in the same publication
[1922, 249; Vischer's brief reply, 286f]. For Vischer (who also mis-
quotes Overbeck), Overbeck was, like his friend Nietzsche, an atheist,

and hostile to theology and church. The main thrust of Barth's reply is stated in his title, "Still Unsettled Questions." Here he writes, "I have a witness for my understanding of the historical Overbeck who really knew him better than Eberhard Vischer. But I do not insist, because I cannot produce a document on it..."

Barth was referring to a conversation he had with Overbeck's wife, Ida, which is documented privately in letters by both Barth and Ida Overbeck. Barth's is in a letter to his friend, Eduard Thurneysen; Ida Overbeck's is in a letter to the editor of *Christentum und Kultur*, C.A. Bernoulli. Barth's words are not entirely clear; they say she depicted her husband in a way that precisely agrees with his and Thurneysen's understanding.[78] The documentation by Ida Overbeck is more interesting. The editor of *Christentum und Kultur*, C.A. Bernoulli, had heard about the conversation with Barth by way of Thurneysen, who had mentioned it to a group of pastors in Basel. He asks her in a letter, dated Nov. 11, 1927, what she had told Barth. There are two versions of her reply, a first draft and the final copy. The key sentences are, first, in the draft: "I felt for a moment a unison [Zusammenklingen] of souls, but lifted myself quickly to honor the other truth: that my husband's point of view [Betrachtungsweise] certainly [allerdings] presented Christianity from within [von Innen heraus], yet with an objectivity that corresponds to this outside [die dieser Aussenseite entspreche]." In the final version this sentence reads, "I felt for a moment the unison of souls, but then gathered myself to honor the other truth, which could not astonish them: that my husband's point of view flowed fully from within religion [dem Innern der Religion], yet wore an objective cloak, an outsider cloak [Aussenseiter-Gewand] ."[79]

These sentences are all the more remarkable in view of the fact that Overbeck entrusted his wife, Ida, with the selection of material for *Christentum und Kultur*. Bernoulli ordered it into sections, fused many notes together, changed the wording as he thought needed—at many points his intervention is all too strong—and added the titles.[80] Traces of Ida Overbeck's work in the late manuscripts can be found, for example, in the Kirchenlexikon under the title "Glauben und Wissen (Vermischtes)," where she writes, "I am not to copy anything old," that is, she was only to copy a selection of Overbeck's late notes for the publication that Bernoulli named *Christentum und Kultur* (cf. X). This is important, insofar as many of the early notes as well as other early manuscripts clearly give witness to Overbeck as a religious person.

There is of course more to the story of the late Overbeck's notoriety in and outside Basel, especially the various and contrary assessments of his friendship with Nietzsche. Two important later works appeared, both based on manuscript material, that supported the view, against Karl Barth, that Overbeck was an unbelieving skeptic: Walter Nigg, *Franz Overbeck, Versuch einer Wurdigung* (Munich: C.H. Beck, 1931), and Eberhard Vischer's edition of Overbeck's late autobiographical notes that Vischer titled *Selbstbekenntnisse* (Basel: Benno Schwabe, 1941). Nigg had used manuscript material—either all or a large part of the Kirchenlexikon—on loan from Bernoulli. Recently published correspondence between Barth and Eduard Thurneysen from the 1930's shows that Barth immediately read the copy of Nigg's book he was sent (prior to publication). He responded to Nigg that it had not brought forth anything new that decisively clarified the different problems of Overbeck interpretation.[81] Barth's reading of Nigg fell in the period when he was making his theological turn to the *Church Dogmatics*, a very different work from that of the 1920's.[82] Whatever the reason, he showed no further interest in arguing publicly about Overbeck, nor did he read in the manuscripts, which became the property of the University of Basel in the late 1930's. He became reserved about Overbeck, neither denying nor affirming his earlier understanding.[83] Broad interest in Overbeck was not reawakened until the 1960's, when the publication of Martin Tetz's guide to the Overbeck archives in Basel invited research by an increasing number of scholars.

Contemporary scholars who think Overbeck divorced himself from Christianity usually do credit him with having "told the truth" about theology. Among those of an earlier generation none is more appreciative than Karl Löwith: "His was an absolutely honest mind... He elucidated the problem which Christianity presents for us."[84] According to Löwith Overbeck's presentations of the problems of Christianity's life in history, his criticisms of theology and church, both liberal and conservative, still ring true.

Nietzsche represented for Overbeck the modern world that theology only thinks it understands and has in hand. It is an interesting fact that the anti-theology of Overbeck's late manuscripts parallels in a certain way the radicalism of Nietzsche's late works. Nietzsche, one of the great masters of style in literature, was also a master of irony. His complex method draws the reader with enticement and offense ever deeper into his labyrinths of reflection. Here too one can be reminded of Clement of Alexandria's *Stromata*. One of the things that makes Overbeck interesting and at times amusing is his use of irony. The following is taken from autobiographical notes probably from the year 1898 [A267a], where he comments on a letter dated in the year 1883 from Nietzsche's devoted helper, Heinrich Köselitz, or Peter Gast, as he named himself. Overbeck writes that in reading what Gast says about Overbeck's "Lebensaufgabe," task for life, he doubts that anyone "has ever been so well understood." He then quotes from Gast's letter: "Nietzsche fights directly against Christianity: in doing this he unintentionally maintains it. In your hand it is given—without causing Christianity pain, without exciting it to counter-action—to make it impossible with time [temporality, history], by taking the protocol of its past." He adds the comment, "The task assigned to me by Köselitz is the only one I have thought myself able to take on."[85]

Concealment in the "Christianity of Theology"

In Chapter 1 [66] Overbeck expresses the book's most important thesis: faith cannot keep the points of attack it necessarily exposes to science away from science unless it wills to do so. This is a motive for concealment, and, if one assumes Overbeck practices concealment elsewhere, the question is raised about the book itself. Certainly some points in the book seem to contradict others. For example, in Chapter 3, Overbeck represents, against the "half-science, half-faith" method of liberal theology, D.F. Strauss' critical perception of the difference between the religion of Jesus and Christianity. Overbeck concludes that such a religion of Jesus "could prove whether or not it has more value ... than that of an historical discovery by being serviceable to us for the establishment of a new religion" [91]. The statement reminds one of Lagarde's and Hartmann's call for a "new religion" and, in Largarde, for a critical theology that will prepare the way for it. But in Chapter 5, in response to Lagarde, Overbeck writes, "one has never heard of a theology preceding a religion," and the course of religion is something "most ungraspable [for science], seen only by ecstatic prophets" [117]. In another place in Chapter 3 he writes, referring to his work on the Acts of the Apostles: "We [sc. I] have recently given the letter its rightful due and based on it above all what we call the historical meaning, in order with its help to determine at most the 'spirit' of individual books in the Bible. But we have given up all scientific-exegetical means of catching hold of what earlier times called the 'Spirit of the Bible' ..." [104]. Here Overbeck both acknowledges such a "Spirit" and withdraws it from science. The text is a parallel to the distinction between fides humana and fides divina in his inaugural lecture, *Entstehung und Recht* [above, 20].

At the end of the Chapter 2 Overbeck states another thesis: the Christian "view of world and life originally sprouted the myths and dogmas [of Christianity] as the stem sprouts the leaves" [88]. The image of the sprouting stem may have been conceived in contrast to Strauss' famous image of the historical Jesus as a dead tree covered by the vines of myth [above, 12]. As one knows from other passages in Overbeck's book, the "view of life" from which the myths and dogmas originate is "world denying," and "world denial is the inmost soul of Christianity" [98]. But in the *Christianity of Theology* Overbeck never explains what the actual agent of the denial is. There must be an agent, insofar as, by itself, a mere negative, denial, can produce nothing. In Overbeck's following work, *Studien zur Geschichte der alten Kirche* [225], he does name the agent. He speaks of the "source of light in whose brightness the first teachers of Christianity let pass away, along with the world, the world's suffering.... Only by holding up no other picture of the world [Weltbild] than their Lord to the slaves, looking beyond all suffering of the world, ...did the ancient church think it could help the slave... Only in lifting masters and slaves into the sphere of peace that the world was not supposed to give..."[86] Here the agent of the denial of the present (sinful) world reality is Christ, the "Weltbild" of faith. This "view of life," of the reality of Christ, is the living stem that sprouts the leaves of the myths and dogmas.[87]

In Chapter 3 Overbeck writes about the result of the "historical discovery of the human being of Jesus": "...even if in the first moment of Christianity's emergence as a universal religion it lifted Christ to the status of divine being, it nevertheless without justification projected this conception of him back into the origins of history... Only [this projection] made Christianity the universal religion we call Christianity" [90]. The "origins of history" ["vorausgegangene Urzeit"] is not, as it at first seems, a reference to New Testament Christology but to the logos theology of early Christian apologetics, which is for F.C. Baur a key moment in the transition of Christianity to world-historical significance.[88] A central thesis of Chap. 1 is that what we call Christianity is a mixture of Christian religion with antique culture, in this case with Greek philosophy. Overbeck's words, "lifted Christ..." refer to post-resurrection belief about Jesus. The context for critical discussion of the resurrection had been set by Strauss, for whom the resurrection was "world-historical humbug," and by Baur's epochal statement that the fact on which Christianity was founded was not the resurrection but the faith of the first Christians in it.[89] Notably Overbeck attaches no statement of "without justification" to the "lifting of Christ to the status of a divine being," the presupposition of which is the resurrection experience.

Overbeck writes about the resurrection in a lecture that bears dates from the years 1867-1870, *Geschichte des apostolischen Zeitalters* [A102, History of the Apostolic Period]. In 1861 a work by Karl Holsten had appeared that gave a psychological explanation of the resurrection appearances; it was soon appropriated by D.F. Strauss. Overbeck incorporates it in his lecture as the "scientific" explanation. It held that the resurrection was nothing more than a subjective vision—not unusual in the ancient world—produced by Paul's excited state of mind in combination with his Pharisaic belief in resurrection.[90] But Overbeck does not simply repeat Holsten's argument. The key to all resurrection appearances, he writes, is not the resuscitation of the earthly body, this is later myth, but "the presupposition of a perceptible reality that somehow goes beyond the earthly." The textual evidence in the New Testament demonstrates the reality only of the vision, not of the presupposition [100-103]. "If the scientific consideration of this subject prevents us from finding here the altogether transcendent miracle the church bases on our sources, science is yet very far from judging [the vision] as a mundane event unworthy of deeper reflection. We are very badly informed about a subjective event of this kind, which is just as deep [tiefsinning] as it is mysterious." Science "is not able to draw firm limits

[Schranken] to the fantasy of the individual" [115]. Later in the lecture he writes that in 1 Corinthians 15 the "reality" Paul experiences is heavenly (himmlische Sinnlichkeit), not earthly, but our "immediate" response to it is to consider it a subjective vision [248]. Overbeck's intention is clear enough: within the framework of what science can determine, namely that the central experience of the resurrection is a subjective vision, there exists the possibility of something having happened that science does not understand. (His word "fantasy"—in German, "Phantasie"—is mistakenly translated as mere imagination; correct is the more original sense of the word, subjective vision.)

The possibility that Overbeck suggests is found in Christian Hermann Weisse, *Philosophische Dogmatik oder Philosophie des Christentums* (Leipzig, 1862), I, III, 437-441, cf. 404f, 682. According to Weisse, resurrection experiences of Jesus were subjective visions in which the visible earthly world played no part; rather, the "heavenly matter" of Jesus appearance (1 Cor. 15) in the "soul" of the witnesses was of an order that it could only be experienced in such a vision. Strauss had attacked Weisse's position as but another example of "half faith, half science" mediation theology.[91] Strauss admits no "limit" to the psychological-scientific explanation of the resurrection experiences. As cautiously as they are made, Overbeck's statements on the resurrection are also exposed to Strauss' criticism. He avoids exposure in the *Christianity of Theology* by withdrawing the resurrection from the grasp of science, by only presupposing the "lifting" of Christ "to the status of a divine being."

In Chapter 5 Overbeck makes the proposal that the cleric or pastor not be bound by any oath of office in his personal convictions and thinking—the cleric's conscience should be free—but only in his preaching and teaching [122]. The recommended oath is further specified as a formula that "binds him in the practice of the office to the need [Bedürfnis] of his parish, whether simply to this need or to certain confessional statements acknowledged in the parish." In 19th century Germany such a proposal had to remind the educated reader of Kant's proposal, in the short writing, *What is Enlightenment?*, according to which official authority is allowed to bind the cleric to the church's confession in his preaching and teaching in the church, but not in his written publications.[92] But Overbeck never mentions Kant (or the Prussian "Religionsedikt" of 1788 to which his writing was related). Instead he cites the example of Origen, who divided the church into simple believers and sophisticated thinkers or gnostics, that is, theologians, as he had stated in Chapter 1 [69]. We have seen this division, between the "exoteric" and the "esoteric," in the theological discussions of the 19th century before Overbeck, where it corresponded to the division between criticism and church. The question is, how seriously does Overbeck mean the parallel between his proposal and Origen's division of simple believers and theologians? What does he mean by the "need" of a contemporary parish? In the late 19th century (after Feuerbach), "need" in religious matters is, without further definition, especially ambiguous. Overbeck knew this, hence he must have intended the ambiguity. But in other contexts he gives clues for how it should be understood. In Chapter 4 he writes that, while Strauss optimistically urges self-reliance, the individual person today is in fact "helpless" [111]. Several sentences in Overbeck's next book, *Studien zur Geschichte der alten Kirche* [67], are noteworthy. He writes that after the canonization of Paul's letters, there were two ways for the church to regain an understanding of his ideas, one being the science of exegesis, the other the "practical needs" of the church. While the former is only "outward" in bringing forth Paul's thoughts, "the practical need of the church" can give them life. "There are moments in the history of the church ... when now this, now that Pauline idea, which before had been a not at all understood dead letter, suddenly becomes a living truth." (Augustine and the Reformation are cited as examples.) In these sentences "need" refers to the Christian doctrine of humanity's need for redemption, its factual helplessness. "Erlösungsbedürfnis," need of redemption or salvation, was common expression of Overbeck's time; one finds it in philosophy as well as in Christian theology.[93] Again one must conclude that in the *Christianity of Theology* Overbeck leaves certain things unsaid, things that only the "attentive reader," as he once writes [82], notices and questions.

As has been noted before, Overbeck clearly makes the *Christianity of Theology* the link between his late and early work. To quote again what was quoted above from Overbeck's late manuscripts: "Since my *Christianity of Theology*, no serious person may consider me a Christian. In the book I explained the reservation with which I wanted to remain a theologian, namely my personal unbelief..." What he explains in Chapter 1 is that theology, insofar as it is scientific—and science indelibly belongs to it—is "unbelieving." No more is said about unbelief than this. In the Afterword of the book's second edition of 1903, he criticizes his understanding of theology in the book in only one sense, namely that he had spoken of "critical" theology as a "better" theology [107]. What he recognizes in the Afterword is that this is no better theology.

"A writing for conflict and for peace"—this phrase stood on the title page and is discussed briefly in the preface of the first edition of the *Christianity of Theology*. In the discussion above [25] a text was quoted from Overbeck's 1879 lecture, *Geschichte der christlichen Literatur bis Eusebius*, that contains the phrase: "the mysterious, all conflict overcoming form of divine revelation." This is the mystery that Clement of Alexandria perceives as characteristic of the canonical literature, but not of that of his own time. In 1877 Overbeck published a seventy-three page piece on the understanding among the church fathers of the conflict between Paul and Peter in Antioch that Paul writes about in Galatians 2:11 ff. Overbeck demonstrates that the theological apologetics of the fathers and, by extension, of today's theologians to resolve the conflict through various harmonizing explanations of Peter's behavior, fails, and he ends the work by challenging apologetics to "recognize itself" in the problematic of the discussion.[94] This is essentially the same failure of theology to harmonize faith and science in the inaugural lecture of 1870, *Entstehung und Recht* [above, 20ff]. In the *Christianity of Theology*, "peace" is represented by religion [122], the corollary to revelation in the quotation about Clement and the mystery of the "form of revelation." At its best science also works toward this end, above all through criticism of bad science and theology.

In the *Christianity of Theology* the New Testament writers are not theologians because they have nothing to do with "Wissenschaft." The language of the New Testament is the language of a non-worldly reality; it is not developed through culture and its sciences. Yet all New Testament language is drawn from the language of the world (Chapter 1). Therefore it is necessarily exposed to the analysis and explanations of science, and the very fact that it is canonized makes it an ideal object of criticism, which acknowledges no sacred boundaries. The angel, so to speak, that guards the gate of the New Testament and the Bible generally, its only mode of concealment against science, is the Spirit. Science for itself must object that "Spirit" is only imagined, as Strauss had objected to fides divina. For Overbeck, for the sake of truth as humanity is given to determine it, fides humana must explain what it can explain. (Overbeck will later call this "profane church history.") Fides divina hears the reality proclaimed in the New Testament in the Spirit in which it was proclaimed.[95] At the end of Chapter 5 Overbeck says that no "theory" brings "Wissen" (fides humana) and "Glauben" (fides divina) together [124]. He rejects any and every "theology of mediation" because mediation is impossible, which is especially apparent in modernity, when every religious statement is grasped and explained by science. The thought is not new: it is Paul's difference between the wisdom of the world and the foolishness of God; or again it is Luther's understanding of the irreconcilable difference between Word, Spirit and faith, on the one hand, and the reason and law of the "world" on the other, as he repeatedly says in his Galatians commentary of 1531.

NOTES

Criticism and Faith, Theology and Church

1. Letter to Overbeck from A.E. Biedermann, dated Dec. 12, 1874, in: Paul Burckhardt, "Aus der Korrespondenz von A.E. Biedermann (1819-1885)," *Aus fünf Jahrhunderten schweizerischer Kirchengeschichte. Zum 60. Geburtstag von Paul Wernle.* Published by the Theological Faculty of the University of Basel (Basel, 1932), 352. All translations are mine.

2. Extant copies of the first edition of the *Studien zur Geschichte der alten Kirche* have the publication date 1875 (Schloss-Chemnitz: Ernst Schmeitzner), but its preface is dated September 28, 1874, and Biedermann's letter shows he received the book in late 1874.

3. Paul Burkhardt, 346.

4. Paul Burkhardt, 347.

5. Harnack, *What is Christianity?* Translated by T.B. Saunders (1st ed. 1900, reprint NY: Harper, 1957), 63.

6. *Die christliche Lehre von der Rechtferigung und der Versöhnung.* The third and last edition (Bonn, 1889) is the basis for the English translation edited by H.R. Mackintosh and A.B. Macaulay (NY: Charles Scribner's Sons; Edinburgh: T. & T. Clark, 1900). Unless otherwise noted, for the following statements of Ritschl's theology I refer especially to the Introduction of Vol. III.

7. With reference to Schopenhauer's philosophy of world denial, D.F. Strauss had compared Jesus and Buddha—both were "world renouncing"—in his last work, first published in 1871: *The Old Faith and the New,* translated by M. Blind (NY: H. Holt, 1873), 69. One may speculate that Ritschl's characterization of the *Christianity of Theology* as "Buddhist" associates Overbeck's book with Schopenhauer's interpretation of Christianity in *The World as Will and Representation,* trans. by E.F.J. Payne (NY: Dover, 1966), I, 383-408; II, 603ff: Buddhism, Brahmanism and Christianity teach essentially the same truth of denial of the will, but Buddhism does so with greater clarity. Overbeck himself later characterized Schopenhauer's interpretation of Christianity as Buddhist and called it "completely wrong": *Christentum und Kultur,* 3.

8. Schopenhauer, *The World as Will and Representation,* II, 187. The source in Overbeck's Kirchenlexikon has the title "Religion und Philosophie," 3f. Later notes in the Kirchenlexikon are discussions of work by Johannes Volkelt on Schopenhauer, esp. the book, *A. Schopenhauer* (Stuttgart, 1900). In a note with the title "Philosophie und Leben" (5), Overbeck writes: "In the human world religion and philosophy exist side by side and so also in Schopenhauer...."

9. An early note in Overbeck's Kirchenlexikon has the title "Gnosticismus und Schopenhauer" and refers to *The World as Will and Representation,* I, 404f. Overbeck's summary comments are: "knowledge [Erkenntnis] alone is salvific [erlöst]," and "approval of Gnostic docetism." On Schopenhauer's translation of traditional Christian doctrines into philosophical concepts see, e.g., *The World as Will and Representation,* II, 166f.

10. *History of Materialism,* trans. by E.C. Thomas, 3 Vols. (London: Trübner and Ludgate Hill, 1879-1881), III, 348f (process), 354 (dogmatism), 360 (symbolic power). Previous references are from III, 281-289, and the Chapter "Standpoint of the Ideal," III, 335-362. Lange's discussion of innate ideas in

their religious significance (II, 224) is more clearly expressed in the 1st edition of 1866, 276f. The English translation is of the 2nd edition of 1873, the preface of which is dated June, 1873, after Overbeck had completed the *Christianity of Theology*. On Lange see George Stack, *Lange and Nietzsche* (Berlin and NY: Walter de Gruyter, 1983).

11. Overbeck gives the reference: "Bd. II, S. 459f, 565 Anm. 12," which corresponds to the 3rd edition of 1877. The content corresponds to Vol. III, 281f. and 287fn., in the English translation, from which the following sentences are taken.

12. III, 345 (core of religion), 320 (translation into philosophical ideas), 287fn (accommodation to culture).

13. *Über Religion. Reden an die Gebildeten unter ihren Verächtern.* Both in German and English its standard version the edition of 1821, translated by John Oman and originally published in 1893 in London but also in later editions (NY: Harper Torchbooks, 1958; Louisville, KY: Westminster/John Knox Press, 1994), see esp. 13f, 21, 35, 87. The first edition of the work from the year 1799 has recently been translated by Richard Crouter (Cambridge and NY: Cambridge University Press, 1988).

14. E.g., Carl Schwarz, *Zur Geschichte der neuesten Theologie* (2nd ed. Leipzig, 1856), 15-19.

15. *Aus Schleiermachers Leben. In Briefen.* Vol. II (Berlin, 1860), 349-353. See R.R. Niebuhr, *Schleiermacher on Christ and Religion* (NY: Scribner's, 1964), 165- 171.

16. From Schleiermacher's "2nd Public Letter to Lücke," from the year 1829. *Friedrich D.E. Schleiermacher, Kritische Gesamtausgabe,* Vol. 10: *Theologisch-dogmatische Abhandlungen und Gelegenheitsschriften,* edited by H.-F. Traulsen (Berlin and NY: Walter de Gruyter), 347. Schleiermacher contrasts, e.g., the Christ of faith with the "wise man of Nazareth" and the "simple country rabbi" of recent biography.

17. The term "Vermittlungstheologie," "theology of mediation," designated in the middle of the 19th century a group of theologians in the tradition of Schleiermacher (e.g., K.I. Nitzsch, F. Lücke, I.A. Dorner) who tried to mediate between traditional Christianity and science. But it was later recognized that almost all theology of the period was in some sense theology of mediation.

18. D.F. Strauss, *Der Christus des Glaubens und der Jesus der Geschichte. Eine Kritik des Schleiermacherschen Leben Jesu* (Berlin, 1865), 23, 220; cf. 40f, 119, 210. English translation by Leander Keck, *The Christ of Faith and the Jesus of History* (Philadelphia: Fortress Press, 1977).

19. The clearest statement on the relationship between Vorstellung and philosophical knowledge (Wissen) is in Hegel's *Phenomenology of Spirit,* VII, C: Revealed Religion. Traditional Christian theology is for Hegel "reflective": it reflects on the biblical material. It does not achieve the higher level of true philosophy, which lifts or transforms the biblical material into pure concepts. F.C. Baur clearly states that dogmatic theology is "Vorstellung": *Lehrbuch der christlichen Dogmengeschichte* (3rd ed. Leipzig, 1867), 18.

20. See R.W. Mackay, *The Tübingen School and its Antecedents* (London and Edinburgh: Williams and Norgate, 1863); Horton Harris,*The Tübingen School* (Oxford: Clarendon, 1975); Peter Hodgson, *The Formation of Historical Theology: A Study of F.C. Baur* (NY: Harper, 1966).

21. Biedermann, *Die freie Theologie, oder Philosophie und Christentum in Streit und Frieden* (Tübingen, 1844), 180, 201.

22. Zeller, "Die Theologie der Gegenwart und die Theologischen Jahrbücher," *Theologische Jahrbücher*, Vol. 5, 1846, 25f.

23. Hilgenfeld, "Die wissenschaftliche Theologie und ihre gegenwärtige Aufgabe," Zeitschrift für wissenschaftiche Theologie, Vol. I, 1858, 10-14.

24. Zeller, "Über das Verhältnis der Theologie zur Wissenschaft und Kirche," Theologische Jahrbücher, Vol. 9, 1850, 101f, 107- 110.

25. *Kirchengeschichte des neunzehnten Jahrhunderts* is the 5th and last volume of Baur's *Geschichte der christlichen Kirche*, Vol. 5 (2nd ed. Leipzig, 1877), 434 (cf. 427ff), 406. On Strauss, see below.

26. Ibid, 416. Compare Baur's "absolute power over everything" with D.F. Strauss' words in the *Life of Jesus*, 4th edition of 1840 translated by George Eliot (Ramsey, NJ: Sigler Press, 1994), 780: Not any single individual, but humanity "is the worker of miracles, in so far as in the course of human history the spirit more and more subjugates nature, both within and around man, until it lies before him as the inert matter on which he exercises his active power...."

27. *Vorlesungen über die Theologie des neuen Testaments* (Leipzig, 1864; reprint Darmstadt: Wissenschaftliche Buchgesellschaft, 1973), 117. For an English translation of the late Baur's interpretation of Jesus see Baur, *The Church History of the First Three Centuries*, translation edited by Allan Menzies (London and Edinburgh: Williams and Norgate, 1878), 24-43. The work in German is *Kirchengeschichte der ersten drei Jahrhunderte*.

28. *Kirchengeschichte des Neunzehnten Jahrhunderts*, 378-382, 398f, cf. 373. Strauss, *The Life of Jesus Critically Examined*, translated from the 4th German edition of 1840 by George Eliot (London, 1846), recently reprinted with an introduction and editorial notes by Peter Hodgson (Ramsey, NJ: Sigler Press, 1994), 779-781, 798-802 (from the 3rd edition of 1838). The work was first published in 1835. On Strauss see also Horton Harris, *David Friedrich Strauss and his Theology* (Cambridge: C. Univ. Press, 1973.)

29. *Schleiermacher Kritische Gesamtausgabe*, Vol. 10, 350.

30. Baur, *Kirchengeschichte des Neunzehnten Jahrhunderts*, 197f.

31. Strauss, 781-784. In the preface to the 3rd edition (ibid, 801) Strauss had defined religion as the "awakening in the human spirit of the relationship between man and God," which develops in an Hegelian process that is completed in the speculative overcoming of their separation. Jesus is a religious "genius" who may be equaled or exceeded by future individuals.—In the concluding section of the 3rd edition of the work from the year 1838 (799, 801) Strauss uses Schleiermacher's language: "in religion alone the divine Spirit touches man in immediate self-consciousness"; "feeling and immediate self-consciousness ... surely constitute the nearest seat and center of religion." But here also religion is comprehended with Hegelian philosophy; the realization of the unity of God and humanity cannot be achieved in any single individual but only in the whole of humanity.

32. Strauss, *Die christliche Glaubenslehre in ihrer geschichtlichen Entwicklung und im Kampfe mit der modernen Wissenschaft dargestellt*, Vol. 1 (Tübingen and Stuttgart, 1840), from the Preface and the Introduction, 1-24. Feuerbach's *Wesen des Christentums* [Essence of Christianity] appeared in 1841, the same year the 2nd volume of Strauss' *Glaubenslehre* was published. Strauss' references to Feuerbach in the *Glaubenslehre* are to earlier works, especially Feuerbach's *Pierre Bayle, ein Beitrag zur Geschichte der Philosophie der Menschheit* [in the German edition of Feuerbach's works, Vol. V (Stuttgart:

Fommann-Holzboog, 1959)].

33. See especially Strauss, *Die Halben und die Ganzen* [The Halves and the Wholes]. *Eine Streitschrift gegen die Herrn Doktoren [Daniel] Schenkel und [Ernst Wilhelm] Hengstenberg* (Berlin, 1865). His criticism of Schleiermacher's life of Jesus follows the same line: *Der Christus des Glaubens und der Jesus der Geschichte. Eine Kritik des Schleiermacherschen Lebens Jesu* (Berlin, 1865).

34. *Die Christliche Glaubenslehre*, 1, 25ff. In all of his works on Jesus and Christianity Strauss rejects Christian eschatology as purely mythical. In the 2nd volume of the *Glaubenslehre* he develops his own modern form of eschatology: the universe is the appearance of the "One" (Spinoza); old planets die, new are born in endless process. At the conclusion of the work one finds these sentences: "Schleiermacher's expression: in the midst of finitude to become one with the infinite, and eternal in every moment, is all that modern science can say about immortality. With this our business is ended for now. The 'beyond' [Jenseits] is indeed in all things the 'One,' but in its form as the future it is the last enemy that speculative criticism has to oppose and wherever possible overcome" (II, 738f). In his final work, *The Old Faith and the New*, I, 161-168, he repeats such use of Schleiermacher. "We demand the same piety for our Cosmos [Universum] that the devout man of old demanded for his God" (168).

35. Ibid., Vol. II (Tübingen and Stuttgart, 1841), 336.

36. Strauss, *Das Leben Jesu für das deutsche Volk bearbeitet* (2nd ed. Leipzig, 1864), 204-209, 180f. Not only is the fantastic eschatology of Jesus unrealistic, but Jesus also gives the modern consciousness offense through the arrogance (Selbstüberhebung) of his messianic consciousness (242).

37. Ibid, 621. The following conclusion of the book (624-627) discusses the transition from Christianity to the modern religion of humanity. Strauss' image of the tree covered by vines can be encountered in later theology, e.g., in Karl Hase's *Kirchengeschichte auf der Grundlage akademischer Vorlesungen* (Leipzig, 1893), 508. With reference to Strauss he writes "what is supposed to remain of history after the tearing down of the mythical vines is indeed a rather bare trunk, but it is still the cross...."

38. Strauss, *Der alte und der neue Glaube, ein Bekenntnis* (4th ed. Bonn, 1873), 139; English translation of the 1st ed. by Mathilde Blind, *The Old Faith and the New, a Confession* (NY: Holt, 1874), I, 161. The translation has recently been reprinted without Strauss' important conclusion (NY: Prometheus Books, 1997).

39. F.C. Baur's successor at Tübingen, Carl Weizsacker, made this point in a review of Baur's *Kirchengeschichte des 19. Jahrunderts*: Baur's form of mediation finds the "essence of Christianity" not as Schleiermacher in immediate religious experience, but in the "power of the absolute and universal." Baur's striving for such mediation gives "the theological, yes, we may even say the religious basis" of Baur's criticism of theology. *Jahrbücher für deutsche Theologie* Vol. 7, 1862, 811f. In his history of theology in the 19th century, Martin Kähler applies "theology of mediation" broadly to the theology of the century: *Geschichte der protestantischen Dogmatik im 19. Jahrhundert*, first published in 1962 (Berlin: Evang. Verlagsanstalt), 86ff.

40. Hase, *Gesammelte Werke* (Leipzig, 1890-92), VIII.l, 356f, 359. Perhaps the most important critique of the methods and results of the Tübingen School to appear during Baur's lifetime was Hase's *Die Tübinger Schule* (Leipzig, 1855), which was addressed to Baur. Baur's answer is *An Herrn Dr. Karl*

Hase (Tübingen, 1855). Hase's discussion is notable for its defense of the authenticity of the Gospel of John [8f]: If John is given over to Baur's interpretation (to having been written by a "Mormon-Evangelist"), then "in time not only the whole faith with which the church moved victoriously through the centuries, with which it believed in the one born clothed in purple from eternity and the one who opens all access to the Father, would collapse, but also we would lose with it all those traits of highest spirituality that we have loved in him and all those promises with which we have been comforted that are based on the witness of this Gospel." Yet practically in the same breath Hase can say, "if you [Baur] can demonstrate that this Gospel is not written by an eye witness, cannot at all have been written in the apostolic period nor be historical, then we must yield to your demonstration, for it would be a foolish love of the divine Logos that would be greater than the love of truth." —Hase is particularly critical [49f] of Adolf Hilgenfeld's thesis, in *Das Evangelium und die Briefe des Johannes* (Halle, 1849), which argues that John is part of the development of Gnosticism, against which Christianity, as Hase points out, seriously struggled for its own existence. He also says that according to Hilgenfeld John's God of the Old Testament is the Gnostic demiurge, the father of the devil.—This perhaps partially explains why Hase consistently blocked Hilgenfeld's promotion to the rank of professor at Jena, where both men were on the theological faculty. Cf. the Chapter on Hilgenfeld in: Horton Harris, *The Tübingen School* (Oxford: Clarendon Press, 1975), 113ff.

41. *Die Tübinger Schule*, 93f.

42. Paul Burkhardt, 352. Letter of Dec. 4, 1874. In *Christentum und Kultur*, 217, Overbeck briefly discusses the reference to Hartmann's book in his *Studien*.

43. Hartmann takes this point from the work by Paul Lagarde discussed in the following section.

The Religious-Political Situation

44. Karl Kupisch, *Die Deutschen Landeskirchen im 19. und 20. Jahrhundert* (2nd ed. Göttingen: Vandenhoeck & Ruprecht, 1975), 72-78. Karl Hase, *Kirchengeschichte auf der Grundlage akademischer Vorlesungen*, III/2/2 (Leipzig, 1893), 863f. Hase offers a lengthy discussion of the history. A complete statement of the new legislation on religion in this period is found in: *Die kirchlich-politische Gesetzgebung der Jahre 1873, 1874 und 1875* (Berlin, 1875).

45. On Hengstenberg (and Dorner and Ritschl) see Emanuel Hirsch, *Geschichte der neuern evangelischen Theologie*, Vol. 5 (Gütersloh: Gerd Mohn, 1960). D.F. Strauss gives an important assessment of Hengstenberg in *Die Halben und die Ganzen* (Berlin, 1865), 66ff.

Fides Divina, Fides Humana. Overbeck at the time of the "Christianity of Theology"

46. F.C. Baur, *Kritische Untersuchungen über die kanonischen Evangelien, ihr Verhältnis zu einander, ihren Charakter und Ursprung* (Tübingen, 1847), 50-76. On Acts: *Paulus, der Apostel Jesu Christi* (Stuttgart, 1845), 1-14. In his "second" life of Jesus, *Das Leben Jesu für das deutsche Volk bearbeitet*, Strauss concedes that Baur's source criticism must be combined with mythical interpretation.

47. *Kurze Erklärung der Apostelgeschichte*, by W.M.L. de Wette, 4th edition revised and enlarged by Franz Overbeck (Leipzig, 1870), 487pp. Over-

beck argues that the only truly authentic part of the work are the "we" narratives, that it is otherwise an attempt of the Lucan writer to reconstruct the history of the early church from a particular point of view. While Peter is made to represent certain Pauline views, the more significant change from the actual history of the early church is that Paul is made to represent the Jewish-Christian viewpoint. This misrepresentation of Paul (esp. Acts 21:23-26) signals the lack of understanding of Paul in the later Hellenistic community, which tended to legalism. In this interpretation Overbeck departs from the usual view of the Tübingen School that Acts is a conscious attempt to reconcile Jewish-Christian and Hellenistic-Christian points of view. For Overbeck the Hellenistic-Christian community of the Lucan writer (early 2nd century) is inherently more Petrine than Pauline.

48. The lecture was published in Basel in a limited edition in 1871 and has recently been reprinted in *Franz Overbeck Werke und Nachlass*, Vol. I, *Schriften bis 1873*, edited by Ekkehard Stegemann und Niklaus Peter (Stuttgart and Weimar: J.B. Metzler, 1994), 75-106. References to the work in my text refer to this edition.

49. The most significant and instructive theological hermeneutics of the Vermittlungstheologie [theology of mediation] is Richard Rothe's *Zur Dogmatik* (Gotha, 1863), which is in its entirety about the relationship of fides divina and fides humana in exegesis (see esp. 140-157) and New Testament theology. The mediating intent is obvious in the following (290): "In Scripture we have an infallible and errorless report about divine revelation, but not in such a way that it is immediately given. Rather the immediately given report [in Scripture] must be reworked by us ourselves into an infallible and errorless report— by means of unceasing research in Scripture, which is expressly to include the historical criticism of Holy Scripture." How Rothe thinks this "toilsome" [mühsame] work is to be done—the subject of the book—is still worthy of theological attention. Rothe, whose theology is a mixture of deep personal piety, criticism and speculation, was a founder of the Protestant League [Protestantenverein], mentioned in Chapter 3 of the *Christianity of Theology*. Overbeck copied and paraphrased extensively from an an article by Rothe, "Zur Debatte über den Protestantenverein," *Allgemeine Kirchliche Zeitschrift*, 1864. (Kirchenlexikon, "Christentum (Gegenwart) Entzweiung). Here Rothe speaks of the unavoidable present power of secular science in theology, in which time belief in Christ and his resurrection is a gift of grace. —Another significant theologian of the time who represents the mediation of fides divina and fides humana, and a teacher of Overbeck's at Leipzig, is Christian Herrmann Weisse: *Philosophische Dogmatik oder Philosophie des Christentums* (Leipzig, 1862), III, 506.

50. *Die christliche Glaubenslehre*, I, 114-136 (esp 136), 224f, 354f. Strauss frequently comments on the matter in other places in the book.

51. A good example is Edward Zeller's dicussion in his article "Über historische Kritik und ihre Anwendung auf die christliche Religionsurkunden" in: *Theologische Jahrbücher*, 1846, 297f. What tradition calls the "witness of the Spirit" is at most an impression one has from reading the Scripture, and one can be deceived by such feelings. (Strauss had made the same point.) Zeller discusses the doctrine completely in the frame of Orthodoxy's claim that the witness of the Spirit authenticates the credibility of Scripture, i.e., makes criticism superfluous. Baur discusses it with the same limitation: *Lehrbuch der christlichen Dogmengeschichte* (3rd ed. Leipzig, 1867), 300f., 364-367.

52. Cf. Schleiermacher, *Der christliche Glaube* (7th ed. Berlin, W. de Gruyter, 1960), §130.2. A theologian more closely associated with Hase than Overbeck, R.A. Lipsius, who became a member of the faculty at Jena, has the same understanding of fides humana and divina that one finds in Hase: *Lehrbuch der evangelisch-protestantischen Dogmatik* (Braunschweig, 1879), 143.

53. It is noteworthy that Overbeck gives Luther prominent mention also in the *Christianity of Theology*, Chap. 3. Luther's famous Commentary on Galatians (1531) sets a clear limit between Word of God and its work, faith, and the "world's" law and reason, which comprehends neither Word of God nor faith. For Luther each has its rightful sphere of action and influence in human life. Overbeck's understanding of the existence of faith and science in the same person is similar: see the last two paragraphs of Chapter 5 in the *Christianity of Theology*.

54. See e.g. Baur, *Church History of the First Three Centuries*, II, 11ff. In the inaugural lecture, *Entstehung und Recht*, discussed above, Overbeck writes (23): "As is known ... Baur dissolved the New Testament canon into a product of about the first hundred and twenty years of the church." The German word for "dissolve," "auflösen," is Strauss' word throughout his *Christliche Glaubenslehre* for the dissolution of Christian doctrine into its historical components.

55. Overbeck, *Über die Anfänge der patristischen Literatur* (Darmstadt: Wissenschaftliche Buchgesellschaft, 1966), 36. The work originally appeared in the *Historische Zeitschrift*, Vol. 48, 1882, 417-471. My citations in the following text are to the Darmstadt edition. Overbeck's corrections and additions are given by M. Tetz in *Overbeckiana* II, 160-162.

56. Ibid, 36. Overbeck considers only the form of the Gospel new; the other forms are interpersonal (letters) or adopted from earlier, esp. Jewish literature (apocalypse). The canon that Overbeck here means is not the final collection, but the generally accepted writings at the turn of the 2nd century. "Urliteratur" and "Urgeschichte" are parallel concepts designating the contrast between the New Testament period and later church history. See e.g. *Christentum und Kultur*, 20ff.

57. *Stromata*, I, 1. Overbeck (60-62) quotes similar statements in VI, 1 and VII, 18. (He refers also to a related text in Augustine, *De Doctrina Christiana* [On Christian Teaching], IV, 3.) Clement is not writing for the person of "simple faith" but for the educated new Christian who seeks understanding. This point is made in Chapter I of the *Christianity of Theology*. In this book Overbeck will cite other instances of patristic apologetics directed to Christians. In the *Anfänge der patristischen Literatur*, 53, Overbeck writes: "Since the 3rd century the practical aim of Christian apologetics is directed not toward paganism but toward Christianity, that is, ... a Christian public that is treated as heathen. This is the peculiar characteristic difference between apologetics since the 3rd century in distinction from earlier apologetics. It is most clearly seen in the most important apologetic writing of the 3rd century that we have, Origen's *Contra Celsum*, and indeed already in the preface." In the preface Origen says the work is for "weak" Christians. See the translation by Henry Chadwick (London: Cambridge U. Pr., 1965), 6.

58. In *Anfänge der patristischen Literatur*, 29, Overbeck writes that the canon is the "death notice" of the literature it contains. In a book Overbeck clearly read [A 12], Christian Herrmann Weisse discusses the "death" of a literature that becomes an historical document by leaving its living existence as

present event and becoming an objective form of the past, for the consideration of those who now read it. There is "no true historical tradition without the transition through this element of death." *Über die Zukunft der evangelischen Kirche. Reden an die Gebildeten deutscher Nation* (2nd ed. Leipzig, 1849), 152.

59. The work was posthumously edited and published: *Titus Flavius Klemens von Alexandria, Die Teppiche (Stromateis)*. Deutscher Text nach der Übersetzung von Franz Overbeck. Im Auftrage der Franz Overbeck Stiftung in Basel herausgegeben und eingeleitet von Carl Albrecht Bernoulli und Ludwig Früchtel (Basel: Benno Schwabe & Co. Verlag, 1936).

60. A verse Overbeck apparently wrote to his bride in 1876 may also be a sign of Clement's influence. It is in a copy of *Studien zur Geschichte der alten Kirche* located in the Overbeck Archives [A343]. The verse is printed in Tetz, *Overbeckiana* II, 158. Literally translated it reads: "Not just in the garden of the bride / has this plant grown up / but all gardens are open to her / because the beloved risks hoping / that she discovers him in all of them / even where he has very well concealed himself [auch wo er sich noch so sehr versteckt]." One of Clement's images of the *Stromata* is of a garden in which the ripe fruit is hidden, as Overbeck notes in *Über die Anfänge der patristischen Literatur*, 60.

61. Overbeck, *Über die Anfänge der patristischen Literatur*, 70f. In a later work (published in Basel in 1892) on Eusebius of Caesarea and the beginnings of church-historical writing, Overbeck argues that church history also begins as apologetics: *Über die Anfänge der Kirchengeschichtschreibung* (reprint Darmstadt, Wissenschaftliche Buchgesellschaft, 1965).

62. Weisse, *Die Evangelische Geschichte kritisch und philosophisch bearbeitet* (Leipzig, 1838), II, 482-484. In the last, 1895 version of Overbeck's lecture, *Geschichte der Literatur der alten Kirche. Patristik* [A105] the language is more reserved, but the concepts are the same: Although certain New Testament forms—esp. John and Acts—are in some sense addressed to an "ideal public," they are peculiar forms that, after canonization, are not repeated in the church. Overbeck addresses the composition of a Gospel in distinction from (world) literature: its peculiar form is derived from the recognition of only one "master," Christ, and the corresponding equality of the members of the early Christian community. In (world) literature the author is the master of his ideal public. Matthew's use of the of "logia" or sayings of Jesus for his Gospel is typical: "Nothing justifies the assumption that in this work, if one wishes to call it such, anything depended on letting anyone else speak but Christ himself ... ." It is only the sayings, previously communicated orally, that make the Gospel authoritative for the community. Up to the time of canonization, quotations from the Gospels are not in the form of references to the Gospels, but are solely the words of Christ [223-227]. The community was completely filled by its religious conviction, there was no need to make itself pleasing or plausible to the world beyond itself by means of literature [352-354], until the rise of apologetic literature [387f.] and of gnosticism, which clearly used the literits religious conviction, there was no need to make itself pleasing or plausible to the world beyond itself by means of literature [352-354], until the rise of apologetic literature [387f.] and of gnosticism, which clearly used the literary forms of the Greek world [325, 405]. In another lecture from the same time (1895/96), *Einleitung in das Neue Testament* [A87], Overbeck emphasizes that all in the early Christian community were given the divine Spirit and that no New Testament writer saw himself or was seen as the recipient of a special gift for writ-

ing. "Not one of the Gospel writers in the least shows the assumption that his work is called for through a vocation not given to any Christian who had been sufficiently instructed about the words and works of Christ" [139]. The community was conscious of "living from the inexhaustible source of prophesy" [146].

63. Overbeck's sentence: "Jesus legte eben die rein innerliche im Menschen gegebene Wurzel alles religiösen Verhältnisses des Menschen zu Gott in einer von keiner anderen Religion erreichten Reinheit bloss." [Jesus laid open the purely inward root of all religious relationship to God, which is given in all persons, in a purity reached by no other religion.]

64. These lectures are published in Vol. I of the *Franz-Overbeck Werke und Nachluss.*

The Late Overbeck and the Problem of Overbeck-Interpretation

65. A recent work on Overbeck (whose author concludes he was an atheist or an agnostic) quotes from the unpublished memoirs of Hermann Siebeck, professor of philosophy at Basel from 1875 to 1883: "Overbeck saw the task of human life, as he later once told me, in the ideal of becoming holy [Ideal der Heiligung]." Andreas Urs Sommer, *Der Geist der Historie und das Ende des Christentums* (Berlin: Akademie Verlag, 1997), 149. - There is a portrait of Overbeck, painted late in his life, known as the "weeping Overbeck" because of the sad expression; it hangs in the Aula of the University of Basel. I interpret the portrait with reference to the "melancholy" of Basil of Caesarea about the state of the church, to which Overbeck refers in Chapter 2 of the *Christianity of Theology.*

66. In his lecture, *Geschichte der Literatur der alten Kirche. Patristik,* from the year 1895 [A105], Overbeck writes about Clement's method in the *Stromata* that the "apparent formlessness" has the sense "of a veil for a content that is to be concealed or at least that is not to be given immediately to the understanding" [480]. Clement called the level of the work "gnostic," which according to Overbeck means "scientific [wissenschaftlich]." In the pervasive cultural medium of Greek philosophy, he uses its means to oppose it in the interest of the faith [491-493].

67. It is in this statement that Overbeck writes, as noted above, that he withdrew from church attendance. Other than these comments in A267c, the notes having to do with unbelief are in the Kirchenlexikon under the titles, "Christentum (mein)" and "Theologie (meine)," which were written on the same day, Oct. 17, 1902, when Overbeck was preparing the 2nd ed. of the *Christianity of Theology.* The first note in "Christentum (mein)" begins, "Ich habe kein eigentümliches Christentum," which literally means, "I have no Christianity that is my own possession." The expression is quite odd, and the fact that throughout the note he uses such possessives in denying "having" faith makes it most peculiar. In an early note in the Kirchenlexikon, "Glaube (Vermischtes)," he quoted a line from Ambrose's "Hymn to St. Agnes": fides teneri nescia—faith cannot be held—and adds the comment: "this has to do with the faith that can be held in no limits [Schranken], but breaks through all."

68. It is significant that, when through the agency of Prof. James Donaldson the University of St. Andrews proposed to confer the Doctor of Divinity degree on him in 1903, Overbeck's forthright answer—he had previously sent Donaldson the 2nd edition of the *Christianity of Theology* —presents the severity of his criticism of theology for Donaldson's serious consideration, but never

mentions unbelief. It would have been a simple matter to confide to Donaldson, "I could not possibly accept a D.D. because I am not a Christian." But this he did not do. Rather he welcomed the degree, which Donaldson saw no reason not to confer, and which named him "in Evangelio praedicando diligentem" [diligent in the proclamation of the Gospel]. The exchange of letters is published in Eberhard Vischer's edition of autobiographical notes by Overbeck which Vischer titled *Selbstbekenntnisse* [Confessions], (Basel, Benno Schwabe, 1941), 19-41.

69. *Christentum und Kultur*, 289, from a note in the Kirchenlexikon entitled "Berufsmoral Allgemeines."

70. Finis christianismi: *Chistentum und Kultur*, 289. Theologians as rouge: Kirchenlexikon, "Theologie (moderne) Charakter Vermischtes," 3; published in Walter Nigg, *Franz Overbeck* (Munich: C.H. Beck, 1931), 202. Overbeck's criticism was never simply against liberal theologians. For example, there is a discussion in the Kirchenlexikon under the title, "Reinhardt (L.), Kennt die Bibel das Jenseits? Vermischtes," about a conservative theologian who completely ignores scientific criticism in arguing from and for the biblical text. According to Overbeck what he "proves" is not the Bible, but himself, and the Bible becomes the "pedestal on which finally he alone stands." "His own authority is the only one he establishes, that of the Bible he undermines ... ." That is very "modern."

71. In an early note in the Kirchenlexikon, "Christentum (Gegenwart) Entzweiung," Overbeck copied from a book words that have to do with the need to conceal one's "mystical" religious experience, because the falseness [Unwesen] of a powerful church and its theology seizes upon and distorts all religious life and its expressions. The book is Julius Meyer, *Das Leben Jesu für das deutsche Volk hearbeitet und die Stellung der Gegner zum Christentum* (Leipzig, 1865), 74.

72. Kirchenlexikon, "Theologie (moderne) Allgemeines," §11. In the same note [§1] he writes that an essential mark of modernity is its turn away from Christianity.

73. Quoted by Vischer, *Selbstbekenntnisse*, 47, with slight corrections noted by Tetz, *Overbeckiana* 11, 134f. In the same place Tetz quotes Ida Overbeck's comment on this note, which adds to its dramatic (and ironic) effect: her husband repeated to her that it represented his conviction, then ordered it burned, but she saved it.

74. A note with the same date refers to this same subject matter: Kirchenlexikon, "Jesus (Versuchung) Neuere Ansichten": "Our age—which has so completely forgotten [verlernt] to take the explanation of holy texts ... from spheres beyond the human horizon—will let me, a writing anchorite [Einsiedler], find many an understanding reader ... for the assertion that understanding for holy texts ... is rather to be expected from poets than from theologians, who indeed name themselves theodidakten [taught by God], but as the learned men they want to be—the concept understood in a fully worldly way— are this only in their imagination. If we humans are able to perceive [erkennen] a further foundation of religion than myth and legend—and so also for all that holy texts supposedly tell [bezeugen] us—what can be paradoxical in the opinion that poets will still be the most acceptable ... interpreters of religious things and texts ...."

75. Several lines of this note are published in *Christentum und Kultur*, 48, where Bernoulli has placed it at the end of a similar note, "Jesu Reden über

die Parusie. Echtheit. Kritik. Allgemines." Overbeck writes about the text in yet another note, quoted in *Christentum und Kultur*, 64, cf. 48f. (Johannes Weiss). In an early note, most probably from the 1860's, in a group of loose notes under the title "Zum Begriff der Theologie als Wissenschaft" [A272], Overbeck defines the "consciousness of Jesus" with the following series: "become as children, near end of the world, renunciation of world."

76. Martin Heidegger gives evidence of the conversation about Overbeck with Rudolf Bultmann in the preface to *Phänomenologie und Theologie* (Frankfurt a.M.: Kostermann, 1970), and the work itself is witness to Overbeck's influence. See also H.G. Gadamer, *Kleine Schriften*, Vol. 1 (Tübingen: Mohr/Siebeck, 1967), 82. Bultmann's understanding of "kerygma" is the eschatological proclamation of a reality through which God calls one away from "world." R. Bultmann, *New Testament and Mythology and Other Basic Writings*, edited and translated by Schubert Ogden (Philadelphia: Fortress, 1984), e.g. 13, 54, (cf. 56f. on belief and unbelief). In one essay Bultmann uses the phrase "in mid-air" to give expression to faith's lack of reasoned proof, which parallels Overbeck's use of the image, "sich in die Luft stellen" [put oneself in the air]: *Christentum und Kultur,* 77. Friedrich Gogarten discusses *Christentum und Kultur* in *Die Tat*, 1921, 481f. He writes that one could think, in reading much that is in the book, that Overbeck despaired of his faith and, not being able to say it publically, wrote about it excessively in private. "So one could think, if the vision of this man were not so oddly distant, not at all fixed on the point on which his doubt does its work of destruction. If the doubt of this man undoes Christianity and religion, his vision looks with such intensity beyond what is undone that one is inclined to think that the doubt works with this vision, a vision that moves from the inacessible beyond ... back to Christianity and religion." Gogarten too finds the image "mid-air" meaningful for theology. Important early essays by Barth, Bultmann and Gogarten are found in: *The Beginnings of Dialectical Theology*, James M. Robinson, ed., translated by K. Crim and L. De Grazia (Richmond: Knox, 1962).

77. *The Epistle to the Romans*, translated from the 6th ed. of 1928 by E. Hoskyns (London: Oxford, 1933).

78. *Karl Barth-Eduard Thurneysen Briefwechsel*, Bd. 1, 1913-1921, (Zürich: Theologischer Verlag, 1973), 380. The letter, dated April 20, 1920, is translated by James Smart in: *Revolutionary Theology in the Making. Barth-Thurneysen Correspondence, 1914-1925* (Richmond: Knox, 1964), 49f. In a later letter, dated June 7, 1920, Barth relates a dream in which he converses with Overbeck, who expresses his agreement by pressing their heads together: *Briefwechsel*, 395. Other letters demonstrate Barth's and Thurneysen's continuing defense of their interpretation of Overbeck throughout the 1920's. For one, Emil Brunner opposed it: *Karl Barth - Emil Brunner Briefwechsel* (Zürich: Theologischer Verlag, 2000), 42-53.

79. Bernoulli's letter and both the draft and a final version of Ida Overbeck's letters are in the *Franz Overbeck-Nachlass* of the Basel Library, II, 104-119, Korrespondenz Ida Overbecks. The copy Bernoulli received is in the C.A. Bernoulli-Nachlass of the Library, 157.

80. See Martin Tetz, *Overbeckiana* II, 7ff. 101-103. See also my article, "Der Briefwechsel zwischen Ida Overbeck-Rothpletz und Carl Albrecht Bernoulli über Frau Overbecks Gespräch mit Karl Barth im Jahre 1920," *Theologische Zeitschrift*, 1987. The story of Overbeck's relationship with and choice of Bernoulli as, together with his wife, editor of his late papers, is documented

in letters in the Overbeck-Nachlass. I presented this in an article in the *Theologische Zeitschrift*, 1986, "Zum Verhältnis zwischen F. Overbeck und C.A. Bernoulli." Benoulli's final understanding of Overbeck is given in his introduction of Overbeck's translation of Clement of Alexandria's *Stromata*. In spite of having known Overbeck personally, Bernoulli's interpretation is based primarily, one is tempted to say, completely on Overbeck's manuscripts and publications. Here Bernoulli makes the interesting remark (32f) that the only publication of Overbeck's that is written from the standpoint of Christian belief is the inaugural lecture of 1870 discussed above, *Entstehung und Recht*.

81. *Karl Barth - Eduard Thurneysen Briefwechsel, 1930-1935* (Zürich: Theologischer Verlag, 2000), 63. Thurneysen wrote to Barth about Nigg's book on Nov. 28, 1930: "On the whole it is simply a step backward, reaction ... The Basel humanists and theologians will triumph and say, we always saw it this way...." (66). Cf. further 129, 366.

82. The question about Overbeck's lasting influence on Barth has much to do with the question about the relationship of the Barth of the *Church Dogmatics* to the Barth of the 1920's. In an article from the year 1935 the successor to Overbeck at Basel, Wilhelm Bornemann, included a brief discussion of Barth's relationship to Overbeck in an article on Overbeck in a journal of popular theology published in Berlin, *Protestantenblatt*, 1935, 85-88, 102-104. According to Bornemann, a liberal associated with Harnack, Barth took three key points from Overbeck: the oppostion of the "vertical" and "horizontal" dimension [Word of God vs. history and historical science], the rejection of "culture" within Christianity [cultural Christianity], "and the radicalism that allows no other point of view besides his own." This last point we may translate into Barth's radical "No!" to natural theology or theology of culture. One could add other, related aspects of Barth's theology; for example, the New Testament canon both as human language and conceptuality and as witness to revelation shares in the revelatory event as its unique expression in time.

83. In Barth's *Protestant Thought from Rousseau to Ritschl* (New York: Harper, 1959), Overbeck is barely mentioned. In a brief mentioning in *Evangelical Theology. An Introduction* (NY: Holt, Reinhart & Winston, 1963), 187, he portrays Overbeck as one who pursued the way of historical-criticsm—a modern gnosis behind which lurks skepticism or atheism—to its end and "became wholly disinterested in theology as service." In another late work Barth defends his placing together of Blumhardt and Overbeck in his article "Unsettled Questions" from the year 1920. *Das christliche Leben. Die kirchliche Dogmatik IV, 4, Fragmente aus dem Nachlass, Vorlesungen 1959-1961* (Zürich: Theologischer Verlag, 1976), 444.

84. Karl Löwith, *From Hegel to Nietzsche. The Revolution in 19th Century Thought*. Translated from the German by David Greene (NY: Holt, Reinhart & Winston, 1964), 388. The original work is from the year 1941. See also Löwith, "Die philosophische Kritik der christlichen Religion im 19. Jahrhundert," *Theologische Rundschau*, NF 5, 1933, 211-213, 223-226. Löwith's occupation with Overbeck probably stems from his time as a student of Heidegger and Bultmann at Marburg in the 1920's.

85. The original words of Peter Gast are: "Nietzsche kämpft direkt gegen das Christentum: damit ist er unabsichtlich ein Erhalter desselben. In Ihre Hand ist es gegeben—ohne dem Christentum Wehe zu tun, ohne es zu Gegenwirkungen zu reizen—es mit der Zeit unmöglich zu machen, indem sie das Protocoll seiner Vergangenheit autnehmen." The letter is published in: *Briefwechsel*

Franz Overbeck, Heinrich Köselitz [Peter Gast], edited by David Marc Hoffmann, Niklaus Peter and Theo Salfinger (Berlin, NY: W. de Gruyter, 1998), 147.

Concealment in the "Christianity of Theology"

86. This occurs in one of Overbeck's most important histories, that of slavery in Christianity. As his histories of monasticism and theology, it demonstrates historical Christianity's accommodation to "world."

87. In his lecture of the year 1870/1871, *Kampf der Kirche mit Heidentum* (Struggle of the Church with Paganism) [A107, 3f], Overbeck writes that the ancient (post-New Testament) church fought "with undivided force and complete faith for its religious understanding of the world [Weltauffassung]," even though in many ways it bore in itself the opposition it fought against, i.e., heathen culture or world. - Here the "religious understanding of world" means the "view of life" or "view of world" as the vision of the reality of Christ, a transformed world. In another lecture, *Geschichte des apostolischen Zeitalters* [A102, 245] dated in the years 1867-1870, Overbeck writes that the "new fruit" of Paul's conversion was "revelation, wisdom of God, perception - a new worldview [Weltanschauung]..."

88. Baur, *Church History of the First Three Centuries*, 1, 185f, II, 89f, 138f; *Kirchengesch. der drei ersten Jahrhunderte*, 175f, 330f, 379ff. This content is also in Overbeck's unpublished lectures on Christology and the Trinity from 1865/66 [A108, 678f]. For Baur the final result is Hegel's philosophy of religion, as e.g. his *Christliche Gnosis* (Tübingen, 1835) demonstrates.

89. Strauss, *Der alte und der neue Glaube*, 73. The English translation of these words by M. Blind (1, 83) is not literal. Baur, *Church History of the First Three Centuries*, 1, 42f. Although Baur thought the psychological explanation (hallucination) plausible, his conclusion was skeptical: the information in the New Testament is such that one can make no scientific determination of the resurrection event itself.

90. Holsten, *Zeitschrift für wissenschaftliche Theologie*, 1861, 231ff. See also: Holsten, *Das Evangelium des Paulus, Teil II. Paulinische Theologie*, edited by P. Mehlhorn (Berlin, 1898), 47ff. D.F. Strauss, (2nd ed. Leipzig, 1864), 303f.

91. Strauss, *Das Leben Jesus für das deutsche Volk bearbeitet*, 36. See also Strauss, *Die Halben und die Ganzen* (Berlin, 1865), 58ff.—In the late notes, in identifying with "profane" science, Overbeck agrees with Strauss on "half-half" theology, e.g., *Christentum und Kultur*, 297; Walter Nigg, 143.

92. Imanuel Kant, *The Foundations of the Metaphysics of Morals and What is Enlightenment*, translated by Lewis White Beck (NY: Macmillan, 1990). Kant's writing was a reflection on and critique of laws of the time that bound sermons to church dogma.

93. Cf. Schopenhauer, *The World as Will and Representation*, I, 312: "Man ... is the most necessitous of all beings. He is concrete willing and needing through and through; he is a concretion of a thousand wants and needs. With these he stands on the earth, left to his own devices, in uncertainty about everything but his own need and misery." This misery means humanity's "need for redemption" [II, 170]. According to F.C. Baur, in a discussion of the Sermon on the Mount, the "need for redemption" of humanity "is its own sufficient evidence of the reality of the redemption which it longs for." *Church History of the First Three Centuries*, I, 28f. *Kirchengesch. der drei ersten Jahrhunderte*, 27.

94. *Über die Auffassung des Streits des Paulus mit Petrus in Antiochien (Gal. 2,1 Iff) bei den Kirchenvätern*, 73.

95. The question about the relationship between the "human spirit" and the divine "Spirit" in the New Testament is the focal area of the theological work of Karl Barth and Rudolf Bultmann in the 1920's. In his essay of 1925, "The Problem of a Theological Exegesis of the New Testament," Bultmann asks the question, "at what place can one assert the Spirit of Christ comes to expression" in the New Testament? The question has do with Scripture, in the immediately understood sense, as the word of merely human "spirits" that need to be critically identified, and "only indirectly" as Word of God, which according to Bultmann prevents the Word of God from being a humanly controllable presupposition of exegesis. (*The Beginnings of Dialectical Theology* [Richmond: Knox, 1968], 254f). Bultmann wrote this in response to a text in Barth's preface to the third edition (1922) of *The Epistle to the Romans*, 17, where Barth had written, with regard to the question about historical criticism, that there are no other "voices" in Romans than those of human "spirits," hence the "Spirit of Christ" cannot be thought of as "standing beside" those other spirits in the Epistle. "The whole is litera, that is, voices of those other spirits," but "the whole is placed under the Krisis of the Spirit of Christ" and through this is Word of God. This is the core of the disagreement between Barth and Bultmann in the 1920's. Although their answers are different, the question itself was the same.

ON THE CHRISTIANITY OF TODAY'S THEOLOGY

by

Franz Overbeck

To My Dear Young Friend, Carl Albrecht Bernoulli

My dear Bernoulli! If, according to the Gospels, even the Kingdom of Heaven has to put up with being the booty of the violent, how may this book of mine know only displeasure over your violence against it! For apart from that old theft you have a second title to its possession, namely for the part you recently played in making its re-emergence possible. Take now from my hand, therefore, what you have already once made your own: perhaps as a gift it can serve you for something again. [See Overbeck's explanation in the Afterword.]

Basel, December 15, 1902

Preface to the First Edition

Two recent publications moved me to bring my thoughts together for this book, first of all Paul de Lagarde's *Über das Verhältnis des deutschen Staats zu Theologie, Kirche und Religion* [On the Relationship of the German State to Theology, Church and Religion] (Göttingen, 1873),[1] with its attack on our theological faculties. I hope that our public criticism has made this publication better known. The second is the "confession" of David Friedrich Strauss, *Der alte und der neue Glaube. Ein Bekenntnis* [The Old Faith and the New. A Confession] (Bonn, 1872). The thoughts I have written down for this book are, naturally, older than these recent publications. For a long time now I have felt the need to state my position toward the contemporary theological parties, yet it would not have been difficult for me to have kept these thoughts to myself even longer. There were good and varied reasons for the latter, above all the aversion to endangering a good cause through immature treatment. With all the force of the motives driving me to express myself in a general way about theology, I would not have overcome the reasons for not publishing had it not been for the pressure of my theological teaching office. With this said I do not think I need to excuse myself further for having written the book nor for how it is written, at least insofar as openness must be the first commandment for an author, if the pressure of his teaching office is to be seriously acknowledged. Certainly at the same time I believe that I can perhaps also help other persons, above all young theologians, especially with the discussion of practical matters at the end of the book. They are in situations of great distress that may be ignored neither by any teacher of theology nor by any church authority.

I have declared myself against the practical endeavors of men who count me among their scientific co-workers. With some I have a close personal relationship, with others, a more distant one, and I express my thanks to all of them for their most gracious acceptance of my scientific work. I think the way I have opposed their practical efforts only shows that personal considerations played no part. Furthermore it is by no means my intention to destroy a really existing community. For in all I have said in the book, I have sincerely cherished the wish to secure for science the quiet place in theology that science, by virtue of the very nature of theology, has such a difficult time attaining. But it is my conviction that certain tendencies in contemporary liberal theology very much jeopardize this attainment, and liberal theology has such enormous tasks before it in the whole area of the history of Christianity.

I hope that the reader who can find some merit in the book, despite its sometimes impetuous words, will not contest its right to be called a writing not only for conflict but also for peace.[2] I would like to ask the book's opponents to be aware that the book has to do only with the theoretical solution of the problem of the relation between Christianity and culture, not with the thousandfold practical compromises between them that lie before us in daily life. I ask them to be aware therefore that my judgments have not at all to do with the laity but only with the theologians, above all with those standing at teacher's lecterns and writing books. For I do not doubt that there are many wise pastors who evaluate our theological conflicts for what they are worth and, heeding their practical vocation, remain distant from them. I would not, however, have allowed myself to contest the Christianity of our contemporary theological parties in this way, had I claimed the predicate "Christian" for my own theology without reserve, and were I not convinced that all of us theologians have more serious reasons for agreement than are generally acknowledged.

Basel, May 16, 1873

Preface to the Second Edition

As in April of the current year, to my greatest surprise, I was faced with the possibility of seeing my book of 1873 revived, and as my help was asked for its realization, I was resolved not to refuse it. The book had been very significant for me personally, since the whole conduct of my life, at least insofar as it has been related to the public, has been determined by it. Therefore I could not even momentarily think of completely abandoning it or even of limiting my participation simply to agreeing to a new printing of the unchanged text, which would have amounted to the same dereliction. But the book was almost thirty years old and I myself was in my sixty-fifth year. How was I to perform the help that I, in addition to the request I received from without, was compelled to give? In the distressing situation in which I now found myself I decided to take a great risk, which I now ask my readers to receive from the book lying before them. Because a good part of this risk consists in the fact that I have placed in the text of this second edition [Introduction and Afterword] what normally belongs in the preface, it seems that I have nothing more to do here than to dispatch the most original purpose of a preface as quickly and simply as possible, which is that the author recommend himself to a favorable attitude on the part of his readers. Without my having to say more about it here, they will have occasion to convince themselves how necessary such an attitude is for me.

Basel, December 29, 1902

INTRODUCTION

How I Came to Write My Book of 1873

As the title above indicates, I set out here to write not my life, which is not necessary here, but a chapter or an episode of it. Nor do I have any intention of comfortably writing all sorts of things about my life at my reader's expense or indeed to my advantage. I shall try to be as brief as possible and in doing so I shall be guided constantly by the effort to write only what I can answer for. And because I shall be writing about myself, these should not be difficult to bring together.

On the day after my thirty-second birthday, and completely unexpectedly, I received word of a possible call to be an associate [ausserordentlicher] professor at Basel. I had my youth behind me as well as five academic years as a lecturer [Privatdozent] at Jena. As it developed I allowed it to proceed only under the pressure of necessity. As I moved to Basel in the spring of the following year, 1870, I suffered a great deal from the feeling that in leaving my lecturer's position in Jena I was leaving a paradise, and from the dark presentiment that I, from now on, would have to teach more than I knew, or at least that I would have to be as much student as teacher. And hence I also had the presentiment that I moved toward a task that I might not be able to meet. The presentiment did not remain unfulfilled.

I did not lack any sort of equipment for the task when I moved to the foreign place that had called me. To be a teacher, I had at least come out of a school. In any case I myself knew [wusste] nothing other than that I was a "Tübinger." But what did the "Tübingen School" mean at that time? As anyone can recall, it was a wreck of a ship whose company consisted of a master who had been dead for ten years and a small group of students, most of whom, although still living, had almost ceased to do ship's work. One found shelter at home and continued to teach what he had learned (Adolf Hilgenfeld). Only under the pressure to get back home, a second and third either did the work (Gustav Volkmar) or set about to do it (Karl Holsten). The last of the crew I mention—he was the one to whom the future "belonged"—only "participated" by busily boring holes in the ship (Albrecht Ritschl).[3] I knew, therefore, that I was standing on a ship that could not suffice for a journey into life itself, especially when I had done nothing on the ship for anyone but myself and perhaps for the hopes of a few good friends. But what had I done for myself as a "Tübinger," and what did it mean

for me to think I was one as I left Jena? I could have imagined myself a
strict or even narrow-minded "Tübinger" considering the fact, for example, that I had long possessed that apostate's [Ritschl's] chief work
but had not opened the book more than occasionally. When I did look
into it, then always with the greatest distrust of what I expected to be
taught; moreover I had not yet come to the point of orientating myself
about the relation of the book's "thoroughly revised" second edition to
the first.[4] I readily concede that such "strictness" did not have much
significance, so all the more depended on what otherwise bound me to
the school and kept me in it. It left a lot to be desired.

Ferdinand Christian Baur died (December 2, 1860) in the year my
student period ended. I was never his personal student and I never even
saw him. So I never had any other relationship to his status as master
than a very "free" one, which permitted me to call myself a "Tübinger"
only, so to speak, in a very allegorical sense. Baur's philosophy of religion, which was based on Hegel, remained completely foreign to me.
What I was able to assimilate from his historical criticism of early
Christianity was always limited to what I thought was its completely
victorious struggle for the right to present early Christianity purely historically, as it really had been, against the theological apologetics of the
time or the pretensions of theology to displace that right. But even in
Jena I did not stand all too firmly within these very wide boundaries of
my participation in the school. It was not at all my understanding that
every one of the school's participants had only to do his utmost to preserve the individual chief theses of Baur's construction of early Christianity. I valued too highly the protection against such a coarse misunderstanding guaranteed by the master's own basic principles as an
historian. In all timidity yet very definitely I had already begun to ask
whether or not that construction, even in all its foundations, could continue to stand. When I moved to Basel, I stood on the verge of giving
my co-workers in the field of church history a witness to my doubt: In
the spring of 1868 the printing of my revision of de Wette's commentary on the Acts had begun, and it was to appear in the first weeks of
my stay in Basel.[5] Yet already at that time I was occupied with areas
other than those in which Baur's efforts had especially furthered the understanding of church history (here I exclude his works dedicated expressly to the history of dogma). This was true not only because I had
become dissatisfied with Baur's rather exclusive focus on early Christianity. I had begun to realize from the second, not yet posthumous volume of his church history, published in 1859, that I would be able to
follow his lead in later periods of church history only in a very broad
sense.[6] Another publication made me realize it completely, namely
Baur's *Church History of the Nineteenth Century* [in 1863].[7] This book
is enormously insufficient and one-sided, and with it I became aware
that Baur could hardly remain for me an unconditional model of a
church historian.[8]

I had also let Baur's differences with Bunsen[9] motivate me to get a foothold in an area that Baur had insufficiently treated, the literature of the church fathers, and I was able to habilitate at Jena in 1864 with a small dissertation on Hippolytus.[10] This man of honor was at that time especially obscure, and he was able to give only very minor service in my attempt to gain a mentionable orientation in the literature of the church fathers. In Jena I eagerly continued my patristic studies with somewhat more fruitful subjects. As far as I can remember I had in those years only one opportunity to speak from a lectern other than my own, namely on occasion of the known series in Jena called the "Rose Lectures," which I gave in February of 1867. I chose as my theme "the origins of monasticism," a subject especially distant from Baur's interest in church history and one that at the time I myself was able to treat only separately from the rest of church history. In brief, as I left Jena I could not look back with special confidence on my supposed character of being a "Tübinger" as an immovable guidepost on the course of life opening before me, as tight as the ties still were that bound me to "Tübingen." As I moved to Basel, I did not do so as one who is empty. What I took with me always filled me with indelible gratitude for the teacher I had never met. I had grasped Baur for the enthusiasm that is to be drawn from mere books, and for my vocation as a scholar I had in him an ideal.[11] But I owe Baur even more, namely a task that not only has a great deal to do with my work as a teacher but also goes far beyond me, which I also owe to the freedom I took in looking beyond the horizon of Baur's church history. With no other assistance than his, I undertook to imitate in the whole area of the history of the church what he had done before me in the area of early Christianity. Naturally I did not do this more clearly than usually happens when a non-genius undertakes something of the kind so early in life, but I did it definitely enough to be filled with the undertaking. Certainly I did not realize at that time that I was stretching toward a work I was later to call "profane church history." If that was my goal, the unattainability of it is the surest token of its existence that I still carry in me.

So I followed the call to Basel issued by the "Mayor and the Council of the Canton of the City of Basel" to an "Assistant [ausserordentliche] Professorship of Theology" "with the obligation to give ten to twelve hours of instruction with special regard for New Testament exegesis and older church history." The "Education Collegium of the Canton" communicated the call, accompanying its "greeting of welcome" with "the expression of hope that I will find in my new position a sphere of work corresponding to my scientific inclination, and that my activity in the University may be a blessing for the academic youth."[12]

As encouraging as these friendly wishes were at the moment I left Jena, in Basel they could hardly suffice to help me over a significant gap left by my previous theological education. I have just spoken of be-

ing filled with the historical task I owed Baur: in fact already in Jena I
found no room left in me for any other interest in my vocation as a theological teacher than for the historical-critical understanding of Christianity. I consistently refused every opportunity to draw near to the liberal church-political efforts of my time and environment, neither
harboring expectations of me in this area nor letting them arise in others. Not that I lacked all inner participation in the like. But I never
thought of yielding even to the expectation simply of membership in
the Protestant League that was urged on me, sometimes strongly, from
more than one side. The most I ever did in the way of public acknowledgement of undertakings originating in the Protestant League was my
contribution of less than half a dozen short articles to Schenkel's Bibel-
lexicon.[13] That was very little in comparison with what, from certain
sides in any case, was expected of me in Basel. The position I received
had just been established by the government of the city. Parties had
been fighting about it for years, and the fight had been, as I was called,
so far decided: A teaching chair was to be granted the advocates of radical [sc. liberal] religious reform for the purpose of increasing their representation in the theological faculty. Historical theology was to be
taught according to critical principles, the foremost subject of conflict
in the scientific circles of theology. In the fog of party conflicts conceptions collected about me, who was hardly known to anyone, and about
the requirements I was to fulfill. These had to confront me with deci-
sions as soon as I arrived in Basel, and I was badly or only very generally prepared for them. What I knew of churchly movements that had
recently arisen in Switzerland as parallels to the Protestant League in
Germany was so little that in Jena I was completely in the dark about
what was happening in Basel. This condition persevered even after I arrived in Basel, and that it could do so was one of the first and especially
valuable experiences I had with the civil liberality of Switzerland.

Even today I cannot thank enough those persons responsible for
my call to Basel for the considerate discretion with which they kept
from me the "secret history" of how it came about. Every academic call
has such a history, especially when a new chair is involved, and if they
are usually not so secretive as in my case, they do usually conceal
enough as is advantageous for all concerned. I had the good fortune of
learning at first nothing really enlightening about the doubts of persons
other than myself regarding the call, and what I did learn came only
gradually.[14] I was hired after a seven-year search, for example, which I
learned from a brief and otherwise insignificant advertisement of the
book I am now preparing for its second publication. It appeared in 1873
after I had been in Basel for almost four years.[15] And so it was that for
a long time I remained free in my efforts to find my way in the task entrusted me.

As I now, remembering that distant time, express my gratitude, I
have every reason to include the Swiss "reformers" [liberals] who were

by virtue of the circumstances my first opponents. The way I occupied my chair was the keenest disappointment for them, yet they let me feel their disappointment strikingly little, less than I would ever have expected in any like situation of such tension. Above all I remember nothing of systematic pettiness or paltry behavior toward me that might have unpleasantly stifled the freedom of my thoughts about the basic principles involved in the conduct of the teaching office entrusted me. Especially in what was the decisive question for me, whether or not I would continue to refrain from popular party treatment of religious questions, I was approximately left where I wanted to be by my principal opponents.

There was also a certain process, the least benefit of which was the favor it did for me at first. For me I say, because it forced me to become more unified with myself with regard to the consequences of my scholarly preferences. What was my own relationship to Christianity, whose ways in history I had undertaken to research, as I discovered that a suddenly widening circle of persons was interested in what I was doing? The question arose in my first years in Basel not under ideal conditions, yet under unusually fortunate conditions. I could only wish anyone who has to deal with similar questions such good fortune, if I may intrude into another person's fate with my wishes. What forced me to become more unified with myself was both the conflict between pietism and reform in Basel into which I very unintentionally slipped when I entered office, and the impression I had of pietism in Basel. I would not be saying all I have to say here if I did not give due attention to this impression. Not that the matter could have meant for me any sort of serious participation in this way of thought [Denkweise], for I was already too deeply estranged from it for that to happen. I had been reared in Middle Germany and had altogether breathed its atmosphere in Jena, and it was much removed from all pietism. And yet I was not so completely estranged from pietism as to be totally unreceptive to the new religious climate into which I came. Indeed the thoughts that moved me to my discussion with my theological teaching office, in the book of 1873, arose partly under the influence of pietism. They would probably never have found the exact expression they finally found in the book had I been allowed my wish and remained in Jena.[16]

Yet with all these indications about new influences that came upon me as a theologian in Basel, I have touched on none that I would have to designate as having caught me completely by surprise. Indeed I have touched on none that any observer of the transition I had to make could not have thought of himself, without the information I have given here. However I did meet with one influence in Basel that I did not expect at all. It is the strongest of this kind I have ever met with on my wanderings through life, and indeed *nel mezzo del cammin* [in the middle of the road]. It also helped me write my book of 1873. What I mean is my friendship with Friedrich Nietzsche.

All that I knew in Jena about this extraordinary man—
extraordinary, too, in bearing misfortune—was strictly limited to the re-
ports that had circulated in the German universities since the spring of
1869. They put me in the prospect of having a young colleague in Basel
who had been called to be a professor before his doctoral promotion.
This was nothing that could lead me to expect much in the way of personal acquaintance. Certainly at that time I could not have known that
the indolent way my thinking worked was perhaps what most basically
distinguished me from Nietzsche, but at the moment I was certain that
I, who had been no more than a university lecturer for years, could
hardly match such speed on the academic race track. A coincidence
helped events move differently than first indications led me to expect.
Nietzsche and I were to be not only colleagues in Basel, but also "wall
neighbors," thanks to a mutual colleague who had arranged for my
room and board before my arrival. Out of this situation there developed, in the beginning of our second mutual semester, the habit of taking our evening meal in my room, which was on a lower floor and more
spacious. As one may imagine, at first the pressing obligations of an office to which we were not yet accustomed gave rather modest limitation
to this daily togetherness. But this one hour gradually became the occasion for other hours to join in, and it did not take long for something
like a relationship of inseparability to develop out of Nietzsche's and
my discourse during our four-year *contubernium* [life in the same
house] in Basel, as much as that was possible with the many "official"
occasions that separated us and considering the fact that Nietzsche, especially in the beginning of those four years, occasionally made trips
away from Basel, as is known.

But when we were together the least frequent topic of our hardly
stagnant conversations was given by theology, the beginnings of which
were not lacking in Nietzsche. Our increasing displeasure occasioned
by the great events in Germany, which we now viewed from a foreign
land, provided the topic for our conversations far more often. And we
talked about the innumerable things that persons at our age had to talk
about if they had not sooner been friends and opened their hearts. I
have no intention of asserting that already at this time I understood
Nietzsche, so that in this sense we might have been "one heart and
soul." As so many know today he had long been on his great voyage of
discovery within the broad horizon that opened before him so early.
Certainly just as little do I wish to say that I, seven years his elder,
would have been completely thrown off my own course had I blindly
followed him on this voyage. I did have many an opportunity to realize
that he had hardly arrived at its end, but how should I not listen and
watch that I, too, might learn from what I was being taught in such an
enticing way? The reading of *The Birth of Tragedy* took precedence,
speaking here above all of the public evidence of the thoughts moving
in Nietzsche in those years. I saw the book in the process of being born

before 1872, if I may so speak of a process in which Nietzsche, in the light of our daily conversations, was more than ever a most nontransparent and enigmatic mixture of an overflowing will to communicate and the reserve of a resolute hermit.

But whatever I may or may not have immediately realized of the meaning of Nietzsche's first work in the whole way of thought that was gradually to unfold in his writings, through the wonder [Selbstherrlichkeit] of its richness of thought *The Birth of Tragedy* could only thrive in me as the most powerful incitement to orientate myself more comprehensively in my own academic discipline and to bring more light into this comprehension. This was especially true as I saw how immediately conflicts ensued involving Nietzsche with colleagues in his field, conflicts that actually had more to do with Nietzsche's name than his person. Soon afterwards, perhaps beginning in the fall of 1872, I heard the first outlines of the plan for the *Untimely Considerations*. Here again I had to do with the mere summations that were typical of Nietzsche's communications with friends about such intentions. At first I listened so to speak, with only half an ear and did not reply directly, but by the spring of 1873 they had borne so much fruit in me that I was suddenly ready to follow their lead and courageous enough to undertake the task. The Easter vacation offered the indispensable time for the work. If these distant memories do not deceive me (I never kept notes about them), Nietzsche, when he left for Bayreuth just before Easter, knew nothing definite about my plan to write my *Christianity of Theology* during his absence. I remember with certainty that when he returned a few weeks later I very much surprised him with the information that I was almost finished with it. I did so again just after the middle of May by announcing its completion and reading him the preface.

The book may have taken longer to publish without Nietzsche's assistance. I had originally thought of a publisher much closer to me and less of a paradox to others than the one who finally published the book. When I was forced to give up my original plan for publication, Nietzsche proposed that we publish together: Both my *Christianity of Theology* and the first part of the *Untimely Considerations [David Strauss, der Bekenner und der Schriftsteller]*, which was also approximately ready for printing, should appear at his publisher, who specialized in music.[17] I knew nothing better to do and agreed. Nietzsche's sister has already related what Nietzsche did with his copies of our books when our "twins" lay before us in the binding given them by Fritsch in Leipzig.[18] I too had the two books bound in one volume, and the copy of the "Untimely Consideration" dedicated to me also bears the verse, on the back cover, in Nietzsche's handwriting: "A pair of twins from one house / courageously into the world went out / to tear apart world-dragons. / Two father-works! It was a wonder! / And the mother of the pair of twins / Friendship was her name!" Beneath the verse was written, "from one father to the other!"

Nietzsche's witticism has to do with the publication of the two books and nothing more, so it would be improper of me to carry on with his metaphor and speak of the current status of this strange family that his fantasy once created. Here I am not really speaking of this family at all, but only of one of its offspring, and yet I have had something to say about the "mother." Since she will disappear from life only when I do, she could not be forgotten here. Nor could I leave unsaid that my friendship with Nietzsche was with me as I, almost thirty years ago, wrote from my soul the following renunciation to my theological colleagues and let them know the only conditions under which I wanted to be considered their co-worker. In 1873 it was addressed first to friends whom I could be aware of having among them. Since then I have lost them, either through death, as is the case with most I can still remember, or through no longer being in touch with them. In its present reprint therefore my old and, as already said, unrevised renunciation has to present itself to entirely new readers. For their sakes I thought this introduction necessary, to let them see how it was written. In order that it may now come to an end, I let follow what I wrote in 1873 without delay.[19]

THE RELATIONSHIP OF THEOLOGY TO CHRISTIANITY GENERALLY

In days such as ours, when in the ears of everyone the call rings that not all is Christian that still claims to be, and the right at least to ask whether all is or not, is doubted by no one, theology cannot refuse to recognize the question, as harsh as it may sound, as directecl to itself, for it hardly lives on an island isolated from the rest of the world. Indeed, if it is true that none has the obligation to clairify its relationship to Christianity more immediately than theology, so it is also true that none is more urgently asked this question. Before we attempt to give an answer for our present time, it is fitting to look back in past times with the purpose of clarifying whether or not theology has ever had claim to the predicate "Christian."

Today one often hears that Christianity is inherently "drawn to science." In order to judge this statement, let us first understand in what sense one here speaks of Christianity. In the forms in which it has come down to the modern peoples, Christianity is by no means only a religion but also a culture. In the hours in which it felt its end,[20] GrecoRoman antiquity became Christian and won therewith in death the power to make us its heirs, so that now the modern peoples receive with the Christian religion—at the same time, from the same hands and as a unified structure—also the culture of antiquity. Seen in this way, one can say that Christianity is the embalmment in which antiquity has come into our time. If we understand all this as Christianity, then it is incorrect to say that Christianity is "inherently drawn toward science," bccause Christianity has science within it. If, however, we take Christianity as what it originally is and at first exclusively was, as religion, then this statement is completely false, because Christianity, as every religion, has a thoroughly unambiguous aversion to science. As with every religion: the antagonism of faith and science is perpetual and completely irreconcilable.

When Hermann Schultz tries to determine the boundary between faith and science (in an otherwise instructive and more serious and successful work than is usual in theological attempts of this kind), he still will have us operate, so to speak, with the philosopher's stone: he refers us to the religion "whose object offers no point of attack to science" as the "eternal" religion "that has nothing to fear from science."[21] A religion that really has nothing to fear from science and offers science no point of attack would have to remove its adherents beyond the limits of this world.[22] As long as that does not happen, the area of religion, whatever the origin of the religion may be, is the world. Religion creates its forms out of the material [Stoff] of the world, it has its existence only in these forms, and with these forms it cannot be saved from subjugation to scientific thought. A religion that would really in no way be "worldly" perceptible in its adherents would have to be denied any existence at all by science, and such a religion's fear of scientific thought would cease only with the cessation of its life. In truth, however, every religion has only then been unafraid of science when it has been strong enough to keep away from science the points of attack it necessarily exposes to it.

Hermann Schultz, in the essay mentioned, speaks of the religiously moral life "that is revealed in humanity through Jesus as reconciling and redeeming and that has won expression in those touched by his personality." Schultz asserts that this is "factually present for anyone that can see" and that therefore science can never doubt the Christian religion. But it is not at all necessary for it to doubt the existence of a sum of effects ordered under the name of Christianity. Rather science occupies itself with the explanation of these effects. If it is allowed only the ability to make one doubt "that the expression of this new redeeming life historically originated as has previously been assumed," so has science been allowed all it needs at will to annihilate Christianity as a religion. If the hitherto valid expression of Christian religious life be given over to scientific thought, and assuming that some comprehensible [fassbare] expression of this faith is at hand, it will be subjugated to science. For the expression must in some way have had an historical origin, and so the process of scientific thinking moves on and on as long as it is active and assuming it begins its questioning in the first place. Scientifiic thought can however only have begun and be in action where faith is too weak to remain by itself, where it is in doubt and hence gives over to science what it can no longer keep away from it whether with the intent of abandoning it to science or with the intent of having it supported by science. In either case faith has lost itself, for it has, even in the second case, become superfluous. In this world no really existing faith can withdraw from scientific thought unless it wills to do so; as soon as science is called upon, it will place itself beside faith and remain for all time something other than faith. Therefore the action of every theology, insofar as it brings faith into contact with science, is in itself and in its composition an irreligious action, and no theology can arise where interests foreign to the religious interest do not place themselves beside the religious interest.

Just how foreign these interests are, just how opposed to the interest of faith the interest of science is, can clearly be seen in the fact that the most essential assumptions and pillars of faith are the very first and most undoubted sacrifices to science. For example, no conviction is more essential to a religion than that it is the only true religion, and no conviction is more surely robbed by science. The believing Christian believes that Christianity (with its religious predecessor) fills the concept of religion entirely. He declares other religions false and believes himself bound to oppose them. Science, examining and comparing without prejudice, easily perceives that what Christianity does for Christians, non-Christian religions do for non-Christian peoples and that no religion can contest another without damaging itself—a point that has its most illustrous example in the polemic of the ancient church against paganism. Or, if we take miracles, everyone knows or can know both that they win the religion numerous believers where it rules alone, and that they cost the religion numerous believers where science opposes the religion.

The belief, for example, that the heavens would fall and the earth return to chaos if the Serapis image were touched by human hands, strengthened religious esteem for the image in Alexandria, but it sufficed for the annihilation of this esteem when a common Christian soldier under Theodosius I. destroyed the image with an ax and remained unpunished.[23] What had stood as a miracle under the protection of a belief that withdrew itself from all examination, had entered suddenly into the sphere of objective knowledge. {Among Christians the miracles of Jesus have served as "proofs" for him, but against unbelievers Jesus has had to be defended because of his miracles, for he appeared to unbelievers to be a magician ([for example, the heretic] Goet).[24] Another example is the miracle of transsubstantiation, which was a pillar of the belief of the Catholic Church in the Middle Ages but at the same time was an especially bountiful source of doubt about the church.[25]} Indeed the miracles of one religion work to its disadvantage in the eyes of another, as the Christian apologists demonstrated when they remarked against the miracles of pagan mythology that they were credible only in the first and most uneducated periods of humanity.[26] That is also an instructive example for the extent to which the feeling of commonality can be lost to religions through their oppositions to one another.[27]

Least of all can the fate and the experiences of Christianity cause us to think the relation of faith and autonomous scientific thought is one of lesser opposition. Christianity entered the world with the announcement of the impending end of the world, and just as no sort of earthly history lay in the original expectations of Christianity, so also a theology did not.[28] If Christianity nevertheless developed a theology more quickly than any other religion, then one would vainly search for some congeniality between Christianity and scientific thought in one or another of Christianity's fundamental ideas. The matter may rather be explained completely and easily enough from an entirely different side. Christianity is a young religion that entered a world standing at such a height of culture that one may ask whether today's humanity has

reached an equal height. Even Tertullian, for whom a consideration of
this sort was especially foreign, once noted that in distiction from earlier religious cults a distinguished character of Christianity is that it is a
religion for cultivated persons.[29] In such a world the basic religious
driving forces of Christianity, as strong as they may have been, had to
struggle with the most powerful hindrances, and it was only natural that
those driving forces came relatively soon to the point of compromising
with a world they could not annihilate and of seeking support where
they otherwise found only dangerous animosity.

The struggle between faith and scientific thought once took place
almost in the crib of Christianity, as Gnosticism, with astounding consequences, annihilated all historical presuppositions of the young faith
and transformed it into metaphysics, thereby disrobing it of its popular
character and making it into something other than religion.[30] Despite
this serious experience the ancient church was not able, at least not in
the orient, even for a short time to suppress the desire for a compromise
with the science of the world, which at that time was all-powerfully
represented by Alexandrianism. Instead of simple faith in redemption
through Christ withdrawing all the more energetically into itself, a
Christian theology was placed as true gnosis beside the now defeated
Gnosticism, which was held to be false gnosis. It is true that in this true
gnosis, especially by means of the recently established Christian canon,
a certain sum of Christian tradition was secured under the protection of
faith against the attacks of autonomous thought, but otherwise one felt
required to move from the standpoint of faith to that of scientific
thought. A sure proof of the opposition of autonomous thought to the
purely religious interests of faith is the fact that, even in the tempered
form of this theology, only with a kind of violence was scientific
thought able to press into the church, and it was able to assert itself
therein only under the most jealous control. By every free movement it
was in danger of being charged with heresy. And in fact it proved itself
to be the breeding ground of constant conflicts with the faith of the
Christian community.

Wholly characteristic for the entire development is its beginning,
as represented at the turn of the second to the third century by Clement
of Alexandria and after him by Origen. Contrary to the opinion of some
theological historians, we do not have here to do with philosophy [Wis-
senschaft] making a modest entry into the church through these oldest
establishers of a Christian theology. It was not warmly welcomed by
the older son of the house, faith, so that it could grow ever more beside
him. Rather, at the beginning of this development philosophy [Wissens-
chaft] generally was at the highest point of power it was ever to reach
in the ancient church; in following generations it was pushed back further and further from this initially attained position. In this one can see
very clearly that scientific thought as philosophy broke violently
through the oldest Alexandrians to the door of the church [zur Tür der

Kirche]. Clement rather equated the teachings of Greek philosophy with those of the Old Testament. This was a most brazen change from the standpoint of original Christianity and was shared by no one else at the time except the Gnostics. It could only appear as the worst heresy to the later churchly imitators [Epigonen] of the first Christian Alexandrians.[31] Yet it is just this valuation of Greek philosophy that Clement defends even with ridicule against the simple belief-Christians who shy away from any occupation with Hellenistic philosophy [Wissenschaft].

During his own lifetime Origen was heavily attacked because of teachings that shook the Christian tradition. He did, indeed, enjoy moderately uncontested acknowledgement during the largest part of the fourth century. That was the period when the church, having just been accepted into the Roman Empire, set about expanding its worldly dwellings, and in the midst of that expansion it was not yet able to forget the part played by the creator of its theological system. However, soon afterward Origen was placed among the worst heretics and condemned again and again, although his work had impressed itself indelibly on the theology generally assumed by the church. Hence the ancient church enjoyed the fruit of the audacity of its first theologians but permitted none of their theological descendants such audacity in the least, much less the freedom to surpass them. Nor did the ancient church shy away from forgetting these theologians. One can say this of Clement insofar as, after Eusebius, knowledge of him in the church practically disappears.

In fact the church never reached agreement on the question about the admissibility of a philosophical [wissenschaftliche] treatment of the objects of belief. Origen himself, who often enough asserted very decisively his right as an educated thinker [als Wissender] against simple believers (αρουστεροι, simpliciores) envied them when he remarked, in closing the foreword to his polemic against the pagan Celsus: that Christian is in the best position who has no need of a refutation of Celsus, the "first best" [erster bester] believing Christian who is able through the Spirit within him simply to disregard the objections of Celsus.[32] If the greatest man of learning in the ancient church can speak this way, then it cannot be surprising to see, for example, Athanasius begin an instruction in Christianity, for which a friend had asked, with the remark that the instruction is superfluous because the Christian religion witnesses to itself by means of living facts. Nevertheless he adjusts comfortably to the instruction, namely in order to counter a belittling judgment of the Christian religion and to insure that it not fall to pagan ridicule for want of a reasonable foundation.[33] That is a very worldly reason for giving the instruction. And in consideration of what Chrysostom actually does, it can be no more than a manner of speaking when he, as so many others, once says that there is nothing worse than measuring divine matters with the rule of human thought.[34] But a feeling of the ancient church against its theology comes here to expression from which it never freed itself. Theology fell under the judgment of condemnation that the ascetic ideals of the ancient church placed on all wordliness, especially in the eastern church, where, the more the mixture with pre-Christian culture had taken place, these ideals emerged with special energy. Western Christianity resisted all philosophical [wissenschaftliche] theology more stubbornly and much longer. When it did allow it, it took it, especially in the Origenistic theology, only from the hands of a frivolous literary figure, Jerome, and even then under strong resistance. Jerome was indeed the founder of theological learning in the western church, but in his frivolity he was wholly suited to guaranteeing the harmlessness of the philosophy [Wissenschaft] he brought into it.[35]

Such aversion to theology animated [beseelte] the Christian community at a time when an illusion was possible that, so it seems, should have helped it overcome the aversion, namely that there can be a theology that relates purely apologetically to Christian faith.[36] The illusion really did exist and it was actually possible in the church because it emerged in a period of the most rapid and undoubtable demise of all the sciences.[37] The same illusion was completely possible in the Middle Ages when Christianity, thoroughly mixed with Greco-Roman thought became the religion of those primitive peoples who came in contact with the Roman Empire through the great migrations. The church contained all the sciences within itself. And yet even here the peaceful relation that arose between faith and science was possible only because the ways and means of the state, now subject to the church, maintained it.

Remaining for the moment with the ancient and the medieval church and seeing that in them scientific thought, in relationship to the Christian faith, had clearly only the position of a tolerated magnitude, and recognizing moreover that the aversion to science in all religion is so much sharpened by Christianity's whole view of the world, one should think that theological talk about a "tendency to science" in Christianity could never have arisen at all, were it not for the fact that science is inherent in theology. That such talk could arise is due to the efforts of theology to deceive itself about its own identity. For calm consideration the fact is clear enough that Christianity equipped itself with a theology only when it wanted to make itself possible in a world that it actually denied. Even if one wanted in the most unconditional way possible to derive theology from Christianity's intrinsic religious interest, that statement would still be true, as for example if one were to say that Christianity had to assume theology in order, by looking back at its beginnings and holding to a true memory of its original appearance, to protect itself against degeneration.[38] In this derivation too, theology emerges from an intrinsic weakness in Christianity's existence in the world. But such a derivation would be completely wrong. In the very origins of theology, that is, in the oldest Christian Alexandrianism, it is as clear as can be that the first theologians turned their eyes in a completely different direction than toward Christianity's beginnings: with its theology Christianity wanted to recommend itself to the wise men of the world and let itself be seen before them. Seen in this way, theology is nothing but a part of Christianity's process of becoming worldly [Verweltlichung], a luxury Christianity allowed itself. But, as with every luxury, it was not to be had for nothing.

Just how expensive the luxury was, if it has not already been taught by the confusion in the ancient and medieval church, should be clear in the modern period, when all the illusions about scientific thought that were possible earlier have irretrievably collapsed. Science has emancipated itself from the church completely. It develops its own methods of proof and applies them without regard to purposes lying outside science. Not one of its disciplines orders its work according to the needs of Christianity. They are all completely unconcerned about whatever collisions with conceptions in the Christian tradition may occur, and least of all do they fearfully draw back from the increasing number of these collisions.

Since theology, insofar as it is science, does not possess its own principles of knowledge [Erkenntnisprincipien] but receives them from the other sciences—assuming it is not in a position to dictate them to the other sciences [as in the Middle Ages]—not even the illusion is still possible that theology is Christian science. If we can no longer fail to recognize that there is no Christian science, then theology cannot understand itself as it has heretofore understood itself. That the purpose of theology is not purely scientific is beside the point. It fully suffices to recognize that theology has science in itself, for the nature of what it has from science is not determined by theology's purpose, but by the concept of science generally. If Christianity always has been a scientific problem for theology, then today it simply cannot be overlooked that this means that theology makes Christianity as religion problematical that is, it puts Christianity in doubt. And indeed this is true of every theology, whatever its result may be. Even the result of apologetic theology, assuming the honesty of the process producing it, would not place apologetic theology in a more favorable light than critical theology, because if it could achieve its goal of producing scientific proof for Christianity, it would annihilate Christianity as religion.

Certainly theology most stubbornly resists acknowledging this last point, but it can be doubted only by the false theological idealism we have here opposed. Only this theological idealism can think that religion is indifferent to its own particular forms. Above all modern theology is totally unable to reproduce anything with even a resemblance of religion. A religion can be indifferent especially toward its possession of myths only as long as its myth-generating power is alive, that is, only as long as the miraculous powers that engendered its myth are still ellective in it. As is known, these powers have long since disappeared in the Christian world, basically ever since there has been a Christian theology. Because even earlier the Christian myth entered the stage of rigid tradition, historical interpretation of this tradition, above all of its canonical documents, was pursued early in the Christian community.[39] Yet the ancient church was free of the superstition that religious respect for holy writings can be maintained by the use of historical interpretation, and in allegorical interpretation it had a kind of surrogate for the myth that no longer lived in it. Our theology today, on the other hand, not only recognizes no other interpretation of Christian religious books than the historical, but it also cherishes the almost incredible delusion that it can again attain certainty about Christianity by means of history. Even if it were to succeed, the result would be no more than a scholar's religion, that is, nothing that seriously bears comparison to real religion. It would possess the same truth as the "thinking person's religion" that spooks about in many heads today and that, so one even hears, is supposed to have "displaced forever the religion of faith for all really educated and discriminating persons."[40] In reality nothing brings clearer to light the being of theology that is by nature foreign to the religion it means to serve than the presently so strongly stated overestimation of the historical for the positive [religious] purposes of theology, and the change of the times from the theology's lordship over science to its present subjugation to science. For science today, theology is even less than a maidservant, so far as it wants to offer itself as a maidservant and that is hardly asked of it.

Certainly this underestimation of the mythical forms and overestimation of the historical basis of religion in theology permit theology a sufficiently superficial idea of the relationship between faith [Glauben] and scientific thought [Wissen] to allow it to conceal its own relation to religion. It allows theology to assert, for example, with all too light a heart, that Christian faith is completely indifferent to all scientific discoveries.[41] Such an assertion is refuted daily by life itself, so far as every great discovery of the historical or natural sciences that has a relation to Christian teaching or myth causes conflict about it and makes believers into doubters. With their quieting assurances even good apologetic theologians take the matter very lightly. We give the following example: With regard to the Mosaic account of creation a theologian assures D.F. Strauss that "for a long time now, no Christian who understands the matter has held this religiously poetic picture of the creation idea, which is self-evidently composed by means of the ancient Hebraic knowledge of nature, for revealed natural science."[42] The Christian who regards such comprehension of the Mosaic account of creation as "self-evident" may indeed be understanding enough—it was less so to very understanding people earlier—but it would demonstrate greater understanding if he gave up the idea that such comprehension is religious. For the religious person the Bible does not have to do with natural science, but he also does not reflect on the fact that none is to be found in the Bible.

It is worthy of special note that the same people who so unhesitatingly abandon the creation account to rationalist criticism are also those who today often defend the literal credibility of many New Testament accounts, those of the resurrection for example, as something sacrosanct and with the most vehement invective against everything that is called criticism. They take no note at all of the fact that the shield of historical proof they take into battle is made only of wood. If they trusted this shield less, they would be cautious about making such differences in the canon, since its religious authority rests on equal regard for all its parts. If that is abandoned, one has to establish, for example, why the critical judgment reserved for the creation account is not applicable for the resurrection accounts. To establish this there remains only reflection on the possibility of historical certification [Bezeugung]. Given the temporal distance, one must concede to some extent the greater possibility of providing it for the biblical resurrection accounts than for the creation, but one should not be deceived about the purely scientific and irreligious character of this whole way of viewing the matter, even if the same reflexion at one time supports doubt about the word of Scripture and at another time belief in it. The real believer in Scripture has the same certification for both the creation and the resurrection accounts. One could hardly understand how such apologetic theology can say that the discoveries of science are indifferent for Christianity, if one did not realize again and again how easy it conceives its work of mending the torn places in religious faith to be, a task it sees itself having to undertake because of science.

In order to assure "Christian faith" the same theologian whose statement against Strauss was quoted earlier offers the following as what he would have said if Darwinian theory had really proven its theses: "Then we would only say to ourselves that the unique original miraculous cell, which carried like a seed within itself the whole future plant, animal and human worlds, was certainly the greatest product of the creative majesty of God that can be thought. We would say that the gradual development, according to plan, working its way toward human being, of all the possibilities given in this original cell, belongs to the strongest proofs that not blind chance, but divine thought and will directs the way of things, and finally that the last stage of this development, the step from animal to human being, can certainly only have been brought about by God having breathed his personal Spirit into the most suitable animal figure."[43] Such statements prove that even a theologian can be naive, or rather—on the point here under discussion all theologians usually are. Who does this apologetic theologian think is going to believe these crude fantasies? What serious person in any case; there are certainly enough of the other type who want to be persuaded. The believer takes his conviction about the creation of the world and human being from the Bible, because for him the Bible has religious, divine authority. Indeed he does not need the same kind of authority to shake his faith, but he does to restore it. From where does Professor Beyschlag take the authority to tell us what God did in the creation on the presupposition of Darwinian theory? The Bible says nothing about it, nor does Darwinian theory, which moreover speaks not of a "miraculous cell" but only of an "original cell." Is the sudden inspiration of a theologian really good enough to do what neither the Bible nor Darwinian theory do?

It is obvious that a theology that covers the opposition of faith and science with a disgusting mixture of half-science and half-faith can deceive itself endlessly about its own nature. It is also the most worthless verbiage that has ever existed, because it consists of words that always come up where both autonomous thought [Denken] and faith have ceased. Such superficial attempts at mediation make it entirely clear that science can destroy religion, but never build religion up again. The Christian theology of earlier ages proves nothing, to the contrary, given the atrophy of science in those ages. Recently it is proven not so much through the devastation that science has wrought in the area of Christian faith as through theology's attempt, and through the barrenness of it, to reconstruct the religion of Christianity by means of unbridled science.

We should speak therefore of Christian theology in no other sense than as, and insofar as it is, the *practical* science that works, with particular regard for Christianity, on the task of drawing the boundary between the world-culture and religion and of setting them in relationship to each other. The scientific character of theology has no immediate claim to being Christian. Broadly conceiving the human significance of the matter, support for Christianity is either a matter for all the sciences, as was earlier the case, or for none at all, as is presently the case. For theology today not even the appearance of support can exist. If we have generally ascertained that theology contains an irreligious element, and Christian theology therefore an unchristian element, we are best prepared for the fact—which we now wish to demonstrate in the chief theological parties of the present—that in the hands of theologians Christianity can be transformed into a thing that is no longer Christianity.

2

THE APOLOGETIC THEOLOGY OF THE PRESENT

Today two large theological parties oppose each other in the theological world. They argue the theological conflict of the present for public opinion and, if one obviously has more power than the other, especially in Germany, they share public interest equally. They are now involved in the most vehement feud with one another. We name them the apologetic and the liberal theology. Their conflict turns on the question of how much of the traditional concepts of Christianity should be abandoned to science. It has become more passionate recently, namely since the liberal theology through its chief representatives popularized a series of results of critical historical research about Christianity and the church, and since it began trying to win the laity by organizing associations: the "Protestant League" [Protestantenverein] in Germany and the "Association for Free Christianity" [Verein für freies Christentum] in Switzerland. Here the scientific arguments in the conflict will not be considered, especially the question of whether or not the scientific differences between the parties are as radical as they outwardly appear to be. With regard to this side of the conflict, the way we view these parties' claim to be Christian should be clear from the general view of theology we have already given. We wish rather to follow the two parties primarily in that area where every conflict about religion wins general interest and indeed actual content, in the area of the view of life [Lebensbetrachtung]. Here we wish to evaluate the assertion that in this area they are rather in accord, which is quite surprising given the general tenor of their relationship. They even say that in their view of life they stand fairly close to their bad opponent D.F. Strauss, from whom both have heard nothing worse than the assertion of the incompatibility of world culture and Christianity. Let us begin with apologetic theology as the oldest party and the party that most benefits from its Christianity. the younger party having first been forced by Strauss to affect being Christian.

Possession of power, which is always supposed to be a bad thing, is supposedly the reason for apologetic theology's special lack of self-knowledge and for its complete inability to tell itself with Chrysostom that there would be no heathen if Christians would be real Christians. As a rule it does not at all shy away from deriving the unbelief it finds for its "proof's of Christianity" from the evil will of its opponents, which it does with the most inconsiderate and various expressions. In accordance with the good evangelical words, "you shall know them by their fruits" the character of the polemic that is quite commonly directed by our apologetic theologians against doubters has to reflect badly on the Christianity of this party. However brilliant its traces of heavenly origin otherwise might be (sit venia verbo [pardon the expression] in this case), one may stop one's ears to the creed of a journal such as the *Neue Evangelische Kirchen-Zeitung*, which expresses itself with such poisonous malice and such paltry meanness against persons and opinions it considers heretical. But is the proof of Christianity in apologetic theology really so impressive?

The most worthless of all proofs for a religion, the historical, is by far the most highly rated in apologetic theology. We have already stated why it is worthless, even if it should succeed. Historical proof for religion will always have a bad result, because the origin of all religion is thoroughly nonhistorical and unscientific. Whoever therefore wishes to use science to smooth out everything in such an origin has to make use of a corrupt science. Young Christianity only proved its strength when it, disregarding a contradiction obvious to scientific thought, placed the johannine depiction of Christ beside the synoptic. If, however, the forces are lost that made such boldness possible, nothing can be helped by historical means.

Every more profound apologetic theology knows the weakness of historical proof for religion, or at least it has the feeling, if not the knowledge, that to be effective this proof has to be applied with art. Historical proof of Christianity is as old as theology. Whoever has experienced its bluntness in present apologetics should learn the possibility of its effectiveness in the church fathers. Among them the proof had no isolated effect but rose from the background of their dark ascetic view of life. Pascal's method is less naive and, because it is more consistently thought out, more instructive. One can call him the greatest apologist of Christianity in post-medieval times, whereby it is not to be forgotten that an apologist of Christianity is something other than its preacher. Pascal does wholly without the so-called metaphysical proofs of Christianity, but not without the historical, and not even his acumen is able to make these proofs any better. But he puts them at the end; he knows the matter depends on awakening a certain mood before the success of the actual "proofs" can be expected, and he says himself that one must wish that this religion be true.[44] To awaken the wish, he uses a means so strong that our apologetic theologians certainly never have the power to match it, although they occasionally imagine their works "have grown out of Pascal's Pensées."[45] Pascal tries above all to frighten his reader with the thought of death as the door to dark eternity and of the limited insight of a humanity fluttering helplessly between the infinitely large and the infinitely small. One has to view world and life differently than our apologetic theologians in order to compose, not merely copy, words of such grippingly dark despair as the meditations on death that Pascal intended for the beginning of his work. His subtle and deeply penetrating skepticism is not something for our apologetic theologians either. They prefer his writings on the limitation of human insight. Pascal, who at the same time says that to think clearly is the foundation of morality, may speak of this limitation, not authors who sin on all sides against morality so understood and who awaken the suspicion that they talk about human limitation just to protect this quality in their own arguments. Pascal, who finds the fine expression "to be shaken by reason" (être ébranlé par la raison), may speak of human limitation, not writers who make us constantly doubt that Pascal's statement that this being shaken usually occurs in one's twentieth year has any general validity at all.

What one says and requires be believed cannot just be loftily thought; it must be experienced [empfunden], and so one must experience [empfinden] with Christianity when one defends it. One could almost conclude just how little our apologetic theologians share this experience from the joy they naively express occasionally about "living in an apologetic age." In truth things have become precarious for a religion that has entered *this* period of history among its confessors. More telling is the fact that they are most confidently comforted by that "proof" of Christianity that can most be done without when one experiences [empfinden] what Christianity experiences, namely the historical. Taken by itself it is the most hollow of all and it quite naturally just bounces off the hearer who is not already inclined to believe it. Only one other proof could possibly be worse, the proof on the basis of natural history, of which Pascal happily knew nothing. Yet in apologetic theology today it rivals the historical.

The more weakly apologetic theology speaks from what should be the source of its strength, the more it has to emphasize these exterior aspects of its work. As it does so, as is easily understandable, it occasionally develops into naked impudence, especially with proofs from natural history. It is very impolite of us to express ourselves in this way, but we would like to know how else we should speak of the procedure used, to give only one example, by one of our most respected apologetic theologians, Professor Luthardt in Leipzig. In his well known apologetic lectures in support of his dogmatics, he tries to convince us that the earth is the "spiritual center" of our solar system and the only inhabited planet in it. After he demonstrates this for the planets most distant from the sun, with arguments that only a theological dilettante in the sciences could produce, he seems to suffer a certain anguish with the planets near the earth. He appears to think no one will notice his problem when he simply carries on:

> On Mars existence would be most tolerable, but only because it is similar to the earth, without, however, reaching it. Venus is in its

constitution much like the earth, but, with a 72 degree incline of its axis, its seasonal changes are too harsh. It has also been concluded that its absence of clouds means it is without water and therefore unsuited for organic life. Mercury, however, whose surface is only one ninth that of the earth, is much too small for human life, "whose homeland must be larger." And so we see that only the earth is the true realization of the idea of a planet. The other planets are only stages in the development of the idea of a planet. Earth is the planet, the goal and center of the planetary system, at least as far as we can judge. It is the only body in our solar system suited for the development of higher organic life.[46]

One sees that Luthardt is just as little concerned for the comfort of whatever inhabitants there might be on those planets, all of whom he imagines to be earthlings, as he is for his argument. He is not at all concerned about concealing the fixed idea that determines everything, namely that the earth is *"the"* planet (the emphasis on "the" can hardly press out anything conceivable), and that only that planet can be inhabited that "reaches" the earth, which means finally that only the earth can "reach" the earth. Luthardt's bad conscience is laid bare to his public in the incidental words "as far as we can judge"; the public can make of that whatever it wants. He thinks he can blind the public with a bit of rhetorical art, but can one think of a more paltry and tasteless piece of rhetorical art than the short quotation, taken from trifling small talk, with which he runs past Mercury? In spite of all the words about Christianity how little that is essential need be said in order for Luthardt to lead his hearers into the quicksand of this whole question, and how completely little in order to base Christianity on such shameless nonsense!

One asks us, do the apologetic theologians of the present really base Christianity only on proofs of this kind? Do they not speak of the sin, misery and death in the world? Certainly, but in such a way that no one can believe their diatribes, and one always has the impression that they really feel at home only in the paralogisms of historical and natural historical proofs that they so eagerly pursue. Indeed it is a basic fault of theology that in it there is talk of so many things about which the speakers lack perception [Anschauung], experience or inner conviction, and that its teachers forget to be concerned about these requirements in writings that are intended to convince others. If theologians had a clearer feeling than is usually the case for how easily human language betrays the real state of things, they would speak less of many lofty matters, or at least in lower tones, and fill their mouths less with what their hearts are empty of. But they usually lack this insight, and here too one can say: quem deus perdere vult dementat [whom god wants to ruin becomes demented]. Furthermore the bad habit of defending things that have no inner truth for us produces in them that impure ardor with which one gets excited about things one does not entirely be-

lieve and which is the source of all priestly malice and theological zeal-
otism.

Let us take as an example the idea of hell. As much harm as it has
wrought and as often as it has found its only nourishment in the hate of
the theologian, in the atmosphere of the Middle Ages it nevertheless
served a great poet well as a reproof, and in the church fathers too it
had the gripping character of a really effective and living motif.[47] As is
always the case with Christian conceptions having to do with eschatology (and one can also say it in general), namely that the light Christianity casts on the world beyond serves less to enlighten that world than to
darken this one, so also the conception of hell is completely impossible
when taken out of the context of the dark portrayal of earthly life,
which the church has but our apologetic theologians no longer. Taken
purely by itself, the idea of eternal torment exceeds all comprehension
of head and heart. Thought out with the calmness and rigor required by
science, it leads either to madness or to its own annihilation. That is the
reason for the very particular frigidity suffered by dogmatic expositions
on hell in our modern apologetic theologians. Should their didactic tone
be lifted against an opponent, its lightning bolts are no more than theat-
rical special effects. One has just the opposite of the impression of sublime dread when such a modern rabbi as Franz Delitzsch tells us, in
tones of greatest confidentiality, that in hell "there is not only teeth-
gnashing but also weeping."[48]

On what do the apologetic theologians base their claim to our belief in their proof of the miracles? No one has ever been brought to belief in miracles by means of mere syllogisms. Whoever defends such
belief obligates himself to a certain extent to perform miracles himself.[49] His speech should at least lift us to the world from which miracles are supposed to come. The teachers of the ancient church could do
that through the shadows they cast over the earthly world and through
their constantly repeated practical attempts to give a living presentation
of the existence of a better world. How much worse is the position of
those who, as far as one knows, today arrange their lives as does everyone else, that is, as if there were no miracles, and who, whatever they
say about a better world, constantly remind us that the earthly world
has its own good, and for whom indeed the miracles they do believe
have become something historical [past].

Nothing reveals the character of modern belief in miracles so
clearly as the thoughtless way Protestant theology has accepted the
view [Anschauung] that eighteen hundred years ago a good many miracles occurred in several regions of the Roman Empire but soon ceased
and in our time do not occur. As for the when and why of their cessation, the various answers theology has hatched out will always be particularly telling examples of the absurdity of allowing mere puzzles to
take the place of the world's real problems. When one of these answers,
and it is hardly unusual, states that miracles soon became superfluous,

it is a startlingly naive revelation of just what theologians really think of the miracles they defend and of just how little they are interested in allowing our world to be disturbed by these foreign guests. If the miracles of that former time really soon ceased and today no miracles are worked and above all none just as obvious, then they should rather say to themselves that miracles, as all that no longer lives [wirkt], are dead and can be given over to discussion by science, which theoretically proves there are no miracles in this world. To have the right to dispute science's theory they would have to disprove it in practice, which would spare them a great deal of the crude and self-defeating tactics that they usually expose to their opponents.

What should one say about the following piece of apologetic theology from, again, one of its most respected representatives, Professor Otto Zöckler in Greifswald?

> As we stand over against the works of heavenly beings within our earthly world, these proofs—for human or even English organs [of perception]—of divine spirit and power, these first fruits of the future glorification of the world in the midst of the world's temporal course, we do so exactly and with very nearly the same wonder as the savages of a south sea island first glimpse the triumphs of European civilization and inventiveness, for example, the way a printing press works, or a steam engine, or a telegraph, or a photographic apparatus. And as these raw children of nature only very gradually give up the opinion that these objects of their astonishment have magical, absolutely supernatural, even unnatural character, so do we see that humanity generally only very slowly comes to insight into the true nature of the miracles as emanations of a higher or glorified natural order. But we see that full knowledge and empirical understanding of this higher order is saved up for the end of the world and palingenesis, just as those savages can attain full understanding and complete enjoyment of the blessings of our culture only after Christian education, morality and culture have completed their work.[50]

It is impossible to do justice to all the remarkable things in this quotation, for example to enlightenment about steam engines and such through "Christian education." Remaining with the chief matter, theology, it seems that one judges theologians too kindly when, as is so often the case, one reproaches them for thinking and forming their God in human terms, for here we have to do with a God that is subhuman. What is more painful for the educated, cultured person than the barrier that education and culture erects between him and those of his fellow humans who lack it? It is a feeling that is so strong none stronger stands against education and culture. Would such a person not endeavor as much as possible to equalize the disruption that education brings into the immediate understanding that persons have for another? Would he not feel [empfinden] it his duty, for example, to anticipate all unfounded "astonishment" over a photographic apparatus in those islanders and then to fulfill this duty in the very best way he can? That is, of course, if he does not have in mind exploiting the innocence of his spectators for egoistic purposes. This last situation is similar to that in which Zöckler's deiculus [little god] confronts us poor ignorant inhabitants of the island earth, as if he intended to "astonish" us with his magic tricks, to keep us in such astonishment for thousands of years, and to let us know only with "palingenesis" that all those tricks were basically very simple and natural. And he certainly must not have reckoned with the great cleverness of theologians who would betray his play long before the chosen time. So do theologians today, who speak of the "blessings of our culture" defend the miracles. No wonder one gladly avoids their discussions just in order not to be placed constantly in the position of those astonished savages.

"The blessings of our culture"—an expression one hears dubiously often on the tongues of our contemporary Christian apologists. Christianity once thought very differently about this kind of "blessing," and after having been almost two thousand years in a world that has changed astonishingly little, there is no perceptible reason why it should think differently today than earlier. Our present-day apologists could hardly appeal even to the culture Christians [Bildungschristen] of the fourth century to justify their view, for example, the Great Cappadocians and Chrysostom. There is hardly a picture more insulting of both Christianity and culture than the culture Christianity of the eastern church in the fourth century. In this period, after the peace concluded between state and church, the two opposed powers of heathen culture and Christian faith held each other in a kind of balance. But just for this reason one can see in their union their contradictory natures all the more clearly and comprehensively, and for the same reason they corrupted one another all the more basically. But that is here beside the point. One must not fail to recognize the deep melancholy resting on all those figures of the fourth century, and one must especially not forget that monasticism stood behind and beside them performing satisfaction for their sins—and they were all enthusiastic and practical admirers of monasticism.[51] But who performs satisfaction for our contemporary apologists' desires for culture? Because they do not seem to feel [empfinden] the lack of anyone performing it, not even melancholy is to be seen on the countenances of our modern Gregory and our modern Basil. Those earlier Christians found no comfort when they saw the contrast between their culture and that of the apostles; modern apologists are far more at ease about it.

Only recently one of the smoothest of these modern apologetic culture Christians [Bildungschristen] has found expressed in the words of the Acts of the Apostles, which speaks of Paul's abhorrence on his entry into Athens "because he saw the city was so idolatrous" [Acts 17:16], that Paul, besides this abhorrence also felt "purely human admi-

ration" for the beauty of the Parthenon.[52] Here it seems that, as earlier
faith in Christ misled theologians into making what they wanted of the
words of Scripture [allegory], so today's belief in culture misleads them
into doing the same thing. Here too belongs the almost childlike joy
many theologians feel [empfinden] over the two or three quotations in
the Pauline letters of what at that time were very well known expressions of Greek poets, and here belongs all that these theologians have
built up on the basis of those quotations. Indeed Christ himself is supposed to show, at least in the style of his language, that he was a friend
of culture, and indeed for the inconceivable reason that his style is original.[53] But a view of life hostile to culture, too, can find very beautiful
and distinctive form, as for example in the *Imitatio Christi*;[54] in the
beautiful style and in the views [Anschauungen] of the book disregard
for what we call culture is expressed, and the same is true of the synoptic language of Jesus. But let us leave the cultural needs of our apologists to search for straws to catch at even in the New Testament.

How do they conceive the relationship of Christianity to the culture they strive to have? General Superintendent Wilhelm Hoffmann in
Berlin can instruct us here in a very characteristic way, in a book that,
the more sacerdotal it comports itself, is all the more recommended for
anyone who wants an especially visible instruction on the death of the
real practical ideas of Christianity among its, so to speak, most official
representatives. Hoffmann opposes the [liberal] Protestant League with
the following statement:

> It can be conceded that Christianity and modern culture have to
> move closer together and that this movement does not have to be
> accomplished one-sidedly by the representatives of modern culture.
> A greater appreciation of the peripheral effects of Christianity can
> be required in the circles of the leaders and servants of the church.
> The distinction can also be urged between what really belongs to
> faith and what falls purely in the area of scientific thought. The de-
> mand for the church's restraint in its judgment of science can be as-
> serted. But neither now nor ever may the church, in order to move
> closer to modern culture, give up its belief in the personal Trinitar-
> ian God, the incarnation of God in Christ, redemption through
> Christ's resurrection and ascension and the founding of the church
> by the Holy Spirit. For if the church were to give up these beliefs, it
> would give up not a view [Ansicht] but a religion.[55]

That is clearly stated and really an excellent expression of the position of our apologists toward Christianity and culture, although one
notices, from the whole tone of the piece, that here one of the lords of
the house is speaking, one who has the keys both to the door of culture
and to the door of Christianity and who may allow himself the freedom
to say more boldly than others what he really thinks. Bold, very bold, in
such a mouth, but as the attentive reader will easily have noticed, we
welcome the distinction between a "religion" and a "view" [Ansicht] in

Christianity. As highly as we earlier evaluated the significance of forms for religion, hopefully we have not given the reader cause to think that we might know anything about a Christian religion without a "view" or with a changing "view." Moreover, in the evaluation of what our apologist calls "religion" and "view" in Christianity, we are in the most radical opposition to him, as the reader can also have noticed. What Hoffmann calls a "view" is what we have already called Christianity's view of life, through which one has to comprehend Christianity's judgment about scientific thought, which Hoffmann designates, with an uncomfortably ambiguous and obscure expression, as the "peripheral effects of Christianity"—in plain language worldly life. In this area, according to Hoffmann, the Christian "view" is to be given over to the culture, or it is at least to let the culture have something to say to it. And there could well be a culture that would be satisfied with this success and which could then always boast of having seized the kernel of the matter for itself but of having, with a light heart, given the shell to those who want to amuse themselves with it.[56]

This "culture" would certainly be a strange thing. It would not be allowed to strive for harmony, for if it did, it is doubtful that it would come to a halt before the dogmas the General Superintendent places under the protection of his proud "neither now nor ever." It would have to be a culture of approximately the same level possible in Berlin a short time ago when, in broad daylight, an inquisition having to do with the supernatural conception of Christ was initiated. It could in any case be nothing other than the culture of a sect imagining itself able spitefully to insist exactly on what scientific thought has finished with, which is to say that which, because of its exposed position, first and most surely falls as a natural sacrifice to science.

It is not our intention to follow our apologists' view of life into the different individual areas of worldly living. We wish to mention only one of these because the General Superintendent in Berlin has called it so strongly to mind. We refer first to a German photographer's supposedly unprompted consecration of Prussia's annexation of Hannover in 1866: he compares the annexation to the Hebrews' occupation of Canaan in the Old Testament. The area of worldly life here meant forces itself so strongly on everyone's attention that we can hardly avoid it: politics. Christianity is in its roots nonpolitical, and that is an incontestable truth that would not be overlooked so often if it were not for the fact that in all our histories of the church unclarity and error still rule over the most fundamental points on the relation of the church to the state. At present the representation of this truth seems to have passed, especially in Germany, to the stained hands of the untramontanists, which cannot be surprising considering the fact that the Christianity of the ruling circles of our Protestant conservative theology has taken flight into several dogmas secure in all eternity from every collision with politics and generally with everything that really lives, yet has given up its "views." We wish to give only a few examples in order to make clear the characterlessness of the role only such a "Christianity," in days as are now experienced in Germany, can play. But many other examples could be given.

Among the great and many dangers that a time of such glowing political success can hold for any nation is that of arrogance. If we Germans today are honestly trying to put our whole moral strength into not being conquered by our conquests, then we shall hope above all not to lose generosity and clarity in our judgment of other peoples.[57] What generosity and clarity we have cannot exactly be derived from our current Christianity, but in any case our endeavors to keep them are apparently not being supported by Christianity's preachers. General Superintendent Hoffmann, as he enlightens us "in the light of the Kingdom of God," finds that "the manifold of nations has the right to be in God's great Kingdom," but "first the related Germanic nations, then also the Romantic and the Slavic."[58] The difficulty of showing just how Christianity attributes this greater "right" to the Germanic peoples can be no little one, unless one were to think this is the now discovered allegorical meaning of Paul's words, "first the Jews and then the Greeks." The truth is that here one of Christianity's most original perceptions [Empfindungen] is dead.

Worthy of being remembered is, furthermore, the following course of events that took place at the church conference in Berlin in October, 1871, which in all due pomp united the heads of officially ruling Christianity, especially those in Prussia. An insignificant vicar from Wiedenbruck allowed himself as a Christian to deplore the war that had just ended. He said that wars would no longer be possible if the various peoples were truly Christian. The notes on the conference published by its secretarial office tell us that "the increasing discomfort of the conference participants, who finally made a stormy call for the end of the speech, forced the speaker to desist." And so do the notes have done with it, except for telling us that the next speaker, before turning to his own text, remarked from the podium to the vicar that "as long as there is sin in the world, there will be wars, but God will continue to reveal himself in these wars as the Lord Zebaoth." This remark is a dancing test of balance on the wire stretched between the Old and New Testaments. Theologians have always demonstrated their agility in this act, just as they knew what they were doing when, in the second century, they so bravely defended one of the poles of this equilibrium [the Old Testament] against the Gnostics, who tried to pull it from the ground. But when a conference that calls itself Christian gives no other answer than the one given in the secretarial notes to words such as those of the vicar, its Christianity may be equated with a Christianity in name only, and one gladly turns one's eyes from the Byzantine character of the whole scene. The same would be true even if that representative of Christianity had spoken only clumsily and at the wrong time {which in the light of 2 Timothy 4:2 should not have much significance}.[59]

It is clear from all that has been said that our modern apologists want Christianity, but perhaps it is yet clearer that they want worldly culture. But let us ask what sort of culture do they want? Does at least enough of all Christianity's particular shyness toward the world and its culture live in them for them to be especially discriminating about culture, to appreciate only a wholly peculiar kind of culture, one that corresponds to the individual needs of a Christian view of life? Hardly. Here and there they do hold a small spiritual exercise, in the muted style of a syllabus, against modern culture and modern unbelief, but do they themselves produce anything original? To affirm that, one has to allow the "Christian novel" to count as original that they set in the world here and there and that, as their journals prove, they read along with the novels that everyone else reads.

On the whole one can only be astounded at how much today's culture levels the outer appearances of our most hostile theological parties, which is a sure proof of the actual nothingness of their opposition. If the oppositions that supposedly exist between our apologetic and liberal theologies were serious, they would have to engender basically different cultures. Let us remain for the moment with literature. Do our apologists write differently than their opponents? No. Right and left one recognizes what generally rules in literature today: the newspaper. Are the apologetic theologians more frugal with the treasures they pretend to be the stewards of? Are they more reluctant to carry them to the market place? Given appearances, we should expect an affirmative answer, but everyone knows the answer to both questions is no. At the same podium where a speaker from the Protestant League stood yesterday, an apologist stands today. In print too they are soon found in opposition, but here they have all the more reason to tell the reader quite clearly that what the other side says is wrong, because otherwise the reader might not notice that he—given the great similarity, the coloration of thoughts, the presentation—had read something entirely different in each.

Are the journals of the apologists in their forms edited according to principles other than those of the liberal journals? Here, too, they are essentially the same, although the apologetic side is at times one degree more malicious. One should notice the critical rules with which a journal such as the *Neue Evangelische Kirchenzeitung* measures. The more the character of a work is what one calls "literary" or the more it distances itself from the particular interests of theology, the more certain it can be of being accepted with applause, even if its theological "direction" is not appreciated. But if it has a strictly scientific form, the "direction" alone decides the judgment. A work such as Lüdemann's anthropology of Paul is put aside simply by being called "wrong," while Hausrath's history of the New Testament period is received with a degree of reverence, although every serious theologian, whatever his direction—when he is not involved simply with a mass of facts from which he wants to form his own judgment—can learn far more from Lüdemann's work than from Hausrath's.[60]

Given the narrowness and characterlessness of present apologetic theology, one can give a guaranteed recipe for a good start to the young person who wants to exhibit himself before it scientifically. "Write a grammatical or historical treatment. If you decide for grammar, a theme from the Bible is recommended, because even if you write about Hebrew accents or the use of a preposition in the New Testament, it will appear that you unite theological and scientific interests. If you choose an historical treatment, make a smart choice. If you are not entirely sure of your dogmatics, leave the Bible, especially the New Testament, out of the picture. Do rather a patristic monograph. At present there is a demand for such works, and it would serve your purposes well, especially if you manage to treat your figure no more cleverly than, for example, Zöckler treats Jerome.[61] But something from the popish Middle Ages will always be the best and most certain choice. Not even ignorant persons doubt the ignorance of this period among us Protestants." If the young person followed this advice, he could be sure of moving up in the judgment of apologetic theology.

A pact between apologetics and science having to do with their basic positions would secure the two a long peace, assuming good behavior. If it were based on mutual silence, the ears of the apologists would not be offended, and science, or whatever of science could speak at all, would remain free. And who will doubt that the enormous mass of material piled up by recent work in languages and history suffices for whole armies of living men to conceal themselves behind it? In the works of theology (and if they are worthy of their name they will necessarily have a "tendency"), this kind of pursuit of science will always be such an untruth that it will have only few adherents, as is quite understandable.[62] Having found such pursuit very compatible, apologetic theology has for years suffered the worst sort of unfruitful barrenness in the area of science. One may admit that (for example) the works on the Bible by Johann Christian Konrad von Hofmann in Erlangen are able to conjure up at least a phantasmagoria of science, but how many works even of this sort have been produced by apologetic theology recently? Especially this barrenness should cause apologetic theology to reflect on itself and to take stock of its work. But one cannot hope for that as long as its judgments can be as shallow as, for example again, those of the *Neue Evangelische Kirchenzeitung*. It has done with Keim's life of Jesus with the assertion that "today's science" can "draw a much truer life of him in whom the glory of the only begotten Son of the Father appeared."[63] For several decades now, the "today's science" meant by the *Neue Evangelische Kirchenzeitung* has been seriously challenged to produce such a "drawing," but where is it? In fairness one will not even think of the flood of empty brochures and speeches that apologetic theology has so eagerly produced against recent works on the "life of Jesus." As will be shown, we are hardly an advocate of Keim's work [see Chap. 3]. But where has apologetic theology offered us only one work on Jesus that would be in the least comparable with Keim's in diligence, rigor, learning and richness of thought? Where is the book that could show such obvious traces of serious work, where a composition made up of not only the traditional expressions but of such originality in its comprehension of its object? The *Neue Evangelische Kirchenzeitung* leads us to suppose that at least the desks of our apologetic theologians are full of much better works. They will do well not to overcome their obvious aversion to daylight. Purely learned and polemical works excluded, one does not have to be a prophet to predict that, from the theological ranks of the *Neue Evangelische Kirchenzeitung*, a scientific work on an important theme of original Christianity will never be produced that would have the least significance outside of a small sect. Thanks to the characterlessness of apologetic theology, this future is knowable.

The extraordinary lack of effect of what apologetic theology does produce, especially its popular literature, should also open its eyes to what it really is. Instead it thinks it can boast occasionally about the great success of its writers. It refers us to the lectures of Professor Luthardt already mentioned, which, so the newspapers tell us, were heard by hundreds or thousands several years ago in Leipzig and which are presently published in many editions and translations. Or it refers us to the similar fate of Konstantin Tischendorf's apologetic writings.[64] But one should also speak of a *succès terrible*, of a success of writings that only serves to make evident how empty they are. Especially popular theological writings can experience this success. They appeal to a very lively and general interest, but because of their theological form they are not easily accessible to the people's own judgment; yet basically they are not able to deceive the people. These writings can also be widely sold even when they lack substance altogether. But when that happens their effectiveness stands in opposite relation to their popularity. True, half of Leipzig once heard the great apologetic theologian, but what has changed in Leipzig since then? True, his lectures have been published in both hemispheres and in who knows how many copies, but where does the world really know anything at all about that except from the information listed in the bibliography?

But what can one expect from a theology that is really of the opinion that faith lives in an air castle where it can content itself with a few empty [entseelte] histories and dogmas and has little or nothing to seek on earth? Let us expose this once again by means of the words of a good apologetic church historian. He writes in his discussion of the conflict over Donatism that the ideal of the church "may be realized only imperfectly in a sinful world."[65] With this or similarly banal ways of speaking do our church historians come to terms especially with the great pietistic movements of the ancient church. What person of simple perception [Empfindung], undeterred by the persuasions of Protestant orthodoxy, will not admire, for example, those monks and anchorites of the ancient church who strived to make the impossible possible because they believed in it? Compare the theologians who speak with such tranquility about the impossibility of realizing their ideal and yet want to be regarded in the world as if they believed in it. Certainly those ancient believers were strengthened in their fervent endeavors by that view of earthly life that our apologists have so much lost that they often reject it. Yet one only needs to have that view in order to make the Christian ideal [of life] significantly easier to approach. Even where our apologetic theologians seem to have that view, they only place their credibility in question. Who is seriously deceived by such shoulder-shrugging over the "sinful world" when just this quality of the world spurred those ancients to strive for what was supposed to lift them above it? How much of both tranquility and excuse is needed to leave the realization of the Christian ideal to another world? What they reveal is that our apologists find themselves at home in this "sinful world," that the world's sinfulness has ceased to be a powerful, effective motive. To be judged less harshly the expression of pain that apologetic theology utters about the impossibility of realizing the Christian ideal would have to be more persuasive. Above all, however, apologetic theology forfeits the claim to a milder judgment through the ugly eagerness with which it wants to force on us belief in an ideal that it says is unrealizable. Indeed it is not even belief in this ideal itself that apologetics forces on us, but belief in dogmas, and these are, when separated from the ideal, worthless. One should be silent about an ideal that one admits is not supposed to be realized—whether "imperfectly" or not at all is irrelevant for an ideal—at least one does not speak too loudly about it, and in any case one forfeits the right to force others to believe in it.

In all seriousness Christianity has never been based on anything in humanity [unter Menschen] other than the wretched state [Unseligkeit] of the world. If apologetics cannot again find the strength to do it as its predecessors in earlier times did, it may rummage through heaven and earth with history and natural history all it wants but it will never convert to its myths and dogmas a freethinking or truly perceiving [empfindenden] person who has once gone astray of faith. For if these myths and dogmas belong inseparably to the religion defending them, they do not make up the whole of the religion but are bound with the background of a definite view of the world and of life. This view of world and life originally sprouted the myths and dogmas as the stem sprouts the leaves. If however an apologetics that has thoroughly estranged itself from the Christian view of world and life thinks it has Christianity in the wilted leaves of those myths and dogmas, it may see how long it itself can hold this opinion. Others must be allowed to deny that its theology can still call itself Christian.

THE LIBERAL THEOLOGY OF THE PRESENT

Turning now to the other of the two contemporary chief theological parties whose claim to the predicate "Christian" we want to examine, we see that a large number of rather different theological standpoints can be designated "liberal." For the clarity of our presentation we shall take from among these the one that is most comprehensible, insofar as it is the most advanced scientifically and has recently moved bravely into the light of day in those liberal associations mentioned earlier. As our discussion proceeds other points of view will result that are, as those who know liberal theology will recognize, generally applicable to all recent liberal theology. We shall not deal with actual personal memberships in the Protestant League and the Association for Free Christianity, something that would burden us with reviewing membership lists. Besides, membership is entirely superfluous here, since we are concerned only with the theological views these associations are dedicated to popularizing.

If the apologetic theology has only the shell and not the kernel of the matter it represents, then liberal theology has thrown away the shell of Christianity with the kernel. Liberal theology itself seems to offer us this judgment, given its confessed freedom from the myths and dogmas of Christianity. It must therefore be caught in an even stronger illusion than apologetic theology, namely when it thinks that what it does and effects takes place unconditionally in the sense of the Christian religion and when it protests vehemently, even with the expression "perfidious," David Strauss' attacks on the tenability of its ideas and efforts. Yet this greater illusion in liberal theology by no means justifies the severity of apologetic theology's opposition to it, not only because they both agree in their view of life in distinction from Christianity but also because they both cherish the same illusion in their treatments of the religious forms of Christianity, only with different directions: apologetic theology believes traditional Christianity can be defended by means of science, especially history; their opponents believe that after Christianity's critical dissolution it can be built up again by the same means.

Recently we have heard often enough that today's liberal theology has no interest in "old church belief," insofar as it has brought no charge against Strauss' new book more often than that it identifies Christianity with "old church belief." As we continue to distinguish between the historically developed forms of Christianity and the view of life bound with them, we may point out, as results from our first chapter's discussion on theology, that in the main Strauss is right about the forms. As especially results from that discussion, we can have only a negative judgment about the religious value of the "ideas," "spiritual principles" and other learned abstractions that the liberal school theology is accustomed to substitute for the concrete myths and dogmas it has put aside. We wish to test this theology's comprehension of the relation of scientific thought to the faith of the church by examining only one chief point, namely the liberal appeal to the "Christianity of Christ" and the denial of the divinity of Christ that goes with it.

The Christianity of Christ is for liberal theology supposedly the fixed point for the determination of the enduring essence of Christianity. Even the more progressive liberal theology that talks of the "perfectibility" of Christianity as the result of historical progress has to hit upon it. It also contains an unclarity that is characteristic of liberal theology: here one speaks of Christianity at a point where one actually cannot speak of it, for Christianity is, as the etymology of the word itself shows, belief in Christ and not Christ's own belief. Concealed in the impossible concept of a Christianity of Christ lies another concept, one that certainly does not allow the illusion possible in the former, namely Lessing's concept of a "religion of Christ."[66] One cannot fail to recognize that this concept takes Christianity as religion off its hinges. Lessing knew very well that whoever speaks of this religion and is of a mind to hold to it places himself outside the religion of Christianity, which as a consequence of its whole conception of Christ can know [wissen] nothing of Christ's own religion, in any case not in the sense that his religion could immediately become the religion of everyone else. The conception of a "religion of Christ" is based on the historical discovery of the human being of Christ, that is, on the discovery that, even if in the first moment of Christianity's emergence as a universal religion it lifted Christ to the status of divine being [in Paul's letters], it nevertheless without justification [mit Unrecht] projected this conception of him back into the origins of history and especially without justification based its idea of him as a divine being on his witness to himself. It is obvious that the critical significance of this discovery lies in opposition to the whole Christian religion, and it is just as obvious that it is not usable for the reconstruction of Christianity, because only the projection of Christ as a divine being into the origins of history made Christianity the universal religion that we call Christianity. As such it would never have existed without the projection, while the discovery of the unjust nature of the projection, if we wish to give it practical significance, places us at first only on the so-called Jewish-Christian standpoint [of the first disciples]. If this standpoint could not be lifted legitimately to universal significance by the immediate disciples of Jesus, it has far less prospect of being so lifted by us and especially our learned discoveries. Indeed if we speak only of a religion of Christ, we step behind the standpoint of those first believers in Christ, for they revered him as a human messiah and found far more in him than the ideal model [Vorbild] of his own religion, for naturally his belief that he was the messiah could not belong to such a model [that they might imitate]. Hence when we place ourselves in relationship to Christ's own human religion we have to do with something that, when seen from the standpoint of Christianity, does lie behind Christianity but is indifferent for its establishment, because in reality it was not this religion that established Christianity. Therefore this religion could prove whether or not it has more value for us today than that of an historical discovery only by being serviceable to us for the establishment of a new religion.[67] Therefore we have to say that Strauss is right in emphasizing the extraordinarily problematic significance for Christianity inherent in the modern concept of a life of Jesus, and he is right when he denies that the Christian religion is compatible with it. He writes, in a way that is typical for him: "The thought of a life of Jesus is the snare into which the theology of our time had to fall and in which it had to fall apart."[68]

We cannot see the significance of Theodor Keim's answer to Strauss, namely that the concept of a life of Jesus is produced by a "time in which the old conceptions about divine personage have been left behind and that has won full pleasure in a human Jesus."[69] The Christian religion has had "pleasure" in the human only in the form of compassion, and it has felt compassion especially for the humanity of Christ, insofar as his humanity was believed necessary for redemption. But otherwise the Christian religion has tried in every way to forget this humanity. If recent theology feels "a fuller pleasure in a human Jesus," it should admit that it no longer entirely perceives [empfindet] with Christianity, and if it "has left the old conceptions about divine personage behind," it may have only done what its duty as science requires, but it should not overlook the inner bond that ties these old conceptions to Christianity and that can be broken only in an attack on Christianity.

Certainly one cannot take Keim too seriously when he says he has left the old conceptions behind. He too sets himself the task of glueing the Christ of the church to the Christ of science. And after he has critically annihilated all traditional authorities witnessing to the divinity of Christ, he thinks he can purely historically give us back a Jesus who, although being undoubtedly human—Keim speaks repeatedly of his "personal religion"—is more than human. The most high-flown ways of speaking are wasted on the impossible task. On the whole Keim's work is of great seriousness in its scientific intention, and we have already had occasion to praise its best qualities. One could hardly understand how such a work could contain such error, if one quality of the author were not so noticeable, and it explains a great deal. As Keim says that Jesus possessed a disposition for the greatest variety of vocations, yet the "dictator" of his spiritual being was religion, so one can say of

Keim's work that it betrays a plenitude of the most beautiful disposi-
tions, yet the "dictator" in it is the grandiose expression. One will not
easily find a writer of such rigorous scientific mind who is as helpless
against the sound and flourish of words. Only because of this was it
possible to write one of the most affected works of today's literature
about a subject that requires, as hardly any other, an eminent simplicity
of treatment to bring us nearer to it. We feel the offensiveness of this
judgment and are not inclined to linger with it, yet we find this dimin-
ished rule over the word responsible for the fact that Keim, with belief
in the "dignity of the humanity" of Christ and for its sake, imposes on
the person of Christ a form of veneration that is only possible where
one has forgotten this humanity [i.e., the Christ he venerates has the
quality of divinity].[70]

The free [sc. liberal] theology of the present, with the idea of a
life of Jesus and the way it usually carries it out, has alienated itself
from the interests of Christianity as religion more than it can admit, insofar as it has brought to light what very early disappeared into such a
meaningful and, for the existence of Christianity, such a significant
[historical] darkness. At most the undertaking may contain a kind of
Christian religious interest, for it is doubtful that a science that is given
its character purely by science and investigates only problems that lie in
the scope of the solvable would attempt the biography of a life of which
only a single year is known and even this from scattered facts. Far
more scientifically valuable than the drafting of a story of such thoroughly problematic structure would be an exact determination of what
is known and what is unknown in the life of Jesus and a working out of
the meaning of both in connection with the historical significance of his
person. At least this task is immediately given by the facts now lying
before us.

But let us now set aside the life of Jesus and all the liberty today's
liberal theology takes with the mythical and dogmatic structure of
Christianity while thinking it leaves Christianity as religion unharmed.
Instead let us follow this theology into the area of the view of life,
where we have special cause to examine it. Apologetic theology at least
frequently uses the words that reveal the true position of Christianity
toward all worldliness. Our liberal theology, especially that of the Protestant League, hardly has any interest in the words. It is without doubt
more honest, but it also shuts out the substance of the matter all the
more fundamentally. It thinks it has discovered a Christianity whose
reconciliation with world culture is hardly a problem at all. With liberal
theology we move toward a condition of things in which one will have
to esteem Christianity as that religion above all others with which one
can do what one wants.

Not very distant from this definition of Christianity is the untir-
ingly repeated opinion of apologists as well as non-apologists that
Christianity is peculiarly able to accommodate itself to all possible peo-

ples and cultures or, as one of Strauss' opponents from the Protestant League expresses it, "to live through the souls of times and peoples."[71] This opinion is based on a very arbitrary transformation of the historical experiences of Christianity into an inner ability. In its beginnings Christianity was the religion of dying but highly cultivated peoples. It made a pact with their culture and through it acquired, so to speak, a certain practice in adapting to a culture; in so doing it created the forms that allowed it to attempt such accommodation under new conditions, and these forms now give it the appearance that its very nature is to accommodate. Yet the first experiences of Christianity in the Roman Empire leave the question entirely open as to whether what was possible for Christianity with a dying culture was also possible with a younger culture and among peoples of unbroken strength of life. The history of the ancient church leaves no doubt about the answer: Christianity was able to accommodate itself to those younger peoples to whom it moved from the peoples of antiquity only as long as it held the culture they received from its hands exactly on the level that it itself determined.

If today's popular opinion about the congeniality of Christianity and culture were correct, one should think that Christianity had no difficulty at all entering into that pact with dying Greco-Roman culture. With neither care for itself nor malice Christianity would have hastened to its dying sister and tried in every way to help her regain her strength. Everyone knows that things happened in a completely different way. It is true that the sunken condition of culture in the first Christian centuries called forth Christianity's move toward it, and one may also say that Christianity became the preserver of that culture, but it did so only as it arrested the remaining driving forces of life in the culture. Hence one cannot speak of a "familial" attitude of Christianity toward the culture standing before it. Christianity neither lifted nor tried to lift it from its sinking condition, nor did it save more than its naked life. Christianity allowed it no continuing life of its own; it rather made the culture into a motionless tool and a Christian subject. Christianity was far from being especially world-fleeing in the period of the ancient church, as is commonly thought. In fact it has never again had as great an ability to go into the world, and that is because this world was so weak at that time and very much needed Christianity. But Christianity never gave itself to this weakened and fallen culture without reserve; it never neared the culture without in other places withdrawing into itself. And what it seemed to abandon to culture on the one side, it won back on the other by withholding itself all the more energetically from it.

The most emphatic example of this behavior toward antique culture is monasticism. Catholic theology has long since lost the purity of understanding in its evaluation of monasticism; Protestant theology has never possessed the justice to evaluate it properly. But two facts suffice to convince us of just how very deeply monasticism is fused with Christianity. The first is that we all—especially we descendants of those younger peoples—would know nothing more about Christianity than we know about Greco-Roman paganism, Parsism, Brahmanism and other religions, if the ancient church had not produced monasticism. Even more certain is the second fact: between the fourth century and the Reformation, nothing great lived or happened in the church that did not emerge from the monasteries or that was not in some way connected with them. Having arisen with the elevation of the church to a state church in the Roman Empire, monasticism is derived in one theory, by means of an error lying close to Protestantism, from Jewish legalism. In other theories, which love to feed on empty words, it is derived from an alleged invasion of heathen dualism in the church. But monasticism is actually the institution with which the church, in the moment it seemed to give itself completely into the hands of the heathen state, extricated itself from its iron clasp and for centuries after withdrew from the state and secured for itself the people it needed for its purposes; and these were not the meanest of the lot. Acceptance by the state unavoidably meant the loss of martyrdom, which it could by no means forget and which was foreseen with concern already in the third century by Origen.[72] The church produced a replacement for it in the "martyrium quotidianum" [daily martyrdom] of monasticism and with it saved nothing less than its own life. A theology that thinks the ascetic view of life was only a character peculiarity of a certain period and believes it can reconcile Christianity with world culture without breaking its strength, will see monasticism as something that can simply be separated out of Christianity. Such a theology will make impossible an understanding of not only this institution but also of all the most profound and noble appearances of the history of the church up to the Reformation, with which the productivity of the church ceases.[73]

Christianity has had world-denying character since the apostolic period, and this character lies before us in its sharpest form in that apostle most clearly shown by the light of history, Paul. Liberal theology's comprehension of Christianity forces us to the absurd idea that Christianity had to pass through a 1500-year period in which its real view of life was suppressed by a view of life completely foreign to it. Where does one find the least bit of proof for that? Where must we look to see a Christian view of life amicably disposed toward the allegedly true world and its culture? Original Christianity [das Urchristentum], and indeed in its entire scope, certainly cannot be the place. There can be no more world-fleeing belief than that of the first Christians in the early return of Christ and the end of the present form of the world [Weltgestalt]. And we have to object to another view, recently stated by R. A. Lipsius for the sake of that original Christian belief, that the ascetic view of life is limited to earliest Christianity. Lipsius writes: "The first small group of believers felt itself to be no more than a collection of pilgrims and strangers in the present world, ready at any moment for the call of the Lord. Flight from the world is, therefore, the signature of original Christianity. From the middle of the second century on, however, the church felt itself to be a power in the world and daily opened its doors wider in order to take in the heathen multitude. Exactly that belief in which the secret of its rapid growth lay moved more and more into the background as the houses of prayer were filled."[74] We must object to the assertion that the church, as it opened its doors from the second century on, gave up its world-fleeing view of life.[75] The opening of the doors was rather for the church a cause of the worst conflicts. Even if it did silence the puritanical sects that had risen in the second half of the second century [e.g., Montanism], it neither calmed itself by this action nor modified its ideal of holiness after the assumption of the unholy multitude. In maintaining the ideal the church remained indeed chiefly in agreement with those puritans. While the church could not extricate the ideal completely from the plight in which the ideal found itself, it constantly tried to give the ideal living forms and finally fell into distinguishing between two Christianities, whereby it did not doubt the inferior character of lay or worldly Christianity. We must emphatically deny—and this point is closely connected with what we have just said—that original Christianity's expectation of the early return of Christ after its factual nonfulfillment in the church *only* stepped into the background, and so we also especially deny that the world-fleeing character of original Christianity disappeared in the ancient church. Otherwise one must forever remain with the unsolvable enigma that a belief whose whole view of the world depended on its physical fulfillment was not dashed to pieces on its nonfulfillment. As it had been factually refuted on such an essential point as the expectation of the return of Christ, how could the Christian faith have continued to exist, if it had not found a more ideal form in which it could defiantly conceal the factual refutation from itself? It found this form precisely in the ascetic view and style of life, which is in fact a metamorphosis of the original Christian expectation of the return of Christ, for it is based on a continuing expectation of this return. Christian faith continued to think that the world was ripe for its end, and it moved believers to withdraw from it so that they might be prepared for the appearance of Christ that threatened to occur at any hour. The expectation of the return of Christ—having become untenable in its original form, which brightened the prospect of the end of the present form of the world with all sorts of Judaistic hopes—was transformed into thought about death, into the "memento mori" that already according to Irenaeus should accompany the Christian constantly.[76]

This greeting of the Carthusians, "remember death!" summarizes the basic wisdom of Christianity far better than the modern formula, "no disturbance should intrude between the person and his original source [God]."[77] That is a stale negation, one that has no value beyond the insignificant contention of parties, unless one remembers that according to the view of Christianity the world itself belongs to what "disturbs." Precisely on the point of belief in the return of Christ does our modern liberal theology have special cause to become aware of its false relationship to the fundamental ideas of Christianity, insofar as for liberal theology that original Christian belief amounts finally to a mere illusion—something the ancient church never conceded but tried by the sweat of its brow to conceal from itself. From that belief liberal theology takes only this: "it is a peculiarity of the Kingdom of God that Jesus set in the world through his gospel that it is constantly in the making and constantly coming."[78] If one understands the statement not in the sense of the ancient church as a drive to make present the perpetual coming of the Kingdom by leaving this world, but in the sense of a simple expectation of that coming within this world, so is this understanding rather the same thing as a return to the messianic hopes of Judaism. The generation of Christians that really believed in the return of Christ could not calm itself so easily over its not happening.

We now take up again the question about where Christianity is supposed to have shown us its non-ascetic view of life, after having held the opposite view so early and for such a long time. We have just seen that one cannot make such a claim for original Christianity in general. Finally there seems to remain only the question about the "Christianity of Christ." Liberal theologians have repeatedly appealed to it recently, especially against Strauss's assertion that Jesus' personal model of faith does not cover significant aspects of human life, and against Strauss they have made Jesus into a kind of friend of culture. Here we do not wish to come back to the fact that whoever holds to the personal views of Christ places himself, strictly speaking, outside the limits of Christianity, just as Christianity in speaking of "following Christ" has in mind not so much his personal views as his fate, the drama of his life, which it has moreover considered one of the surest foundations of its ascetic ideals. We also wish to set aside the question about whether and in what sense Jesus predicted his early return to judge the world, and we do not wish to go into any detail on the question of the relation of Jesus to culture. Let us remain for now with the two basic pillars of all human civilization, the family and the state.

Whoever seeks ideals for family and state in the distant past and does not find them in pre-Christian antiquity but in Jesus, will be able just as well to assert that the moon and not the sun lightens our world. As long as Matthew 19:12 stands in the Gospels, it is not to be assumed that the personal views of Jesus could contradict the ascetic view of life in Christianity, not even if they were taken unconditionally as the measure of Christianity's view of life. Occasionally one has difficulty taking seriously the arguments that theologians from the Protestant League present against Strauss on this point. Let us hear one attempt at such refutation—and we have intentionally not chosen one of liberal theology's worst arguments. According to Strauss, so it is said, Jesus is supposed to have "lacked understanding of marriage and family life."

What Strauss actually says is that the model and teaching of Jesus would be unproductive for the virtues of home and family life when regarded through the fact that Jesus had no family.[79] If Strauss really thought Jesus had no "understanding" of marriage and family life because he was not married, his opponent could have rebuked him for a truly strange sort of crudity. Instead, Strauss's opponent goes on, "But he who chose the relation of father and child as the symbol of the highest religious idea must have thought differently about these relationships than Strauss assumes."[80] That misses the point, for here it is not so unconditionally important what Jesus actually thought about marriage and the family, insofar as it is an error to assume that even a very ascetic view of life must exclude a high ideal of marriage and family, whatever shadows it may cast on these relationships. As an example Augustine's view of marriage is to be remembered.[81]

In the same place our liberal theologian will also have Strauss say that "art and scientific thought were alien to Jesus," and the theologian answers, "but a new blossoming of art developed out of this community, and thinking consideration of humanity has found one of its deepest problems in Jesus." We cannot speak in only a few words about art in Christianity, but we can refute what the author says about Jesus as a problem of "thinking observation," assuming what is meant is the *historical* person of Jesus. For a "problem of thinking observation" has to have surveyable dimensions, and there are a half-dozen serious books from yesterday and the day before that do not yet allow one to speak of Jesus as one of the "deepest problems of thinking observation."[82] In any case we do not see what the relation of artists and thinkers to Jesus is supposed to prove about Jesus' own behavior.

One other consideration suggests how essential Christianity's world-denying character is for it. If we consider religion as a matter of daily life and if we compare our time with earlier times in regard to what of religion appears in life, we must only repeat what has been asserted often before, namely that the peoples of antiquity were far more pious than we are. At first glance it seems that Christianity and the Reformation eliminated religion from the world. We do not wish to get into a general discussion of how much religion in the world decreased after the appearance of Christianity, for that is not our business here. One can certainly not contest that the Reformation narrowed the area of religion in life, which will not be surprising for anyone who sees in the Reformation as much a political as a religious movement, just as both of these directions are wonderfully embodied in its greatest figure. But what about Christianity? It did in fact de-divinize the world. It allowed the use and enjoyment of a world it could not annihilate, but it took from them the consecration that antiquity had laid over them. Tertullian once says that we should use flowers as nature intended and not for purposes of a worship service. "I, too, butcher myself a rooster, as Socrates did for Aesculapus, and I burn incense where an odor disturbs me, but not within the celebrations and rituals that occur before the idols."[83] We may also refer to the first Christian emperor's edict that provides for the continuance of customary folk festivals but takes from them their religious significance.[84]

Our examples from Tertullian and Constantine suffice to make conceivable how Christianity prepared a world in which religion can hardly still win visible form—the only important evidence to the contrary being the known efforts of the Catholic Church, rightly seen by church historians as the "paganizing of Christianity." If the reason for this tendency to remove religion from the world is seen to lie in a world-affirming view of the world, then it is incomprehensible how one can continue to speak of Christianity as a religion at all, because in this case it is nothing but the systematic annihilation of religion. The matter is different only when one realizes that world-denial is the inmost soul of Christianity, that for Christianity the world is no longer a possible and worthy place for religion. Connected with this is church history's extraordinary poverty of great and pure characters. In this area [sc. true Christianity] history learns nothing of the greatist and purist.[85]

Since one takes away the whole power of Christianity when one falsely attributes to it any sort of reserve in favor of world culture, just as one uses Christianity to conceal from oneself that one wants world culture but not Christianity, the result of such a view can only be the most disagreeable sort of sentimental, superficial and enervated Christianity. And this is, we are sad to say, what pours in such broad streams over our heads in the popular literature of today's liberal theology. What help is it to speak of Christianity's "eternal enlightened thoughts," "of a love without end, of a grace above all sin, of a blessedness in all earthly pain, of life without death," when one seeks these thoughts in a light in which Christianity teaches us not to find them?[86] Christianity is certainly not of the opinion that one can have all these exalted things so easily in the world that, seen from the midst of world culture, one's search for them hardly strikes anyone as unusual!

We cannot deplore enough the racking general confusion of thought and feeling in these things that has been spread by the way theology has thrown its conflict among the laity. We come to another chapter: the popularization of science and the question of whether its importance and difficulty are not very much underestimated, in spite of all the significant efforts dedicated to the task. But let us remain all the more with our examination of theology. Generally speaking everyone admits that science in its strictest forms is inaccessible for the mass of people not educated for it, that for this reason the form in which a scientific object is to be popularized must be the chief concern of whomever undertakes the task, and hence that it cannot be the purpose of popularization to give the people only loose pieces of information. Above all the one doing it has to determine the uses gained from popularizing. If higher goals are pursued, he must be concerned that the cultivation of spirit and heart grow out of it for the people, that they are given a higher sense of enrichment. As much as all the sciences' current efforts to popularize fall short of these goals, the guiltiest among the guilty is theology, and indeed in both of its two chief parties. Apologetic theology is thoroughly characterized by the thoughtless way it has followed its opponents into the public arena and by the corresponding lack of a churchly sense of propriety, through which it has done its part to promote especially the division of pulpit and speaker's platform. One should think that apologetic theology is called to recognize better than others the ominous significance of this division. But before judging the popular theology of our time, let us remain a moment with the character of the movement that has won it such a visible place in public interest.

No understanding judge of the theological agitation being worked up presently especially by the liberal theological associations in Germany and Switzerland will mistake the fact that a real and very serious state of distress lies at the bottom of it. This state of distress has not rightly been understood, and the theological movement based on it is only seemingly one of the people [as asserted by the associations]. The latter is especially true in Germany where the original cause of the state of distress lies in the truly callous, loveless and thoughtless way the affairs of the church have been handled for years in the most significant political areas of the country. This happened when a barren political reaction put the government of the established churches, which are composed of different elements, into the hands of a sect, that is, of one party in the church. As obviously characterless toward culture as it is, this party imagines that there is no conflict between culture, especially science, and traditional Christianity, and it applies its "insight" without further regard in its leadership of the affairs of the church, as is fitting of narrowness. The state of distress so brought about had to be felt above all among the theologians and especially the pastors. They grow up among us no differently than anyone else, and they receive a scientific education that leads them directly into a conflict that other persons, in comparison with them, learn of only by hearsay. As long as it is given by our universities, this education can never completely sink to the level of education offered in a Jesuit seminary.[87] This state of distress among theologians, especially those in the practical field, the pastors, cannot be overestimated.

Far more questionable is to what extent this state of distress is seriously present among the educated laity, whether or not they experience it at all. Here we have the problem of judging a group that is very hard to define, especially considering the breadth of today's use of the word "educated." But among them too the ignoring of the opposition of Christianity and culture can cause deep conflicts of mind and heart. Disregarding those who help themselves and break from the church altogether, these conflicts are usually suffered in silence. Among the educated laity who are disinclined toward Christianity—which is to say most of them, if these in the majority are not hostile to it—the possibility of avoiding religious questions is so great that the cases in which the present conflict among them offers clear and definite form can almost be limited to two: first, the education of children; second, problems of conscience resulting from the tie between church and state, which both still exists and is constantly loosening. In any case it must be recognized that the basis for a religious movement among the scientifically educated laity, if it is not lacking entirely, is far smaller than the loud conflict that theology fights out before them leads us to assume. If we descend into those circles of the people lacking higher education, no person of insight will deny that the religious conflict of the time is hardly present among them in any immediate way at all, at least with relatively few exceptions. To a great degree the educated have control of whether or not and in what form this conflict enters those circles.

Compare the last great religious movement of the people, the Reformation, and consider the ways and means it had to direct exalted and lowly, noble and common, metropolitan and rural, learned and unlearned, theologian and layman, all to one goal. It is difficult to see how our present religious conflict can be called a "popular" movement at all. The clearest symptoms indicate that it is not. To give an example: Besides the well known Virchow-Holzendorf series of popular lectures [in natural science], there is also published in Berlin a series of similar tendencies made up of broadly understandable theological lectures and treatments mostly from the ranks of the Protestant League.[88] In view of the effectiveness of both series, one really doubts whether the public pays more attention to the one than the other, although one is addressed to the constantly moderate interest of the people in science while the other is addressed to the constantly excitable interest of the people in religion. The point can be made more clearly when we consider what far stronger means than the Reformation our theology today uses to effect results among the people, and what far weaker actual results it attains. The Reformers and their contemporaries uncovered the web of deception and falsification on which papal power had come to base itself during the course of time, compared the ancient church with their contemporary church and called especially on the apostle Paul as a witness against their contemporary church. The result was the greatest act of the Reformation, the break with Rome. We hear that the whole New Testament is a web of fictions, reach back not to the ancient church but to original Christianity and call up not Paul but Jesus himself, and not one thing happens. It may be a good thing that nothing happens, for who can remember all the evil inseparably connected with great issues in the storms of religious history and not wish to avoid new storms?

But what conclusions will a thoughtful theology draw from such mock conflicts? Either it will say that the public has no interest in them, that whatever apparent interest there is does not go very deep, and that in the few cases where interest may be serious there are far more where this interest competes only half seriously with other interests for their time, not to mention all those in the public with no more than simple curiosity. Or it will realize that theology itself has nothing to offer the interest that really is there, either because it is too empty of religious content or of a replacement for it, or because the scientific results it talks about still lack the decisive evidence they need in order to become popular. But let us not go further into what the public really thinks; let us turn again to the character of the theology offered to the public.

If we consider the popular theology of the present in relation to its scientific character, then we may remind the reader that no science for itself is as unpopular as theology. However, because it has at its disposal the most popular interest there is, the religious interest, and since every popular science is directed to practical interests, theology, as it turns to the people, should be inclined to appeal only to the practical interest of its hearers, and to this end mostly not simply veil, but completely give up its scientific character. When therefore theological parties parade before the people a conflict that they have not been able to settle among themselves by means of science, the conflict altogether looses any prospect of being carried out in a suitable manner, and it will never be a sign of the height of culture when theological disputes stand in the foreground of its general interests. Scientific attempts to popularize easily lose all form when they neglect the search for a replacement for strict scientific form, something that especially marks the liberal theology's lectures and brochures. They are often superficial, in their connections of thoughts impenetrably dense and in their scientific consequences truncated excerpts of what elsewhere stands for the scholarly to read in a more grounded, logical and consistent presentation.

However it is the uselessness and lack of cultural value of our popular theology that are the sorest points. Lectures for the people in natural science, for example, whatever educational defects they have, do give their hearers a sum of knowledge that can under certain conditions be useful in the so-called struggle for existence. Popular scientific theology is of no such use, because theology does not elevate and strengthen but lessens and weakens what religion can be for persons in the distress and difficulty of life. What then might be popular theology's cultural value? Chiefly it is the public's religious interest that motivates its interest in theology, but popular theology all too easily confuses the boundary between faith and scientific thought in the public's mind. This is the beginning of all barbarism. What one should think of the cultural value of the specific theologies we have charged with reversing all the concepts of true Christianity needs no wide-ranging elaboration. Moreover apologetic theology deceives the people by offering them in the name of science much that is untrue, whereby the untruth can be fully recognized only by a few; the majority cannot recog-

nize it at all. Critical theology confuses the people through its purely
scientific form, insofar as such a form is not at all suited to satisfying
popular interest in theology, and it confuses the public completely
when it tries to satisfy the public's religious interest with scientific
means. For in this case it confuses their basic impulses by misleading
them about the satisfaction of their needs. This is especially true of all
recent theological attempts at reform: they make into the immediate object of a new belief what was only the criticism of the old belief. In all
these cases the most valuable powers and impulses are worn down and
wasted, and basically all serious and true progress is made extremely
difficult and finally impossible.

Let us glance briefly at the *Protestant Bible*, this most extreme excess among the attempts at popular theology from the side of the Protestant League.[89] It illustrates in several ways the damage done by theology mentioned above. What does the *Protestant Bible* try to
accomplish? With this question we immediately encounter a defect in
today's popular theology, one that is certainly a major defect wherever
it is found in science, but especially when the science addresses itself to
the people: it does not know what it wants to accomplish. This is made
clear in the preface. It is written by a professor in Berlin not unknown
as an expert in law, but he thoroughly places in question his calling to
give Protestants or "the German people" a Bible.[90] Is the purpose religious or rationalistic? At first it seems the purpose is chiefly religious.
He tells us that with this publication the Bible is to be for the people
what the Reformation intended it to be. "In Luther's time our ancestors
read the Bible in the sense of Protestant justification and edification and
in protest against the medieval traditions of priestly rule." Assuming
that this adequately characterizes how our ancestors read the Bible, we
point out that it too presupposed a certain view [Anschauung] of the
Bible's nature and origin [Wesen und Ursprung]. What was this view?
The editors of the *Protestant Bible* will surely not risk asserting that
they share it, and even if they are able to show that Luther's belief in
Scripture was different from that of Protestant scholasticism, hopefully
they will not say that they believe the same thing about Scripture that
Luther believed. While they exercise more freedom in their judgments
about Scripture than he, who is known for it, nowhere does one see evidence that they believe it as he did.

If Prof. Holzendorf's introduction is characterized by an uncom-
fortable ambiguity through its appeal to Luther, he does not go so far as
to tell us that Luther himself speaks from the pages of the *Protestant
Bible*. Because he has to represent the religious significance of the new
undertaking, he feels the need to add his own confession of belief about
the Bible. He tells us that only those who "judge unhistorically" speak
of "unreconciled contradictions" in the New Testament. "What we
openly concede to be contradictions in the Bible are no more than
waves upon an ocean unmoved in its depths." This statement is com-

mon property among our apologists and popular critical theologians and, as with most of this common property, it is meaningless, although it appears to strike the face of the scientific thought that the *Protestant Bible* pretends to represent. Recent scientific discoveries in the Bible, which cannot be summarized adequately under the category "contradictions," have churned up the Biblical "ocean" in its deepest depths. If the editors of the *Protestant Bible* had really been of a different opinion, they would have to have spoken with the people of the ocean themselves, because only the ocean interests them, and ignored the play with the waves: if they are truly only waves, they interest no one. Were it not for the fact that the Lutheran text is reprinted in the *Protestant Bible*, that the ocean therefore speaks for itself, one would not easily catch sight of that ocean in its pages.

With the sentence about the ocean the reader has reached the first of the high points in the preface of his juristic leader, the one intended to convince him that the *Protestant Bible* has a religious purpose. He now has to climb the second peak, from which it appears that the *Protestant Bible* is a rationalist undertaking. Before he gets to this peak, however, he has to struggle through an area in between, where he hears the following oracle: "Not in the mystical darkness of the supernatural but in the light of history does respect for the Bible grow." It is possible that in the mystical darkness of the supernatural a basis for such a completely untrue assertion can be found, but in the world of light one looks vainly for it. No wonder, then, that the following sentence cancels it out: "Historical experience teaches that the eyewitnesses of a fact are indeed the best reporters, but not the surest judges of its nature." Naturally one does not increase respect for authors when one places the surety of their judgment in question. We at least do not wish to give the impression that we here pursue the purpose of increasing respect for the editor of the *Protestant Bible* as a theologian. But now to the second peak.

Here we are told, after having been prepared by the just-quoted oracle, that the *Protestant Bible* is supposed to lead us "to the understanding of the Bible" and indeed to its historical understanding, and it is to do so with the means given by recent "Protestant scientific thought." We must concede that the view from this peak is clearer than the view from the first one, although it is still far from sunlit clarity. In fact clouds begin to gather when we hear the following sentence: "Formerly the letter of the Bible ruled; today we look for the Bible's indwelling Spirit." This is a sentence that once more both inverts the truth and reveals a bad confusion of thought in questions that are, for an undertaking such as the *Protestant Bible,* questions of principle. For the truth is: formerly one sought in the Bible the indwelling Spirit; today the letter rules among us. As dark an area as the history of scriptural interpretation is, anyone can know from it that the church's interpretation of Scripture is based on a theory in which the letter is indifferent and only the spiritual meaning is of value. A chief complaint against this method of interpretation by the theology that intends to represent the *Protestant Bible* is that it is far too free of the letter. We have recently given the letter its rightful due and based on it above all what we call the historical meaning, in order with its help to determine at most the "spirit" of individual books in the Bible. But we have given up all scientific exegetical means of catching hold of what earlier times called the "Spirit of the Bible"—and we do not see any means the *Protestant Bible* has to bring it back to us again.[91] One should also not think that what we have said here is superfluous because, in Holzendorf's view, the letter of the Bible no longer has for us the holiness it needs to be the vehicle of a "Spirit." For even if we all agree that this expression of his opinion was perhaps not usable in the preface of the *Protestant Bible*, this does not justify him placing a completely misleading statement in its place.

If we climb down now from the preface to the text of the *Protestant Bible* itself, we may do without examining the scientific value of what the commentaries offer, for it would hold us up too long. Let us only ask briefly if what has been published thus far achieves the intended purpose of increasing respect for the Bible. We have no objection to the printing of Luther's text of the New Testament, as we said before; it does respect for the Bible no harm. The commentary on the synoptics could perhaps considerably further respect for the Bible, if certainly in an unintended way, through the contrast with the text it interprets. The contrast is especially evident in the superstition governing the entire commentary, namely that what the texts says naively, vividly [anschaulich], inimitably, but completely understandably, must be and can be made clearer through an abstract, imageless recension. That the historical commentary to the fourth Gospel and the Acts is able to increase religious respect for these books can only be the conclusion of one sharing the opinion of the preface of the *Protestant Bible*, namely that to increase respect for the Bible the "light of history" is needed.

All that we have said here against this modern undertaking certainly means nothing for the reader who, as one commentator writes, possesses the secret of reading the Bible "for edification and in a critically reflective way *at the same time.*" (He comes up with a finer word than Bible: "the classics of our religion.") The *Protestant Bible* will not lack such readers, nor may one fear that it will ever become a book of the people. And there can be no doubt that it will not be entirely able to resist the peculiar taste of our time: one often knows not whether, in its desire to possess all, it will take at least something of everything, and where it has two irreconcilable wholes will rather take half of each than the whole of either; or whether it is so apathetic that it no longer asks about the whole of anything and prefers a mixture of halves. Whichever one assumes is the case, desire or apathy, either would explain why our culture today is so lacking in resolve.

It is also not resolutely for enlightenment. Only one plant has grown up in the world that can be used to cure obscurantism, and that is enlightenment. It works its healing best where, to the greatest possible degree, it is unmixed with anything else. Where would we be today if the great figures of the Enlightenment in the previous century had placed their light behind the screen with which their contemporary epigones in theology love to dim it? If obscurantists wish to refuse reason and threaten to extinguish the light of truth, let them see what science, without timidity and without being veiled, can accomplish. The necessary courage for this conflict may still be drawn best from a view of life like that of Christianity, even if one confesses unbelief. But one should deceive no one, neither opponents nor oneself nor anyone else, about the nature of one's weapons by drawing a sheath over them that does not let their sharpness be felt.

If liberal theology believes it must continue its efforts in the forms it has previously chosen—after all that has been said here, this is certainly not recommended—it will finally have to go one step further and give itself with greater abandon to science. If it does not, it will lose the ground beneath its feet and cause a confusion that will hinder all real progress. It already owes science what independent power it has. And liberal theology must more seriously consider to what extent it can still call its efforts Christian.

CRITICAL THEOLOGY
AND ITS POSITIVE RELATIONSHIP TO
CHRISTIANITY IN THE PRESENT.
STRAUSS' CONFESSION

If there is a better theology than the apologetic and liberal, then it can only be the critical theology, which has to demonstrate its critical nature above all in itself by being absolutely clear that its goals are not purely religious, that in their pursuit it by no means serves Christianity alone but also the need to make a place possible for world culture beside Christianity.

Such a determination of its task excludes the thought that critical theology could relate to Christianity only negatively or indeed with hostility. As free as it is toward Christianity, it will be able, first, to protect Christianity against theologies that think they represent it when they accommodate it to the world, theologies that, through indifference to Christianity's view of life, either dry it out into a dead orthodoxy that banishes it from the world, or draw it down into worldliness and let it disappear therein. Critical theology will prevent such theologies from dragging through the world an unreal thing they call Christianity, from which has been taken its soul, namely the denial of world. Second, without identifying itself completely with the Christian view of life nor failing to recognize the excessive character that Christian world denial has for human existence—without whose factual acknowledgement there would never have been a theology in Christianity—critical theology will feel and perceive deeply enough with Christianity's view of life in order with courage and good conscience to reject attempts to extinguish it entirely, as D.F. Strauss' new book tries to do.[92]

Strauss did theology as science such an essential service in his early work that a critical theology cannot be indifferent about finding itself at odds with him. Furthermore we welcome his new book's rejection of certain damaging but at present very much alive "half this-half that" practices in theology's dealings with the laity. Yet our emphatic contradiction of Strauss' "confession" cannot here be based on a comprehensive evaluation of its good qualities and its far greater weaknesses. Instead we shall concentrate only on a few of the book's fundamental and interrelated ideas.

One could think that the opposing theological standpoints today are all silently agreed that Christianity consists only of a definite sum of historical or mythical facts and dogmas and that one's relationship to Christianity is determined by whether one accepts all or half or none of these. They seem to agree that it has no definite view of life or that this is its most insignificant aspect. Corresponding to what we observed in the apologetic and liberal theologies in this connection, Strauss thinks he has done with Christianity when he critically annihilates a series of fundamental Christian dogmas and especially the church's traditional comprehension of its earliest history. He skips over Christianity's ascetic view of life with two or three deprecating and very incidental remarks. As we have already said, Strauss is hardly alone in this, but here it is especially offensive because the claim is loudly made that Christianity has been done away with. One should think that an historical appearance of this kind could only be fully perceived and judged from the whole of its effectiveness, that it could not be so simply restricted to a few empty forms nor limited to a single and moreover superficially comprehended period of its existence, while all the things that the powers it loosened brought forth in later periods are ignored. Indeed one could have easily done without the whole criticism of the apostolic symbol and the life of Jesus with which Strauss begins his book, if he had offered us instead a well ordered presentation of the church's view of world life [Weltleben] in its chief appearances in church history, showing how it belongs to a Christianity still able to resist world culture. Were such a presentation rich in facts and conceived with spirit, it could fill one of the sorest gaps in our church histories; what Strauss offers us instead he himself has given us far more rigorously and instructively in other works. The missed presentation of the church's view of worldly life would also have placed us at the right standpoint for judging the arrangement of life Strauss proposes for a world in which Christianity has been done away with. It would certainly have cast a far more dangerous light on this conclusion of his work than his conception of Christianity does, the only clear conception of which is given by its beginning [Anfang].

There can be nothing more foreign to Christianity and its feeling of compassion [Mitleidsempfindung] than the ideal of culture that Strauss unfolds in answer to the question about how we are to order our lives without Christianity. But where does it place us? Approximately on the standpoint of the narrow-minded citizen of imperial Rome, who had his religion in the "mysterium" of the chief of state. In the tranquil enjoyment of his wealth he had the army to protect him from enemies outside Rome and the severity of the law to protect him from enemies within. He whiled away the gloomy hours with a dead art, which the order of the state could not keep him from. Insofar as he had the possibility of becoming Christian and refused, he is perhaps the most anti-Christian figure that history shows us. This standpoint is so base that we hardly need to call on Christianity to prove its meanness, nor even pre-Christian Greco-Roman heathenism, which would truly provide only the most shaming parallel to Strauss' ideal of life. The heathen of imperial Rome suffice, for they, or at least the thinkers among them, knew [empfanden] the bitter fruit of every state that has arrived at its goal: uncontested and unconditional rule. They knew that here all the powers have disappeared from the world that helped to found, transfigure and uplift the state. Plutarch and Tacitus recognized this bitter fruit with sadness and fright: Plutarch, as he declared the no longer poetic form of the Pythic oracle to be appropriate only for common questions of little significance, which were the only ones that could still be asked of the oracle under the regulated conditions of the time; Tacitus, as he found no place for the great political eloquence of earlier times under the effective police of Trajan's Rome.[93] Strauss on the other hand seems to be of the opinion that nothing is lacking in the happiness of a people that has let itself be locked in the cage of such a "finished" state. He seems to think—incredibly—of the happiness of the Germans in a way we Germans certainly would never have thought ten years ago and hopefully still do not. If we did, it would have to be easier than it usually is to forget that we are human. Strauss would have us forget it: he tells us that "one climbs only on the feeling [Gefühl] of nationalism upwards to the feeling of humanity" [Strauss, 264; B II, 78]. Is it possible that such gymnastics of feeling is necessary to be human and to perceive [empfinden] it?

Strauss also takes the matter all too lightly when he speaks of cosmopolitanism. He himself knows that it does not have to mean disinterest in one's own people, and not even he can simply ignore the noble forms of cosmopolitanism that our great thinkers and poets present. He can, how fair of him, have nothing against it when these thinkers and poets "encompassed the whole of humanity with feelings of empathy and wished to see their ideals of fine morality and reasonable freedom gradually realized in all peoples" [Strauss, 266; B II, 80]. Yet instead of reflecting on the meaning of this and telling us where to look for the evidence that "we do not forget" those noble models of cosmopolitanism, Strauss knows nothing better to do than to use these models for a sudden attack on internationalists. He may be right in saying that "this sort of world citizen" may not find support in Goethe and Schiller, but may Strauss?

But we want to speak about Christianity, which Strauss often enough refuses to mention when presenting his ideal of culture. Yet with his ideal he cannot avoid this question: is it possible to win a people such as the Germans for a culture that is not only free of Christianity but that would be unwise enough really to act as if there never had been a Christianity in the world? What was Christianity? Was it a bad dream from which humanity had only to waken, a confusing drunkenness from which humanity had to attain sobriety, so that afterwards it could be completely forgotten? One finds it difficult to be convinced of that when one simply compares what Strauss says about the state, war, the political power of punishment, and the working class, with the Christian parallels in Augustine's *City of God*: In Augustine all is so much more profound and more humane and therefore much truer. One simply resists the thought that what Strauss tells us is all the wisdom that can flow from Christianity—the deepest experience of the part of humanity to which we belong—for a people that neither stagnates nor simply ignores the experiences of times past but uses them for its own good and the good of others. Christianity long ago dealt with and left behind the culture Strauss paints for us. A humanity that has gone through the school of the antique world, which ended in Christianity, will always ask whether such a culture deserves to exist at all. And especially in Christianity this humanity will find cause to strive for a culture that would be noble and sublime enough to think it could rightly supercede Christianity. It would in any case have to be at a higher level than the one Christianity came to rule.

Strauss would not have opposed his own ideal of life to Christianity so inconsiderately, if he had tried less to paint Christianity in terms of current trends and events and had tried more to lift it into the light of a general view of life, and if he had tried to move toward deeper and more serious needs with his moral-religious depictions and advice. As it is these only scrape that surface of human activity that newspapers write about. What should one think, for example, of the fact that a question of such immediate practical significance as education is given no attention at all? Or one would have to refer here to Strauss's proposal that in the country "Nathan the Wise" and "Hermann and Dorothy" should take the place of the Bible [Strauss, 301; B II, 121 f].[94] The timidity of the proposal allows us to refuse to take it seriously.

What should we think of the confident way Strauss opposes his ideal of life and its optimism to Christianity? As he tells us himself, it is inclined "to make its work too easy." Why then should he make it difficult again by being of the opinion that pain and evil in the world "play a role," indeed, a "powerful" role, but still only a "role?" [Strauss, 147; B I, 167]. In Strauss' world, certainly, every day one can spend in decent entertainment can lift one to the peak of happiness and "leave nothing to be desired" [Strauss, 300; B II, 120]. And at the end of his book he can happily concede that its course may have been a bumpy one but it will have been enjoyable, if one's chest swells with the proud awareness of traveling the "highway of the world's future" [Strauss, 375; B II, conclusion]. This happy confidence is not convincing. As jovial and as loud as it sometimes is, it cannot prevent tones of a completely different kind from reaching our ears, and these resound far stronger. It is above all the tone of heavy, unfruitful and hence false resignation that this confession cannot suppress as it looks back one last time on its destructive work [Strauss, 372f; B II, conclusion]. An aimless "striving" is to comfort us for the lost belief in miracles. For the lost belief in providence we are to be comforted by the insight "that our state of being receives only its form from the world outside us, but its content of happiness or unhappiness only from within us"—a statement that hardly gives foundation to the ethics Strauss develops in previous sections [Strauss, esp. 241-244; B II, 51-55].[95] For the lost belief in immortality everyone is completely left to fend for himself: "Whoever cannot help himself in this cannot be helped, he is not ready for our standpoint." Everywhere one finds the same visionless withdrawal of the individual into himself, a withdrawal that contradicts the factual helplessness of the individual, makes all truly human existence impossible and therefore can escape the reproach of naked egoism only when paired with complete denial of world.[96]

If this is the goal to which this "new faith" leads us, we have to be allowed not to share the haste and lack of consideration with which it teaches us to tear apart the bond of the community of the old faith. A better striving would be to ponder forms that, in spite of all the difficulties of changing times, still secure this community its continued existence to the widest extent, especially in the distress and difficulty of the present, into which Christianity's view of life still lets many a redeeming idea shine. In our time, when the various peoples so openly move apart from one another, social classes only too malevolently threaten to close one another out and individuals suffer from a serious indifference toward all community not based on mean interests, it is yet of inestimable value that at least the name of Christ still hovers as a kind of categorical imperative over this whole disastrous dissolution, condemning it.

In such a time nothing could be more deplored than the splintering off of a sort of religion whose own proclaimer sees nothing wrong with the fact that for the foreseeable future it can only be a religion of the middle class.[97] Certainly not even this strange religion should be prohibited, and one can share Strauss' wish that the state permit a "number of citizens" the freedom "not to belong to any church at all, not even only outwardly" [Strauss, 296; B II, 1 16]. But the gain that we are supposed to have from the "appearance of such a group" is difficult to see as long as the "number of persons" belonging to it has such a dubious right to call itself a "group." One cannot yet say whether or not this new religion of Strauss' too will require a theology. But it is certain that a critical theology will have the greater possibility of serving a real religion than a mere construction of ideas such as this cult of the "universe," whose most enthusiastic prophet is none other than our most sober critic [Strauss, 147; B I, 168].

Even if we have succeeded in making clear that also[98] a critical theology in many ways has the possibility of protecting Christianity against misunderstanding, we know well that we have not dispelled all doubt about whether or not a theology such as ours, which relates to

Christianity with so much freedom, has the real possibility of serving practical needs. In conclusion we shall have to address this question.

THE POSSIBILITY OF A CRITICAL THEOLOGY
IN OUR PROTESTANT CHURCHES

We wish to take our point of departure from a work that is an attempt to prepare a place for a scientifically free theology. Although we shall have to oppose this attempt, we are very thankful for it, for it is based on a sharp insight into the difficulties of the task, it uncovers them with clear decisiveness and is seriously concerned about showing us a way out. It is the proposal for the reform of the theological faculties that Paul de Lagarde has recently made in his stimulating and intelligent brochure, *On the Relationship of the German State to Theology, Church and Religion.*[99] (See above p. 63.) Lagarde intends his proposal for Germany, but the situation is essentially the same in Switzerland. The basic outline of the proposal is as follows. Through their theological vows and obligations of office, which have to do with the methods and results of their work, our professors of theology forfeit the right to be considered servants of science. The faculties to which they belong have the task of educating clerics of specific confessions, hence each of them is bound to a confession. The state cannot support any of these confessions because they are mutually exclusive and none has the prospect of becoming a church of the whole nation. Therefore the state must completely withdraw its hand from them and declare them sects, hence the state must also withdraw its support for the presently existing theological faculties and give them over as seminaries to the individual churches. However, because no nation can do without religion and therefore the state has no choice but to have to do with it, because the existing churches do not satisfy the state's religious need, and because finally the state cannot create a religion of the nation, the state should at least prepare the way for the coming to be of a religion of the nation. To do this the state must above all provide enlightenment about religion. At this point the state again becomes interested in theology, but only in a theology free of all confessional ties and based on knowledge of religion generally, for only this theology can be the pathfinder for the coming German religion. Accordingly the state must replace the existing theology in the universities with this theology and equip it with whatever it needs. Enrollment in this new theological faculty must naturally have no confessional conditions but be completely free in this regard, and in particular it must not be required of the future clerics of the existing churches, as much as this would be desirable even in the self-interest of these churches.

It is not at all our intention to evaluate all aspects of this proposal, which is based on very complex presuppositions. We shall also leave aside the difficulties involved with its practical realization under the special conditions of the present, especially since the recent enactment of new laws on religion in Germany. We shall only consider the proposal's most important basic theoretical ideas and its most general practical thought as these relate to our own proposals.

On one point we must dispel all doubt about agreement with Lagarde; on the basis of this agreement it will be possible to engage in an honest disagreement with him on another point. We mean agreement with him about the vows required of teachers of theology on attainment of their licentiate [permission to teach] or on assumption of office. Lagarde's comprehension of these vows is not free of a certain exaggeration. He establishes the incompatibility of the vows with scientific work by referring simply to the nature of science's results: science does not know at the beginning of its investigations where they will end, therefore it cannot be bound by a vow. The problem is that Lagarde presupposes a concept of strict science that was not presupposed by the lawgivers who originally formulated the vows, and none of the vows originally had the sense Lagarde gives them. He thinks that the vows impose on theology a definite limit on the presupposition that correct and not arbitrarily restricted thought [Denken] would automatically go beyond this limit. The case is, rather, that an illusion about the limits of scientific thought underlies all the vows, namely that these limits exactly correspond to the needs of faith, that by its own nature thought has to remain exactly at the point that is the condition of its compatibility with faith. If the reverse were true, if these vows were based on Lagarde's insight into the contradictory natures of faith and scientific thought, they would be products of the most extreme perfidy.

That the mentioned illusion underlies these vows can be seen in the fact that in many universities changes have been made to accommodate the vows to changes in the relationship of faith to scientific thought. That means the illusion is still there, and in recognition of it one could agree with Lagarde that there is no conceivable need for a vow. Certainly it must be admitted that the illusion is not based on a clearly conscious theoretical statement that the area of scientific thought exactly fits with the area of faith. Such a statement would itself presuppose a clearer distinction between the concepts of scientific thought and faith, and hence a clearer concept of their relationship, in the minds of those who wrote the vows than actually was the case, and the continued existence of the vows continues to be based on a theoretical unclarity about these concepts. Only too often however no unclarity was needed for the first introduction of the vows: as a particularly ugly side of the history of Protestantism shows, in earlier times naked force suffced.[100] Such vows have always had a bad root, and our remarks here against Lagarde are not meant in their defense. We only want to enlighten one point, to which we shall return. We have no wish unduly to sharpen a question that is already painful enough.

For the moment we have to concede to Lagarde, as a simple consequence of our earlier statements, that today every theology that binds the scientific freedom of its teachers with vows abandons its scientific character. This is true because today those illusions about faith and scientific thought, as possible as they may have been earlier, have evaporated. Every scientifically educated theologian, at least every such Protestant theologian, knows with every scientifically thinking person that science seeks its methods independently, and that as a consequence it can acknowledge as result only what it has proven with the unlimited application [Anwendung] of these methods [Lagarde, 5]. Today therefore the theological vows do in fact threaten to become a conscious falsification of science—Lagarde only attributes them a falsification in too broad a sense—and the elimination of the vows is a requirement of public morality, that is, insofar as they really set limits to theological research that contradict the nature of science and do not have exclusive application to the practical task of the theological teacher, which is to educate the clerics of his church. For the theological educator, at least for the sake of peace, may continue to tolerate a formula that obligates him to dedicate himself to and generally to be mindful of this his practical task with zeal and fidelity. Yet if any scientific obligation exists for the theological teacher, then it can be none other than to make known the truth that he has found out and that he is convinced he can prove [Lagarde, 5]. A [university] theology that is more than only vaguely suspected of suppressing truth under the cover of its proclamation must soon suffocate under the burden of general contempt. As things stand today, the continued existence of vows that in effect limit scientific thought will close the theological faculties to all persons seriously active in scientific pursuits, and they will make impossible the presence of the faculties in our universities, for two reasons. First, the other faculties are based on a concept of scientific thought that prevents vows of this sort. Second, although theology is not simply [bloss] science but an application [Anwendung] of science, it does not have special sources out of which it may draw from science only what it needs [cf. below]. Lagarde is right in saying that vows that bind science to a confession shake the scientific character of our theological faculties. We disagree with him by wanting to remove only the vows, not the existing theological faculties, from the universities. The right to such disagreement will result from our further considerations, which we shall here limit to Protestantism.

Lagarde's proposal would have two theologies instead of one in need of improvement. Both are impossible and will always be unrealistic. Let us turn first to Lagarde's idea [47] of moving the present theological faculties into purely confessional seminaries. Not even the most orthodox faculty would let itself be forced into seminaries as Lagarde conceives them. For example, however strict a Lutheran faculty may be, it will not admit what Lagarde [7], again only by means of a certain exaggeration of existing concepts, wants to attribute to the concept "Lutheran," that is, it will not admit that it has nothing other to teach than "knowledge about the Lutheran religion." For essentially the same reason no faculty will presuppose that beside its own confessional theology there may legitimately exist an entirely different application of theological scientific thought, a theology, for example, that teaches "Catholic knowledge." For his concept of new seminaries Lagarde [2, 6] quite incorrectly refers to the "peaceful coexistence" of faculties of different confessions in the universities. The coexistence that exists among them is based in its greater part on the structure of the universities, not on the theoretical presuppositions of these faculties. If this is clearly true of Catholic theology, it is no less true of Protestant theology. According to its presuppositions the theology of one's own confession stands in an especially close relation to scientific thought, and its application of this thought is of a purity possible in no other confession. Therefore even in a purely confessional seminary, Lutheran theology, for example, could not give up the claim of being the truest theology in the area of science. Whether or not Lutheran theology would be correct in its judgment of itself and other theologies is beside the point. Every theology lives from this claim, and, contrary to Lagarde's belief, there neither is nor can there ever be a purely confessional theology without it. No confessional theology can admit that it makes merely formal use of scientific thought for the treatment of its object, or that its object has no claim to objective truth determined by scientific thought, or that its relation to such thought is no better than that of any other confessional theology.

Lagarde, in his judgment of the theological faculties, overlooks the element of true scientific thought that is present in every theology, and he wants to bind the faculties rigidly to the task of handing on a specific confessional content to their students, something one finds nowhere in these faculties. In their place he sets a discipline that one must doubt has the right to exist under the name "theology" at all.

For a long time now Lagarde's basic ideas have led to related proposals that have to do with the future of our theological faculties. When the necessity of separating the faculties from the purpose of educating clerics for their confessions has been seriously discussed, the proposal has usually arisen that these faculties, as purely scientific, be absorbed into the philosophical faculties.[101] That would be the only really consistent thing to do. The discipline that Lagarde would have as theology in our universities is to be indeed not philosophical but exclusively historical. It would give a scientific knowledge of religion, "insofar as it gives a history of religion." The historian would learn through theology "religion generally and come to know the laws of religious life; it would do this in observation of all religions of which it could have certain knowledge" [Lagarde, 50]. But with all these determinations nothing has been said that would warrant excluding such a study of religion from the philosophical faculties.

When Lagarde nevertheless insists on having a theological faculty for his theology, this is based on a conviction that we do acknowledge, namely that even a seriously scientific theology has a practical task that could not be met if theology were absorbed into the philosophical faculty. We have to doubt however that such a task can really be found for Largarde's new theology. He assumes he can assign it the practical task of being the "pathfinder of German religion." But theologies have always followed their religions, and indeed the more energetic and uncontested the original impulses of these religions were, the later did theology appear on the scene. One has never heard of a theology preceding a religion, and it is hardly to be expected that something of the kind could ever happen. Lagarde [50] thinks he has the "presentiment" that his new theology "will be able to calculate the curve on which religion will move in the future from the course the beneficent star of religion has taken to this point." But one may certainly say that such presentiment is possible only through an excess, a kind of mania of scientific rationalism that wants to wrestle into its possession [an sich reissen] even what is most ungraspable [das Ungreifbarste], to be seen [das zu Schauende] only by ecstatic prophets. With regard to the understanding of the past, theology, as a consequence of its practical direction, has produced divisions and confusions of immense proportions. It must really be in for an adventure when its object is supposed to lie in the future, assuming of course that we take this new theology's goal seriously. But there is another concern about Lagarde's new theology. Considering the entirely historical character of its task, the lack of any prospect of it reaching its final goal and the overwhelming power of the historical direction of scholarly studies in the present, Lagarde's new theology would very soon lose sight of its goal and itself in the historical material and become a purely historical discipline.

One sees therefore that Lagarde's attempt at separating the two basic elements of theology, scientific method and practical direction, from their present union and having them re-form in a new structure fails both theoretically and practically. Its result is the division of the two basic elements into two disciplines, whereby the practical element falls to the confessional seminaries and the theoretical element to the new theology. But these seminaries would not want to be reduced so completely to the practical, and the new theology would be so purely theoretical that practical concerns would escape it entirely. Judged from Lagarde's own scientific point of view, his confessional seminaries would be absurd. Absurdity knows how to help itself powerfully enough in this world, and it is always a bad thing when one offers it a helping hand and calls it forward, even where this is supposed to further something smarter and better. In such cases it is far too easy for the means to remain the only attainable goal.

But even if Lagarde's proposal for confessional seminaries contained fewer difficulties and problems, one would find it difficult to join him because of what he dissolves. When he tears apart the bond that brings our churchly theology and our highest scientific institutions together, he destroys one of the most valuable things we have inherited from a wise past, a foundation stone that cannot be easily replaced. On it hopes for the future of the affairs of the church may be built, insofar as such hopes can be related to theology at all. In any case what theology can still do for us depends above all on the right relation of theology's scientific and practical elements. The practical direction is the soul of theology, and because of its relation to the practical needs of life theology cannot easily alienate itself from practice completely. Yet it must see to it that it not become a mockery of science, and in its connection with the universities it has the most lively reminder one can imagine to guard against such a danger, the most effective defense against the degeneration into which every sectarian or seminary theology quickly falls. We may however refuse to hear proposals of even such radical reform as Lagarde's only when serious doubt about existing university theology can be dispelled on two other points.

The first is the separation of church and state. The problems we think would arise from the separation are difficult to evaluate because [in Germany and Switzerland] separation has been realized only to the smallest degree, and for the time being we are unable to see what is going to happen in the future. In fact we do seem to be moving rather rapidly toward separation. One can only wish it will come about and indeed in as honest and complete a way as possible, in order that truth and honesty may finally enter into a relationship that has been ruled by deception and ambiguity since its inception, and indeed through the guilt of both sides. One unavoidable consequence of separation would seem to be the removal of the present theological faculties from the universities, yet we do not think it has to be unavoidable. As we argue for our position in what follows, we shall disregard the fact that in Germany such a consequence is removed to the distant future by the new laws having to do with the church, since these laws also control the theological education of clerics.[102] It is undeniable that the rights assumed by the state in these laws could not exist on the presupposition of a consistent separation of church and state; but the state has asserted its right to issue such laws on the basis of circumstances that are momentary, and the situation can change.

But let us assume that the worst, in our opinion, comes about, that the state refuses to require that the theologians of any confession attend the state's highest scientific institutions. Would our existing university theological faculties still have the possibility of continued existence?

Certainly not if the consequence of separation were the ruin of the Protestant churches. One hears often enough that the separation would only strengthen the Catholic Church but threaten the Protestant churches with dissolution and lead them toward "American conditions," as one is accustomed to say. Then we would have to expect that the large communities of the present established churches would split up into sects—and Strauss' "group" would take its place among those who declare themselves free of every church. Certainly it would be a bad sign of the poverty of the churches, if they really were seriously threatened by this consequence as soon as the state withdrew its power of holding things together. Assuming the threat is real, after separation the state would have an interest in retarding the process of dissolution, because an excessive development of sects would seriously endanger our culture. Even the development of Strauss' group would hold little promise of usefulness for this culture as long as one knows nothing more about it than, as Strauss says, "it will have nothing at all to do with the church."

For purposes of retarding such dissolution, above all the theological faculties in the universities would have to serve the good of the state, and in maintaining them the state would have to hold open at least the possibility of a thorough and serious scientific theological education for as long as possible. Could the state expect help in such an endeavor from the former established churches? In Germany and Switzerland, yes. Considering both the level of general education in Germany and Switzerland and the attachment to the large church communities that has developed over the centuries, not to mention the force of habit, one should think that significant powers would arise in these communities to stem their dissolution and that after many factions had splintered off at least a very strong core would be held together by them. And the interest of this core church community in the theological faculties would correspond to the state's, so that the attendance of them would be assured without the state having to make requirements. But whatever actually happens, one can say that whether or not the theological faculties fall victim to the separation of church and state will depend above all on the character of leadership that the affairs of the churches have at the critical moment of separation. At present these things cannot be judged.

The second point requires a solution far more urgently than the first and also has to do with doubt about the continued existence of the scientific theological faculties in our universities. It has to do with the objection that, contrary to purpose, the result of the education given in the theological faculties is a deficiency in the number of pastors. Lagarde writes [52]: "The Protestant churches (as far as we can still speak of their existence) have been brought to the point of soon not having any pastors by the sincerely well-meant efforts of the governments to provide for their scientific education. As dubious as the science of the Protestant faculties is, with the minimum of criticism they do have they have caused a good number of the youth enrolled in them—and not the worst—to leave theology for the study of philology or medicine. The problem arises when these youth are placed before the question about whether or not they want to take vows of ordination and enter the service of a definite and ordered church. Given the choice, they prefer to leave theology than to be made liars." This is correct, this is the situation in theological education today. Furthermore a theology of such a thorough scientific attitude as Lagarde wants would seem to have to depopulate our clergy entirely, but this is insignificant at this point. If the "half-scientific" theological faculties now existing have the result Lagarde attributes to them, correctly we have said, then these faculties are ripe to meet their end, unless a means can be found to prohibit such a result.

The two means we shall propose give a strictly scientific faculty the same possibility of continued existence in the university, with the same traditional purpose of educating clerics, that it gives a "half-scientific" faculty. The first of these means is a change in the vows of ordination. The second is the acknowledgement of both a personal esoteric standpoint of the scientifically educated cleric and an exoteric standpoint that he assumes in relationship to his parish.

The vows of ordination bind the personal beliefs of the cleric to Christianity as an historical religion and to the historical facts with which it presently is usually established. No understanding person familiar with these things will doubt that the vows keep many persons from service to the churches, and these are persons who would find a vocation in the church if they were not faced with the vows. Those who are not indifferent to winning these persons too for such service—and only they have here the right to find fault with the existing faculties—will want either to eliminate the vows or to modify them.

Our vows of ordination bind in two ways: first, they bind the personal belief of the one to be ordained; second, they bind his official statements [e.g., from the pulpit]. If the vows were changed so as to allow freedom in both areas, the vows would naturally be altogether eliminated. Max Krenkel in his proposal for reform completely overlooks this in his otherwise laudable book, *Religious Oath and Confessional Obligation*.[103] He reduces the obligation of our clerics to the Scripture alone, but not in a literally and legally binding way. He wants the obligation only to be "a reference to the duty of every Protestant preacher to research industriously and conscientiously in the venerable documents of the Christian faith, to strengthen his morally religious life continually from the Spirit revealing itself in them, and, in pious dedication to them, to form for himself a firm independent conviction that he can preach to his parish with complete inner truthfulness." This essentially eliminates every vow of ordination, just as it ignores the single purpose of such vows or makes their fulfillment illusory. This single purpose is the protection of the community against the individual. If one misunderstands this purpose or if one does not acknowledge it at all, the only consequent result is the requirement to abolish every such obligation of clerical office. Others do in fact require the elimination of the vows. Typically they say that "the open acknowledgement of the right to individual religious convictions would be nothing but the urgently necessary elevation of a factual condition to a legally justified condition."[104] This is entirely correct, and yet if the vows are completely done away with, one should not be blind to the fact that every church community will be dust, every church order will be impossible, and a condition will arise that Lagarde [52] correctly describes: thanks to theological education, the cleric's gown will have become "only a cloak under whose folds as many Protestantisms and Christianities are crowded as there are Protestant pulpits."

Certainly the purity of individual conviction deserves protection. But to accomplish this while not harming the community there is only one possible course, and it is to free the cleric's individual conviction but to bind his official utterances. That with this limitation the currently valid form of the ordination vows would really be changed for the better, may be seen in the fact that our proposal secures the true purpose of the vows while sparing them a lamentable excess. The excess is the intent to make vows into a chain that binds what by its nature cannot be bound; the attempt to do it is often effective enough to produce the most ruinous conflicts of conscience. The enactment of ordination vows in accordance with the limitation we propose certainly requires acknowledgement of a distinction that is very foreign to modern and especially modern Protestant conceptions, but without it our religious confusions have no prospect of a tolerable solution, at least not when one realistically considers possibilities of the current situation. This distinction is again that between an esoteric and an exoteric standpoint of the scientifically educated theologian.

The first theologians of the ancient church were more enlightened than we are about the inevitability of this distinction, and it needs no more detailed an argument than the one we have already given at the beginning of this book on the relationship of scientific thought [Wissen] to faith [Glauben].[105] The essential difference between one who scientifically thinks and one who believes is rooted so deeply in the essence of things [im Wesen der Dinge], it is so certain that the theologian views the objects of belief that he has thought through scientifically differently than does one who simply believes, that in practice every theologian will behave exoterically in thousands of cases. He will keep his theology to himself and leave a belief that does not need it undisturbed.

A powerful basic error in the world of Protestantism stands in the way of a principled and unconditional acknowledgement of this twofold position of every practical theologian. It is the opinion that in his parish the cleric has to represent his personal views and the convictions he has won through scientific thought and can preach them to the parish with "complete inner truthfulness." As seemingly correct as this statement is and as worthy of acknowledgement as its basic perceptions are, it is in fact one of the richest sources of the dilemmas and confusions of the Protestant churches. For one thing, nothing empties our churches as much as the situation in which parishioners have to listen so much to the personal views of the preacher in worship services. His personal views, as those of anyone else, will naturally be of highly questionable value in their largest part, and because of the lack of freedom in them today brought about by current ordination vows they will be especially worthless. Furthermore nothing wears our clerics down as much as the fact that their office makes such a constant claim on their person, that in their office they are able to forget themselves so little, and that especially in their chief function, the sermon, they are so exclusively teachers and not at all priests.

Certainly the strict concept of the priest is so totally uprooted in Protestantism that its reinstatement is inconceivable. Protestantism does have a just criticism of Catholicism based on very rich experience, namely that the complete priesthood, the complete sacrifice of the individual to religious office, cannot be required. Yet the concept of the priest is so essential for every religion that it can never be completely lacking in any religious community that has any life left in it. If the "priesthood of all believers" is not the rule—and it is always and necessarily an unreal ideal in such large communities as our established churches—nothing remains but the emergence of priestly individuals who present religion in itself [Religion an sich] for the others.[106] They cannot do this as natural individuals but only as bearers of an office that is given them. If the position of the clerics in the Protestant churches is still based in any way on religion, then at least so much of this priesthood must adhere to them that they relate to their parishes neither exclusively nor first of all as individual persons, and that especially their personal convictions take second place to regard for the religious needs of the parish. First importance should be given the task of taking care that the religion of the parish is what it should be for it: it should comfort, elevate and better it, and cause peace to rule in it. If the cleric has to place this task above everything else, if in certain circumstances he must suppress his personal scientific convictions, nothing stands in the way of placing him in office with a formula of obligation that frees his personal conviction completely but binds him in the practice of the office to the need of his parish, whether simply to this need or to certain confessional statements acknowledged in the parish.

Adherents of complete freedom for the cleric will object to our solution by protesting the self-denial here required of him. The denial we mean is not at all a complete renunciation of the cleric's own conviction or of its use (about which we shall soon speak), although renunciation is certainly required of him. But insofar as every community limits the freedom of the individual, least of all can the head of a Christian community wish to withdraw from every such requirement, for if he did one would have to ask what significance Christianity still has for him. Moreover it must be asked whether or not the denial here expected is not richly repaid by the gain it brings the cleric, assuming he knows how to appreciate ideal benefits. In any case the freedom of his scientific convictions is more clearly assured than when his relationship to his community is based, whether with or without a binding vow, on the freedom of his scientific conviction. And otherwise, too, in the position here assigned him the cleric will perhaps forget himself only to gain himself again [Matth. 10:39].[107] For having always to be himself in the practice of his office is the most oppressive slavery weighing on the Protestant cleric.[108]

Critics will also find in our proposal gate and door open to untruthfulness and hypocrisy. We resist the charge of encouraging hypocrisy. It should not be forgotten that, because of the emphasis on the person in clerical office, the most complicated and subtle forms of hypocrisy are at home in the Protestant world. And it is easy to understand that the cleric who never forgets himself yet denies himself, involves himself most deeply in falsity. As for untruthfulness, it certainly cannot be denied that the setting aside of personal conviction required by the presuppositions of office that we advocate can become a bad habit. The best protection against this will be the honesty and warmth of zeal with which the cleric is concerned for the well-being of his parish; the more these are present, the more genuine will be the setting aside of personal conviction in the practice of office. Vocation for caring for the well-being of a parish, the ability to love its people, is naturally assumed here.

The possibility of disharmony between the convictions of the cleric and the belief he represents in the parish will seem to many intolerable. But this possibility is in truth not as bad as it easily seems when viewed through the eyes of theology. Let us imagine the worst possible case, that the personal convictions of the cleric agree with no letter of the parish's belief. But let us also assume that the cleric in the practice of his office puts his own convictions aside, that he dedicates himself exclusively and honestly to the need of his parish and in this sense proclaims to the parish the belief that is holy for it. He will have attained everything that at least human sight sees as necessary, and in any case more than can be enforced by a vow.

Should we go further into the subject of the priestly vices one could see here looming on the horizon: love of domination over others, vain theatrics and the like? Discussing these would not be very useful. What institution can stop the sources of human perversity? Protestant laity are secured against many kinds of such offence by their greater rights, the full acknowledgement of which is very probably imminent even in Germany, although these rights too are subject to serious misuse. But beside this we have a curative medicine in mind, one that is certainly not infallible, but neither is it completely contemptible: a serious scientific education free of outside constraints. We would have equipped with it those theologians whom we, above all, want to help.

As we speak of this education, we return to a point made previously. After all that has been said, we need present no further proof that our idea of a formula of ordination is as compatible with the practical needs of a parish as it is with the most rigorous and free theological education of its cleric, and such an education is especially desirable in the present. If we have ranked the conviction of such theologians below the need of their parishes, this hardly means renunciation of conviction, nor does it mean in the least that this conviction is supposed to be a dead personal possession, so that the parish would have nothing of it. Rather, all the cleric's convictions of every kind should be at the parishioners' disposal. The cleric should only not introduce them in the wrong place and without being asked.

Christianity has very different degrees of inner truth in our parishes, both when these themselves and when their individual members are compared. But however this may be, the goal toward which our theologians are educated is to be able to be, if not all things, yet something to all persons [cf. 1 Cor. 9:22]. This goal will by no means be reached in all cases nor does it need to be, because here the only thing that is important is that the cleric fulfills his task only in one parish. But it must be strived for, as long as culture and Christianity are not wholly to separate in practice as well [as in theory], and as long as there is serious interest in preventing from being completely torn apart, without replacement, the ideal bond with which our churches still bind together persons of the most different levels of culture, the most different ways of thinking and even in their forms completely different beliefs. Nothing will be able more suitably to produce the ability to fulfill this task of the theologian today, in some adequate degree and with dignity, than a deep scientific education that opens insight into humanity and world and that really lifts its student above the conflict of parties.

Here we should like to end these remarks about the possibility of a free-thinking theology in our Protestant churches. The reader who has participated in our development of this book would not expect from a longer discussion any reconciliation of the opposites [Wissen and Glauben] that would be theoretically sufficient and exclude all doubt. Because they are founded eternally in the essence of the world [im Weltwesen], no theory brings them together. Their possible union can be presented for us therefore only in living persons.

We are also aware that our proposed formula of obligation also puts rights into the hands of the authorities having jurisdiction over the clerics, rights that can make all betterment of relations expected from such a formula illusory, if they are handled by imperious personalities guided by the attitudes of church-political parties. Here it makes no difference whether or not these authorities are of the contemporary mixed state-church kind or the pure or purer church kind of the future. If, however, our churchly affairs are again to be led onto more peaceful paths and to be kept on them, this will depend above all on the insight and love for persons that rises above parties in those authorities who have chief responsibility for leadership in these matters. It will depend on the insight with which they perceive the depth of the oppositions that fill the whole history of the church and the seriousness of the conflicts arising from them for theologians today. It will depend even more on love for persons filling the authorities with the purest and most unerring will not to sharpen but, in every admissible way and especially for the younger clerics in their charge, to mitigate the conflicts to which the clerics are presently exposed. Only few emerge from these conflicts as victors; the vanquished, as broken persons. We will have taken a respectable step further on the path of peace in the church, when especially the leaders of the affairs of our churches have opened themselves to the perception that scientific thought inheres in all theology as an element destructive of and limiting religion. But as long as we cannot do without theology, and as long as we wish to limit the effects of its irreligious tendencies, it is wrong for theology only to play at science, make counterfeits of it and entertain impossible ideas about its consequences. Rather, theology must apply [anwenden] the results of science temperately and wisely.

AFTERWORD (1903)

What I Have Experienced With My Book

In the Introduction I reported how the book came to be written in order to clarify it and to excuse this second attempt to present it to the public in its original form. This Afterword is a continuation of that excuse. In all that I have experienced with the book, I have found no reason to regard its essential thoughts [Grundgedanken] as mistaken, and I have stood by it in all dangers it has brought me.[109] I divide what I call experiences here into lesser and greater. The lesser experiences are so to speak our, my and my book's private experiences. The greater experiences are those I have had with the book out there with all the world in the general course of things and in the development of theology, as that is the one thing my book is about.

I wish to close the Afterword with these greater experiences. When I do so I shall not have to provide for public interest nor for the space in which this interest could show itself, since it covers almost thirty years. The matter is different in the first two sections of the Afterword, at least as regards the public character of interest. It is most undoubtedly different where I shall have to speak of the personal consequences that I have experienced as the author of my book. In order not to fall into an all too private sphere, I shall limit myself to the consequences that I have experienced as a person of public office, as a teacher of theology. But also with what I now begin, that is, with what I directly experienced with the book, I shall acknowledge analogous limits: I shall only be able to speak of judgments of my book that were made known to me through publications. What will not be considered at all is what was said to me about my book privately by personal friends near and far, or by distant persons whom I have never known but who made their sympathetic understanding known to me. And there really have been such persons, as little as I may have deserved it.

The Public Criticism of My Book

The following public judgments of my book are the only ones I know about.

1. *Neue Evangelische Kirchenzeitung* 1873, No. 41, 646 (where I am discussed together with Lagarde's work.)

2. *Volksblatt für die reformierte Kirche der Schweiz* : 1873, No. 43-44, 170f., 174.; 1 1874, No. 7,26f. In these two articles I am again discussed together with Lagarde. They were written by Rudolf Kündig.

3. *Im neuen Reich* 1873, No. 45, 734f. The article is written by one of the editors, A. Dove, who gave it the title "An Unwilling Theologian."

4. Daniel Schenkel, *Deutsches Protestantenblatt* 1873, Nr. 44.

5. Hans Herrig, *Magazin für die Literatur des Auslandes* 1873, No. 45, 662-664; in addition the editorial afterword, No. 46.

6. William Purdue Dickson. *Introductory Lecture Delivered at the Opening of Divinity Hall at the University of Glasgow on the 10th of November* (Glasgow, 1873), 11ff.

7. *Reform. Zeitstimmen aus der Schweizer Kirche 1873*, No. 24, 32f., by C. Hörler.

8. _____, No. 25, 451ff., an article by H. Lang with the title "Two Odd Fellows." The title refers to Nietzsche and me.

9. *Litterarisches Zentralblatt für Deutschland* 1873, No. 51, 1611f.

10. *Saturday Review* 1873, 793.

11. *Westminster Review* 1874, 251ff., where T.K. Cheyne also discusses me together with Lagarde.

12. Adolf Hilgenfeld, *Zeitschrift für wissenschaftliche Theologie* 1874, 296f.

13. *Beilage zur Augsburger Allgemeinen Zeitung* 1874, No. 35.

14. H. Ewald, *Göttingische gelehrte Anzeigen* 1874, No. 1, 12ff.

15. F. Nitzsch, Jenaer Litteratur Zeitung 1874, No. 5.

16. *Protestantische Kirchenzeitung* 1874, No. 8. 171ff, written by H. Holzmann and P.W. Schmidt.

17. C. Fuchs, *Musikalisches Wochenblatt* 1874, No. 13, 163.

18. *Die deutsche Predigt: Homiletische Zeitschrift vom Standpunkt des wissenschaftlichen Protestantismus* 1874, II, Heft 1, 61f.

19. *Blätter für litterarische Unterhaltung* 1874, No. 30, 473f.

20. H. Schultz, *Jahrbücher für deutsche Theologie* 1874, 44.

21. Palmer, *Jahrbücher für deutsche Theologie* 1874, 333f.

22. A. Hauck, *Theologischer Jahresbericht* 1874, Vol. 9, 308ff.

23. Albrecht Ritschl, *Die christliche Lehre von der Rechtfertigung und Versöhnung*, Vol. III (1874), 540f.

24. Eduard von Hartmann, *Die Selbstzersetzung des Christentums* (Berlin, 1874), 24 (and often).

25. F. von Hellwald, *Culturgeschichte in ihrer natürlichen Entwicklung* (1875), 791.

26. J. Bach, *Die Dogmengeschichte des Mittelalters*, 2. Teil (Vienna, 1875), preface, ix.

27. H. Reuter, *Geschichte der Aufklärung des Mittelalters*, II (1875), 346, where, with regard to the 13th century conflict over Aver-

roism, I am named and quoted with the addition of single and double question marks. Cf. 348f., fn. 2, fn. 11.

28. Julius Räbiger, *Theologik* (Leipzig, 1880), 201 ff.

29. C.A. Bernoulli, *Die wissenschaftliche und die kirchliche Methode in der Theologie. Ein encyclopädischer Versuch* (Freiburg i.B., 1897).

30. Eberhard Vischer, *Ist die Wahrheit des Christentums zu beweisen?* (Tübingen and Leipzig, 1902). 18f.

Before I begin my discussion of this list, I must ask the reader to exclude Bernoulli's book (No. 29). It is a unicum, one of its kind, and I shall have better occasion to remark about it later (in the second section of the Afterword). So the reader will see what I have to say about it.

I begin with an introductory remark about my source for the list: it is a loose page kept in my copy of the book on which I noted all utterances about it that I happened upon in my reading. Whatever one may think of its value, I assume that no better source will exist for the study of its reception. I can support its claim to be complete at least with the explanation that nothing has been intentionally omitted. The list contains all that I know of what has been published about the book to the present, and this means all that I have known about earlier and all that I know about now.[110] But enough preliminary remarks, I have no cause to remain here longer. If I continue to speak as I have begun, that is, with the title of this section of my Afterword, with the long list of publications my book called forth, and finally indeed with the expression "study of its reception" that has just flowed from my pen, I shall be on the best way toward completely misleading my readers about the interest I have for the book's reception. I hasten, then, to abandon it, and I turn now to the question about what the list is supposed to mean for me and the reader.

To give a very brief, at least approximate yet comprehensive and not entirely false idea of what I call "the reception of my book," I say, first, that the list is strictly chronological. If the reader realizes this, then he can almost read simply from the list what sort of success the book had, namely a momentary one. For not quite two years all sorts of circles and even theological celebrities of the time were interested in it, and after that it was hardly mentioned at all. As for the few latecomers on the list and how much they may be considered signs of a significant awakening of what has been soundly slumbering interest, I leave them aside for the moment. I have already said I would come to one of them, Bernoulli, later. Otherwise, I have absolutely nothing against the reader ceasing to have any interest in the reception of the book. And in truth the reader has nothing more of special use to expect of it. I say this only to disperse, as convincingly as possible, all concern that my list is intended to challenge anyone to "study" the literature in it. The reader may also be assured that I have no intention of conducting such an unrequested study here myself. The reader's impression of the list is also my impression, and, accordingly, I limit my interest in it. Yet I do not wish to be misunderstood, and I offer the following further explanation.

In this discussion I have spoken of my experiences with my book. I have distinguished therefore between my book and myself, and friendly readers will already have excused me for that. Without this distinction I would not seriously speak of the reception of my book. Especially its invective character had to call forth criticism that had to do partly with the book's theses and partly with its author. Accordingly I have to speak about each. I begin with the author, with the criticism of my person. I wish to be as brief as possible, as required by the fact that, of the critics on my list, only a disappearing few are still alive. What I might have to say about the praise and censure they gave me has ceased to have public interest and, so to speak, sunken into the series of my private affairs, about which will not be spoken here at all, as I have said. But what sense would it have in these pages to express what I still feel obligated to express, namely my gratitude for the consideration and acknowledgement I experienced! There is hardly anyone left to accept it. And if judgments of my book have perhaps given me more cause to defend myself than to be grateful, I always neglected the right time for such defense, and I have maintained my silence. Even disregarding all respect that one still enjoying the light of the sun owes the *manes* [the spirits of those who have died], I myself could only deplore tearing out the grass I have let grow. I wish to say no more than the following about the personal treatment I experienced in the judgment of the book: it was as it had to be and approximately what I expected. I allow myself to say this because I know that no resentment is hidden in my words, just as there is none hidden in the warning I have given my readers about not letting themselves be misled by the list into undue occupation with the book's reception. Here there is nothing else expressed but the sincere opinion that there is not much to be gained from it. How sincere this opinion is and how little I am inclined to claim the interest of my readers for more than a very summary glance at the list, will be clear in what follows. I shall from now on put aside all that is personal and turn immediately to the question about the fate that public judgment determined for the book's content or theses.

My purpose is still to convince the reader not to pursue the criticism. As I consider what could be helpful, I see myself prompted, first, to remove from the list the very few voices that have spoken without reserve for my view. The numbers 5 and 7 on the list have done so, but as like-minded persons who do not discuss the questions I raise.[111] Hence they fall out of consideration when it comes to ascertaining the real result that the discussion of the book had for my theme. For similar reasons I must immediately remove from the list the names Eduard von Hartmann and von Hellwald (numbers 24 and 25). They are not at all like-minded even if from their own standpoint, which is far different from mine, they do give my standpoint limited acknowledgement; my book's encounter with them is only incidental and as it were accidental. What remains after these have been dropped from consideration is the theological part of the criticism of the book, the criticism that should be most important for my readers and for me. This criticism is altogether negative, yet in such a peculiar form that it has been completely unfruitful for others no less than for myself. I could judge the matter differently only by means of a serious self-deception. The book totally failed at calling forth an interesting discussion of its content or questions that in any way really furthered perception of things. The response it had, especially from its theological judges, was above all surprise and puzzlement. Persons in these circles have often said that they did want to understand me, so I cannot accuse them of not wanting to, yet it is certain that they did not. And they took from this misunderstanding the liberty not to take me seriously. For I have heard nothing more often than that I am hardly intelligible, as has been said also indirectly in my readers' reservation regarding their understanding. With no other weapon have I been more often opposed than simply with questions about the religious confusion of our time and the situation of distress arising from it for theology, for which the questioners themselves had no answer and hardly tried to conceal their lack. If the last of the voices on my list understands no more than that "much is to be learned" from the book, but nothing really right, then I have heard nothing from theological criticism as constantly as this. It is the motif running through all the different variations, and it lets one see best the way in which "modern theology" places me among the holy gathering of those it still considers worthy of being heard. In the few years in which my book still had a certain circle of readers, this was the public opinion that formed about it, and this public opinion provided "modern theologians" with a comfortable way of thinking about it. It also gave the book the room in which gradually and completely to disappear.

One will perhaps think that such an at first glance rude valuation of the judgments of my book obligates me all the more to show, by discussing the literature on the list, how I arrive at this valuation. I withdraw from this requirement not at all because of the difficulty of the task but because of the delay it would cause here, a delay that not only I would feel, but especially my readers. For I have already given them an indication from which they should draw completely opposite advice. The readers will ask, why continue a discussion when I have already shown myself convinced that it would be unproductive? Why not break it off ? This advice pleases me much better, and I shall try to follow it.

The indication I have just mentioned consists in the fact that, in the whole difficulty I have described, I myself may be the guilty party. I do not deny this, and I can briefly make my opinion on this understandable by saying that my book is a monologue. As such it found the only understanding that such lucubrations can find in the world, namely nearly none at all. Having said that, I have only to show that my book is a monologue.

First, considering the process of its birth, as related in the Introduction, it could not have been anything else. I do not think I need to go into this; the reader may judge it for himself. Second, its monologic character is shown in how the book was received. I do not want to go into this, for if I did, I would have to discuss individual points that I did not make clear enough in the book.[112] I wish to offer only one excuse for not entering into such a discussion, and that is my regard for the patience of the reader. I shall, rather, hold as narrowly and as strictly as possible to the character of the whole of the book in order to make firm the notion that in it I really think only of myself and work only on matters that have to do with my own needs, and therefore that in the book I deliver the very model of a monologue that is difficult for anyone else to appreciate.

But of whom or what should I think in the book than of myself, and whom should I help with it but myself? Certainly not Christianity. At the end of the book's first preface I disavowed the calling and the pretension of showing Christianity the way out of its present distress, which I neither misunderstood nor denied. I intended to help theology even less. In the book I expressed only a bad opinion of theology and indeed of every form in which it represents Christianity present to me at the time, both the "apologetic" and the "liberal." I did once let slip the expression "better theology" as the goal I pursued (see p. 115). But the perceptive reader will not have been misled by this *lapsus calami* [slip of the pen]. He will have seen that what I know of a "better theology" is exactly nothing, or at least something only very relative, but not at all enough to nourish myself on the least bit of desire to be something like a reformer of theology. For this "better" theology that I named "critical theology" is simply the theology that brings the right awareness of the damage I charge theology with doing. Such a theology may be able to keep itself alive, but not Christianity, which theology by common reputation serves. This self-conserving theology is also the theology I needed for myself when I wrote the book, as the Introduction of this second edition shows. What I wanted to do with the book was certainly anything but confess my love for theology. From the moment in which I dedicated my own thought to this discipline, I *never* felt [empfinden] love for it. Yet beside all the disinclination to it that theology itself instilled in me, I had gradually found a place in it, for here I could learn church history better than anywhere else and so occupy myself with a life's work. And with this interest I tried with my book to conserve theology for myself but for no one else.

But is it really true that I thought in the book only of myself and my needs, when I, in more than one place in the book (p. 132 and in the Preface), let the intention be known of also helping others? With this question a hostile reader might finally carry my interpretation of the book ad absurdum and charge me with trying, by slandering the book, to idealize it or to make it more interesting than it really is. I would have to answer that I have not completely forgotten that I, from page 140 on, have had no intent of idealizing my book but have attributed responsibility for the seeming injustice it experienced to its own deficiencies. Nor have I applied the diabolic arts of dialectic in my advocacy of it, as this last charge suggests. Exact reading of the places in the book that I have cited will show I was not of the opinion that I myself had to do with persons in need of help: I rather refer them partly back to themselves and partly to the help of other persons, namely of the authorities over them. And that could be enough said about my readiness to help in the statements I made. I would like to concentrate the rest of what I have to say on this question in the discussion of a single point, one that has especially occupied the book's critics and therefore has become one of the book's special problem areas. In discussing this point I think I can best illustrate what I mean by its monologic character.

Hardly anything has been found as offensive as the proposal I make in the concluding paragraphs (pp. 129-133), and hardly anything has given more strength to the critics in their opinion that the book is strange and ambiguous. The proposal was to make the concept of accommodation respectable again in theology's representation of the church, in accordance with the example given by the ancient church. Among all the heresies in the book, this proposal is the only one about which I expressly confess (p. 130) both an awareness of its paradoxical character in the present and a certain concern as regards difficulties that I might cause myself in the reception of the book. And yet truthfully no thought in the book is so carelessly just thrown out, so to speak, as this one. I expressed it with the conviction that an idea that once had such great and lasting significance for the theoretical representation of Christianity could never disappear from the church completely without shaking the very foundations of the relationship the Christian world had to its religion. I considered it to be something like a truth that no one questions because life itself represents it. The entire proposal corresponds to this conviction, and I have never found any reason to abandon it.[113] I refused to establish the proposal with any sort of reasonable discussion (132) and I expressly presupposed that the clerics already had the wisdom I proclaimed to them (toward the end of the first preface). In the representation of my theses in the book's last pages, I even went almost so far as to take the standpoint of subservience or of the maxim, "the first duty of the citizen is not to disturb the peace" (esp. p. 133). That is to say I almost sank to what is acknowledged to be the lowest form of abdication in the use of one's intelligence there is. My book is just that monologic, and it is just that far from thoughts of helping anyone but first of all myself.

I think I can now summarize what I want to say about the reception of the book or the criticism given in it. Yet I shall not do what the direction of my discussion seems to indicate. As ready as I am to accept the situation I have described, I have no intention of saying a *pater pec-cavi* [Father, I have sinned]. I should not make the book any better than it is, but I should not make it any worse. I do not doubt that it is not without fault in appearing non-transparent to its critics, so that something like a shimmer of ambiguity and deceit has remained hovering over it that they have not liked nor could like, something that prevented them from understanding it. But this fault of mine does not make their criticism of me and my book any better or especially any more productive. Yet I did not judge my critics so meanly that I could have left the matter with the simple statement of that result that I have given above, namely that the criticism was unfruitful, and I have tried to correct that impression in what I have conceded about the book's own fault. I did so in hopes of another concession, one from readers willing to grant me something of a fair judgment, namely that not only conceited obstinacy is my motivation when, disregarding all the criticism of the book that I have heard from theologians, I continue to hold to its essential percep-tions [Grundanschauungen]. And I hope for the same concession when I state that I am still of the opinion, now as then, that we live in an age [Zeitalter] that is about to clarify its relationship to Christianity, that is, to free itself from Christianity, and that theology is not the last thing re-sponsible for our having come to such an issue.

The Consequences of my Book for Me

It would be a bad sign for the book if I had nothing here to say about its consequences for me. For that would amount to admitting that the author regarded the book with as little seriousness as he was regard-ed, because he had, inconceivably, so written it as if it had to do with others but not himself. This was not the case at all. The book is not a monologue in this sense, so that in writing it I had, so to speak, placed myself beside it. When I wrote it I knew very well that I was writing against myself, and I have always accepted the consequences that it in-flicted on me. Whether willingly or not is beside the point.

Indeed in the beginning I overestimated these consequences. When the book was finished, I thought it might cost me my theological teaching office. Yet I was never in the least given the idea that anyone in Basel considered removing me, and I remained completely uncon-tested in the office entrusted to me until I resigned it twenty-four years later. Basel has remained the "asylum" for my "theology" that I have held it to be from the moment I entered the city, and it deserves there-fore my just as constant gratitude.

I was to be less deceived by another presentiment that accompa-nied me as I wrote the book, one that had a far greater character of cer-tainty, namely that with the book I had disqualified myself for every theological lectern in my native Germany. That this country—or

"Reich" as it has become since I left it in 1870—has been in a state of war with me since 1873 is something that it supposedly has not known until today. And even I could not have actually intended the book as a declaration of war. But I betrayed so much in it that I rather knew it would involve me in an irreconcilable conflict with the theology thriving in the German Reich and that the conflict would condemn me to banishment. And this is what happened. There was only one exception, in which old contacts with the university suggested my name, and even so there were no more than a few dim indications. Other than that, since I left Germany I have not had the least knowledge of anyone in a German university uttering a wish to have me on its theological faculty. Naturally I do not say this for the purpose of calling anyone to account, nor do I think anyone should give an account. I say it only in advocacy of my book, for the sake of which alone I have undertaken to report on how I reacted to its consequences and to show how it indicated the direction my relationship to a theology I rejected were to take.

As I look back on all my actions and omissions that come here into consideration, I discover only a single point that could be considered a contradiction of my indifference toward "getting somewhere" in theology, toward my theological "career." I mean something that, in the eyes of someone other than myself, could be so construed, insofar as he could consider it an effort to maintain relations with theology in Germany: my contributions over an eleven-year period (1876-1887) to the *Theologische Literaturzeitung.* These contributions never amounted to a "stream" of publications, and toward the end they were like a small brook running dry. But the journal is a chief organ of "modern theology" and I have already conceded that my contributions to it could be construed as a maintenance of relations to theology in Germany. If I do not immediately counter this idea with evidence to the contrary, then for two reasons. First, by defending myself against a charge that is possible but not probable, I could be doing something superfluous, and these pages are already so overburdened that they tax my reader's patience, which is the second reason. Before entering into such a discussion I would like to hear from the editors of the journal doubt about the complete freedom of my relationship to it.[114] I sincerely hope to avoid this both for my sake and that of others, and in this hope I refuse to be pushed unnecessarily into giving an account of my participation. If I may set this aside now, I repeat that I have never experienced a weakening of my conviction that with the book I wrote myself off as a teacher of theology in Germany. Thanks to the emergence of "modern theology," no one will find my conviction surprising who considers how soon what at first was a presentiment had to become reality.

There is another point that is truly more in need of an account from me, one that calls me away from the more or less "speculative" sphere of talking about an offer I never received. After I wrote the book, how did I conduct myself in the teaching office with which I was entrusted in Basel? This is without doubt the first question my readers will ask me here. And I answer: after the book no differently than before, only that what before was half-conscious and instinctive became conscious with constantly increasing clarity and, accordingly, determined my behavior more and more definitely. My conduct as the author of the book was actually no different than what it would have been had I not written it, only had I not written it, I would not have to give the account I am now giving. But there is more that needs to be said about this.

I have already (see p. 141) given special mention to the last part of my book, which has been a special point of offence. It gives the book the appearance of pushing good advice chiefly on the clerics, advice that I hold to be purposeful in the difficulty and distress of the time, while I myself, as an academician, silently pretend to be elevated above the problem. I believe I have already said a good deal in this Afterword to prevent such a misunderstanding, but truthfully I think I stated my position on this in the book itself. Toward the end of the first preface, I expressly state that I hold exactly the clerics to be those who, in comparison with us academic teachers, have the very least need of the advice. In 1873 I did not think so childishly about the questions of life that come to bear here that I could have forgotten there is no difference—none that could in any way be important for us Protestant bearers of a teaching office in the church—between the teacher's podium and the pulpit in the proclamation of our wisdom. Nor did I hold us academicians to be a group of teachers less exposed than pastors to the danger of becoming alienated from the needs of life, for which needs our universities, too, exist. These needs are only so much [von Haus aus] closer to the pastors.[115] So I not only had the academic theologian foremost in mind, but I drew the general figure of the theologian that I needed simply to formulate my advice from none other than myself. And the advice was intended for no one more directly than for me. For some time before I wrote the book, I had not taught my hearers [sc. those hearing his lectures] what I accepted of Christianity, but what on the presupposition of *their* faith I held to be purposeful in letting their faith be. The publication of the book changed nothing in this. With regard to my hearers' relationship to the book, I began immediately with the bold fiction that they knew nothing about it. I never mentioned the book in lectures, and no discussion of it with my hearers ever took place on my initiative. As for me, the book's publication only meant that I was conscious, in my *forum internum*, of having made known the secret of my teaching. And then, as the years passed and I made progress in the object of my teaching, and as I saw what transpired in theology in the rest of the world, I saw the gap between that object and me rather widen.[116]

And so I performed the duties of my teaching office twenty-five years long without interruption, from the spring of 1873 until the spring of 1897. I offered a two-year cycle of lectures. In the first year I dealt chiefly with church history to the end of the Middle Ages, with exegetical lectures in addition. In the second year I treated the exegesis of the New Testament and additionally held lectures on individual chapters of general church history.[117] Should I now, apparently having begun to report on the general constitution of these lectures, try to illustrate what they were like? Presuming that the general conditions of what is to be said here are still the same, the answer is no. The idea that still gives form to what I relate here is that, in all I have experienced with the book, I have never found cause to judge its essential thoughts wrong, and that I have stood by it in all dangers. Hence this report is a literary undertaking of a common kind. Its form does obligate me to allow no problem to impede the reader's comprehension of the stated idea, or said differently, it obligates me to include whatever serves to insure our necessary accord. I think I have met that obligation in what I have said about the general constitution of my lectures; I think it suffices completely to produce the necessary accord. What I have said about the lectures has no doubt given the reader the strong impression that they were very problematic, and I have no intention of correcting it. I have no desire to defend these products of a difficult situation against the judgment that they can only have been models of how a theologian should not deal with such a task. Accordingly every further attempt to give the reader a clear picture of my lectures would be entirely superfluous and to no good purpose. This is all the more important when one considers how complicated such an attempt would have to be. In fact it would be so complicated that, as agile as I might try to be, I would have to be concerned about constantly hearing, from the midst of my readers, the admonition that I enlighten them beyond all measure of proper discretion about my private affairs and claim more interest than they have for distressing problems that I myself had created. Hence I should break off the discussion of my theological lectures and move on to something else that I might have to communicate about the book's consequences for me. And yet, if I were to close this discussion now, I would demonstrate blindness toward an important fact, which at this point no one should or even could see it but I. It is the change that occurred at the moment I entered into a discussion of my lectures, a change that has to do with my readers and that takes this report out of the sphere of a literary undertaking of the common kind that I originally intended it to be. In explaining what I mean I would like to say something about the sphere of common literature.

In every literary undertaking in the strict sense of the word, the public to which the author turns is a dark chasm into which he writes with the awareness that neither is he personally known nor does he know anyone personally.[118] If he directs his words to a future time, then this is certainly obvious. But the matter is no different when and as far as he directs his words to contemporary readers, in which case nothing connects the author and his readers but their belonging to the same time. This may give the author an advantage, but by itself it hardly suffices to produce a relationship between author and reader of personal acquaintance. It is just this natural relationship of remoteness between author and public that ceased to be when I took up the subject of my lectures. I began this report without thinking of the hearers of these lectures, which allowed me to ignore the possibility of their presence among my readers. That has now ended. As I now write about the lectures, precisely my former hearers have completely ceased to be a part of my public that I might overlook, and indeed however small their number among my readers might be. Of course not all of them will be a part of this public, not even a noticeable number of them. But by no means will they be completely lacking, and even the smallest number of them suffice to take the character of remoteness from the public. It was this character that I had in mind when I spoke above of seeing no need to go further into unveiling the nature of my lectures. But such an assumption about the public collapses as soon as I catch only a glimpse of my hearers among them. If I were to continue to speak about the lectures without concern for those who heard them, how could I ever get those hearers out of sight? Must I not see that a concern I spoke of earlier is now altogether meaningless, namely that if I remain longer with these lectures, I would have to hear the admonition that I speak of things that concern me more than others? I now have far better reason to be wary of a completely opposite admonition, one from my hearers: "Most honored teacher, your talk about breaking off your discussion of the lectures we heard seems to us to betray the dubious notion that you can rule over property that is not yours. Are these lectures not as much our concern as they are yours? You gave them to us. Should we now not even ask about the true character of the gift and what value it has, after having just heard things about it that make its value highly questionable?" I can only acknowledge these questions without the least hesitation. As imperfectly as my hearers and I may have gotten to know one another, I hardly wish to persuade them that we were only strangers and certainly hope I could not. The only question is how I am to answer. I think I need not abandon the idea that a long discussion of the lectures would be superfluous, and I think the theme of my lectures has been sufficiently presented in what I have already said. Yet in no way do I wish to deny my hearers' claim to further explanation, and I see no possibility for accomplishing this than to put aside the previous form of relating what I have experienced with my book and to move with my hearers to a short "*a parte*" where I can speak with them about my behavior as their teacher. I ask only one concession from them before we, so to speak, move aside together: neither the place nor the occasion is suitable for a confidential conversation about our remembrances. Hence in what I have to say here I shall not be able to avoid holding strictly to the chief matter, even with the danger of seeming improperly brief.

Without further delay I uncover the basic flaw of the whole relationship between me and my hearers by saying that I persistently withdrew myself from them as a theologian, that is, as the advisor that they above all sought in me. This theologian was missing in our togetherness, and I was not able to produce him. He was not only missing at the lectern. There a teacher stood who tried, for students who were to be instructed in Christianity, to interpret the New Testament and church history as neutrally and without *Tendenz* [as objectively] as possible. As corresponded with the duty of his office, his intent was to communicate this subject matter in a form that enabled the students to meet their immediate need, which was to pass their examinations. But my students also had to do without the advisor in all questions with which young theologians are accustomed to turn to their teachers outside the lecture halls, which questions I would like to designate very broadly as questions of conscience. What I have just said suffices to guarantee that I have no illusions about the theft-like character of my understanding of my office. I know very well what I owe my hearers, who undoubtedly suffered a serious loss through my behavior, and that is an apology. My apology is here expressly given.[119]

In my own mind I could not honestly make this apology, if I could discover in the memories of my relationship with my hearers something that would have to convince me that the apology is a hopeless or useless gesture. Nor could I honestly mean it if I thought the memories of my hearers contained impressions that would have to make my now unveiled behavior toward them unpardonable. I am fairly confident that they do not think I ever "hoodwinked" them, or that animosity or indeed contempt ever played a role in my relationship to them, or finally that I was the only one to gain anything from my behavior and they were the only ones to carry its cost. Nothing of that sort stood between me and my hearers. I say this with regard not only to my own judgment but also to that of my hearers, for none of my observations of them over the years contradicts my conviction that their impressions are the same as mine. And in fact I never deceived them, neither those among them who entirely correctly missed edification in my lectures, something that sounded like the influence of belief in the object, for here it was missing, nor those whose critical attitude "from house out" [von Haus aus] may have brought them nearer to me, who heard nothing from me that might have misled them about the difficulty of the task of life toward which they moved.[120] These latter hearers too might have had grounds to complain about a help I did not give. But if someone were to say that animosity was the reason that help was not given, I would surely deny it. I have not forgotten how often I thought of them with completely different perceptions [Empfindungen] than ill will or disdain. Certainly they heard very little about these perceptions; I gave little notice of them. But there was certainly nothing to notice of ill will or disdain.

Finally, with regard to the fair distribution of the loss suffered by them and me through my understanding of my teaching office: at the time they were still hearers this was not a point that could properly have been raised by me, because our relationship was not yet based exclusively or even chiefly on our remembrances. And it is probably not a point that my hearers have thought much about. But it is not a point that I might have to avoid, not even after having confessed—toward the beginning of the Introduction of this book—that I learned from the preparation of my lectures more than they about the exegesis of the New Testament and church history. For I was not my hearers' last teacher, and I have not been their last teacher for a long time now. Another completely took my place whose way I certainly did not prepare and with whom I have never thought of comparing myself. This teacher is life and the experiences one gathers in its school. I can only assume that, even for my most recent hearers, these experiences have taught them sufficiently to enable them to understand my protest against the notion that they were the only ones to suffer loss in our former relationship. I think I need only briefly refer to the sacrifice involved in renouncing the best part of personal satisfaction that a teacher usually has from the relationship to his students. In spite of the shadows cast over our relationship, I think my hearers will not simply discount the sacrifice and have nothing left for me but condemnation.

The question I am now dealing with—about how much the book's problematic consequences burdened me in the conduct of my theological teaching office—has moved us to the edge of what I intend for this report, in which my main concern is to represent my book. I acknowledged without hesitation that this question is of special interest for my former hearers and that they, accordingly, have the right to special regard from me on this subject, which regard I have now given in the apology above. I certainly allowed myself to adjoin to this apology the expression of my trust that our common memories of our former relationship can stand the offence I could not avoid giving them.

I am now at the end of the *"a parte"* having to do with the consequences of my book for the conduct of my teaching office in relationship to my hearers. What I have to say further about these consequences in part goes far beyond the horizon of my relationship to my hearers, and it no longer belongs to what especially concerns them. I can now take up again the chief and basic thread of this report.

Tradition dictates that we university professors in the German-language area be, at the same time and equally, both teachers and authors. Whether this is problematic for the work of education can be disputed. In any case I have worked entirely within the scope of this tradition, and I hope that no power with pretensions of reforming the structure of our universities will ever succeed in limiting the academic freedom rooted in the tradition and the two kinds of activity it has produced without meeting the most extreme resistance of the university teachers. I say that here in order that my following discussion not be taken as a complaint about this traditional dualism, insofar as I have not had the best experiences with it.

The academic teacher's public, which he in the practice of his office has before him in the lecture hall, is basically different from the public to whom he turns as an author. The teacher, who speaks to the closed circle of his scholars, does not have to seek his public, while the author does. The teacher has to do with seekers and he helps them find. In helping them attain their goal it is his responsibility to determine how much he wants to communicate; indeed to a certain extent he has to limit himself and choose from what he has within himself. The matter is entirely different with the author. He does not know the persons to whom he speaks but must seek them. What prospect does he have of finding them if he does not above all let himself be perceived entirely? The purpose of the teacher presupposes in certain circumstances the limited perception of his person for his hearers. The purpose of the author in relationship to his readers presupposes the opposite; the teacher can be silent where the author is prohibited silence. One hears it said that the author too has to educate his public, yet only a select few are allowed such a presumptuous comprehension of the author's vocation. Apart from them, such talk always has the character of an allegory: real experiences of discourse between teachers and students are carried over to the ideal experiences of the discourse between author and reader.

However that may be, I did not completely lack insight into the stated differences between the two vocational areas of the university teacher when I wrote my book, even if I had an imperfect understanding of its consequences. I have already tried to show how early I felt the chains the book imposed on me in my relationship with my hearers. When one considers the "fiction" that I state above, namely that I never mentioned the book in my lectures nor on my initiative in personal conversations, then one should think I had to have been aware that the situation created by the book predicted a future in which my theological publications would fit very poorly with the purpose of the academic teacher. And how could I avoid realizing that what I concealed with the book in the lecture hall, namely that I was not a theologian, would irresistibly press out of all pores in the whole of my future writings? Yet in the years immediately following the book's publication I indulged in illusions about this which are now difficult to comprehend. Completely under the impression of the multitude of historical tasks for which my book paved the way, I not only thought in 1875 that I could publish a first volume of *Studien zur Geschichte der alten Kirche* [Studies on the History of the Ancient Church], but I did so expressly in connection with the book of 1873 and with the most definite advocacy of its essential ideas. Accordingly the form in which I treated church history in the "Studies" was rather exactly the form I thought I had to prohibit myself in the lecture hall. I need hardly mention that my lecturing soon led me to recognize that I could not proceed as I had thought in 1873: it would have been all too comical for me in my lectures on church history to have ignored altogether the three parts of the "Studies," all of which had directly to do with the subject of my lectures (the letter to Diogenes, the Roman emperors' laws on persecution, and the church's view of slavery in the Roman Empire). And I did not ignore them at first but referred the hearers to them at the proper place. But as time passed I made such references ever more unwillingly and always with the attempt to blunt the anti-church barbs of these treatments, hence making them not clearer, as I should have done, but unintelligible. This effort steadily increased, but so did its difficulty and the feeling that my continuing theological publications irreconcilably contradicted my teaching. It is no wonder then that the first volume of the "Studies" remained not only without its promised successor but also, strictly speaking, the only book I published after 1873. The next was no more than a publication for a specific occasion, and without the occasion it probably would not have been written.[121] None of my following publications had the form of a book. In all of these I tried to make myself as understandable as possible, also as a "theologian," and yet here too concealment is at work, or at least the will to emerge only at a chosen place and occasion and, above all, for a limited public. This characterizes the few reviews and articles I published until 1882 in the *Historische Zeitschrift* and until 1884 in the *Göttinger gelehrte Anzeigen.*[122] The same is to be said especially for my *Basler Universitätsprogramme* from the years 1877, 1892 and 1898. In the journal publications, everything depended on the non-theological character of the journal.[123] My relationship to the *Theologische Literaturzeitung*, which I mentioned earlier, existed from the beginning with constant thoughts of cancellation. As the reader will understand, I did not want an increase of such relationships. In the late fall of 1899, the editors of a theological journal—the *Zeitschrift für die neutestamentliche Wissenschaft,* which first appeared in 1900—asked me to be a co-worker, and with a program that could have enticed me some years earlier. But by then I was too firmly decided to renounce all theology, also publicly, before letting myself be seen again among its co-workers. My refusal was expressed with the strongest regrets, but I can only assume that it was hardly understood.

The *Basler Universitätsprogramme* had to serve my stated purposes much better than any journal, and they did so more durably.[124] I seized the advantage of the natural concealment of this literary form, and it served me as a small contribution toward paying the debt to the University that I was aware of having incurred through the way I conducted my teaching office. These *Programme* had the disadvantage of being especially accessible to my students. I was even given copies to distribute among them, so I could hardly think of keeping them secret. However, when I distributed them I avoided everything that might have encouraged interest in them.

I fear I may have included too much in making clear the consequences that my book had for me as a theological author. What I basically wanted to say in all of this was that only the power of the simple facts pushed me to the insight that, with my book on the Christianity of theology, I had not only put a difficult hindrance in my way as a teacher, but I had also reduced myself to silence as an author. That being said, I can be all the more brief about the conclusion that my course as a teacher of theology had: the resignation of my office. That happened in the spring of 1897, after I had let the office become a very heavy and hardly endurable burden, especially in the last two years. I had suffered ill health and was especially under the pressure of depression. No doubt I felt the traces of age coming before their time, and these made me into an invalid in office. They moved me to submit my resignation in the summer of 1896, before the completion of my fifty-ninth year of life, to be effective in the coming spring.

A certain experience convinced me of how ripe the time for resignation was; it uncovered the whole danger of the situation in which I finally found myself at the teacher's lectern. It was Carl Albrecht Bernoulli's "encyclopedic attempt" that I name at the end of my list in the first part of this Afterword and that I designate there as "one of its kind" among the public judgments of my book. I introduced his name for my present readers in the dedication of this second edition of my book. Certainly Bernoulli hardly needs my introduction to today's general public, and he has needed no such introduction for a long time. He is well known to the theologians, and not only through his "attempt." To wider circles he is known through his novel, *Lucas Heland*, now in its second edition, and through similar literature. But if an introduction is here not necessary, what is needed is an explanation of what I mean by "one of its kind" and why I dedicated this book to him. What I have to relate now is not only my experience but also Bernoulli's, so only a little of it stands at my own disposal.

Bernoulli had for some time become closer to me than others among my hearers. In the beginning of 1895 he complimented me with the dedication of his work for the *licentiate*, a book on Jerome's catalogue of authors that I had suggested. If I remember correctly, soon after I resigned my office Bernoulli began to mention something about a book in which he intended to use my *Christianity of Theology*. He wanted to improve theology, to show its scholars more useful ways. (I write this not without awareness of how very offensive it is here.) There was not much said between Bernoulli and me when his project was mentioned. That was not only his fault, and perhaps the fault is least of all his. I listened with only half an ear to his hardly comprehensible indications, which was my usual attitude toward all mentioning of or inquiries about my book, and there were such from my hearers even if they were few and far between. At the time Bernoulli was no longer a hearer but a lecturer at our university. When my former student spoke of a task whose solution I myself had found impossible, he did cause me to listen. But then he told me it was no longer a project but a work already completed, and this persuaded me to remain evasive, as was my habit. I received the published "attempt" in June of 1897. Bernoulli did not give me a personal introduction to the book, so I had to find my way through it by myself. This was not very easy, even if it was perhaps good to have to do so from the beginning. I think it is known that Bernoulli's book has to do with a new theological method. Two branches of theology, named by him "church theology" and "scientific theology," are to be forced together into a single tree, and in the shadow of this tree all who endeavor in this discipline may rest. I also assume as known that I am among the four learned persons Bernoulli treats with such distinction that they have been called Bernoulli's four great prophets.[125] As I saw myself called upon to be the patron saint of a plan for the reform of theology, what other feeling could I have but sudden terror? My book and I could not have been misunderstood more fundamentally.[126] I do not think I need to give any further explanation about why that is the case. When I first recognized the damage Bernoulli had done, I asked myself whether the time was right to set the matter straight. It was not.

First, when his book was published Bernoulli had not yet completed his fourth semester as a lecturer in theology at our university. How could I seriously think of showing him the blunder he had made without risking the possibility that he lose the ground of his effectiveness as a teacher from beneath his feet? It would have meant letting a scholar achieve his goal only to ruin him. Second, as his former teacher, it was hardly proper of me to consider his work only from the point of view of the value it had for my work. His book was, for me as for others, a most respectable first work that could by no means simply be dismissed; it rather led to the expectation that it would give the author more than only momentary satisfaction. Certainly the work suffered an overabundance of youthfulness, but who at my age would not think twice before taking offence at just this sort of overabundance? If I did have my reservations about our time's immature crowd of reformers, whom the "theology of the day" encourages in their self-consciousness of being modern, it was not Bernoulli who was especially suggested as a subject for my pathological studies in the just mentioned suffering of our time. Third, a particular prejudice spoke for this youth, and here I come to my designation of the book as "one of its kind." As hurriedly or out of such an abundance of youthfulness or with whatever other defect he read my book, he was its only reader known to me who really did something with it, certainly not something "right" in my understanding, but in any case more than anyone else had succeeded in doing. Fourth and finally there was a very special reason dissuading me from a rash judgment of the unintentional disservice done me. Bernoulli was "lucky" as far as the point of time of his publication is concerned. It was as if he had waited for the hour when I was no longer in office. Had Bernoulli's book appeared while I was still at the lectern, there may have been a kind of catastrophe. It would have been far, far more distressing, and I could hardly have avoided a public defense, at least one that would protect my hearers against a further spreading of such misunderstanding. How much more free was I after leaving office! I could be sure of having withdrawn from one danger through a completely unambiguous act of free will, namely from the danger of being charged with an irresponsible carelessness toward a confusion in my students that I could have prevented. After I retired nothing forced me to move in that direction. I preferred to temporize, which succeeded beyond expectation.

All this does not mean that I, even for one day after I read the book, left Bernoulli in doubt about our disagreement. And yet what I wrote in my copy of his book, and only for myself, a few weeks after reading it (July, 1897), namely that an abyss separated us, remained unknown to him until more than five years later, in January of 1902. Being surer that we understood each other better, I read him the comment. How all that happened is a matter I may speak about only with reserve, as the reader will understand. I shall permit myself to say further only that, while I have remained restfully "sitting on my age" in Basel, my "wild" student, who left his home city at the end of 1897, has been in constant motion from one distant place to another. In doing so he has not only learned more, but also found time and opportunity to move a good distance away from my "school." This separation of our ways may have insured that a collision would not happen. Yet we were never seriously at odds and in the past few years we have become even better friends. So I could ask his permission to dedicate this book to him, which dedication the reader will find at the book's beginning.

What I have said about Bernoulli should make clear how little reason I had to delay the resignation of my theological teaching office, which, as I said, became effective in the spring of 1897. With this last episode in my report, I have twice exceeded the limits I set for myself. For I have stepped into the experiences of another, and I have related personal experiences that go beyond the time limit set for them. Something else demands that I stop these excesses, namely the thought that I still have to write a chief section of this Afterword, the section I designated at its beginning as having to do with the "greater" experiences I have had since the appearance of my book in 1873. So I turn now without further delay to this last chief section.

The Modern Theology of Contemporary Protestantism and What Has Resulted from It for Me as the Author of My Book[127]

This title and its statement of the extremely limited point of view that will determine my discussion of modern theology should disperse clearly enough all expectations about the quantity and scope of the following communications about this magnitude of our day. The title indeed indicates that here modern theology will rather move into the background; what I shall have to say about it will only serve the task of furthering the understanding of my book. As I reflect on all that I have said in these pages about the book, I remind the reader that I have no intention of claiming any sort of success for it. Especially when one speaks of books, success usually means the winning of influence on the further development of the things evaluated in them. Assuming all I have said about the book is correct, then it was not supposed to be successful, certainly not in the sense stated above; for I wrote it for my own liberation. Furthermore I lacked the qualities and talents that are indispensable for overcoming such a hindrance to success, so perhaps the book never could have, and in any case never did, become successful. This will not in any way be questioned in what follows.

Should I now plunge into answering the very simple question that remains for me to answer? I refer to the plan I sketched at the beginning of the Afterword: I said that I would change the sphere of my discussion from the "lesser" to the "greater" experiences. In the first and second sections I had to speak without knowing whether or not I was speaking among good friends and sympathetic readers. Certainly I could not allow myself fantastic ideas about their agreement, but at least I had done nothing to make my readers hostile toward me and hence even unlimited illusions about them were not entirely excluded. But now! after having stated the term "modern theology" in my title— "modern theology," this "magnitude of our time!"—I shall have to abandon any thought of pushing such a distinguished lady "into the background" of my book and indeed of forcing her to serve it. Unavoidable considerations of this kind make it necessary for me to say more about this before I come to my actual subject. I shall have to answer two questions: What right do I have to attribute to my book a relationship to modern theology at all, and in what way has the book "experienced" modern theology?

To attain clarity about these questions one must above all come to an understanding of the prophetic character of my book. I have no need to deny it all such character. I do think I remained in the book rather strictly within the boundaries of an historian in speaking about theology, and accordingly I had to deal chiefly with the past and present of the discipline. But I was occasionally extravagant and assumed at least something of a prophetic mien in speaking about the future of theology.

What calls itself "modern theology" is a product of the time that has passed since I wrote the book, so it is not due to some sudden fancy when I bring them, my book and this theology, together for the reader's attention, as problematic as this may be. That "prophetic mien" is not a completely unwarranted attribute may be noted for some places in the book; (e.g. p. 95). Surely it was not wholly false, and precisely with regard to modern theology, when I wrote (p. 100) that, with the theology I contested, "we move toward a condition of things in which one will have to esteem Christianity as that religion above all others with which one can do what one wants." But without bringing up all that I myself might have to say in the way of criticism of such clairvoyance, and even if there are those who do not doubt its accuracy, what does it actually mean? With dozens of such hits in the target of modern theology I could pass as something of a fortune teller. But as a prophet? a person who has read and seen coming things out of the "signs" of his time? By no means! After I wrote the book I saw things develop entirely differently than I could have thought, insofar as in 1873, doubting theology's ability to fulfill its task, I recommended silence. Instead, as I have been well taught by "modern theology," theology entered into one of its most prolific periods. It has so much to say that it almost has the appearance of marching at the head of our whole period of history and leading it toward a restoration of Christianity! Hence I have asked where my wits really were when I uttered the oracles in my book. With this admission I believe I can break off this excursus on my prophetic character and the complete contradiction I experienced through the course of events, the rise of modern theology and indeed the recent discovery of the "essence of Christianity" by modern theology's acknowledged master.[128] Before I state my opinion of modern theology I would like to summarize the most important concessions I have to make to it beside the one just made.

What I have said up till now should secure me against the charge that I deny modern theology any merit, but not against the absurdity that I limit this merit to the reproof modern theology has given me as a prophet. Even I have "learned" far more from it. I can mention first the praise that my book, in a manner of speaking, sings to it, for who caused the two theological parties I contest in it to have almost disappeared from the public arena they once filled? No one will say that I am the cause, and I could hardly take the least bit of credit for it without abandoning myself to public laughter. And no one thinks so mythologically as to believe those theological Cadmeans of the sixties and seventies of the previous century had killed each other off. No! If one scarcely still sees them today, this is due without any doubt to the hand of modern theology alone. Things are different in theology today than they were thirty years ago. "Modern theology" has changed the face of the whole discipline—who would doubt this once he has looked around among us? When I was a young graduate, things had not yet arrived at the point where a theologian as theologian could write a brochure that in no way betrayed the fact that he was not an agent of a railroad or trade company, not even if he indicated that he had another profession by putting something like an SJ on the title page and something like an SDG at the end.[129] With this remark I shall have touched on an area of recent progress in theology that probably appears problematic not only to me. In so arguing ad hominem, i.e. ad me, I have even more to feign about modern theology's achievements of generally acknowledged value. If it is matter of fruits that ripened too late for me to enjoy, that is no reason to mistake them.

Thanks to its enormous industry modern theology has produced a greater treasure of newer and better historical information than any one person can survey. How much sour work in this new wealth would have been spared me (to name only one) had I still found my dream of a profane church history possible and, dreaming, imagined myself beginning again with my first work on the Roman Hippolytus![130] But aside from that, if I were to try to imagine just how much I might have to thank modern theology for the help it has given me, I could easily fall victim to the danger of rebelliously refusing any acknowledgement, even if I could hardly fall victim to this danger entirely. I could do it most easily in the area that long ago pushed Hippolytus out of my mind, an area to which modern theology has already dedicated whole libraries: original Christianity. With all these libraries I cannot see that modern theology has built anything out of it but a heap of ruins. Hardly anyone can find his way among them, in any case no two persons in the same way. And, as usually happens with ruins, even the most important and interesting problems are being buried. I also cannot agree with the contemporary authorities of modern theology when they say that this state of things is so indifferent for the existence of Christianity (Harnack, *Das Wesen des Christentums*, 119).[131] By no means do I intend to find edification in the belief that nothing more has been learned about original Christianity than was heard thirty years ago, especially from the "Tübinger." Considering the tower of paper that has been erected since then, I could be so impressed that I might blindly fall into a state of reverence. I could seek the strength to do that in right strange words of strength that I find among the works of the theological *doctor gravis* I have just cited: "The work decides."[132] And if all that states my readiness to acknowledge the work really done in original Christianity by modern theology, how much less is my willingness to acknowledge what modern theology has achieved in enlightening other, less controversial periods of church history.

But it is time to bring this excursus to a conclusion and to move to the "simple question" that is for me the only question implied in the title of this last section of the Afterword. How does my attempt to revive my thirty-year-old book relate to the events that have occurred in the history of theology since its first appearance? Can I, especially after such a long time, think it fitting to leave the word "today" in the book's title? I have already stated how little I hold modern theology to be an historical "nothing" and how much I, especially with regard to my book, have had to find it a very noticeable "something." So I can turn now to my "simple question" and in answering it allow myself all the freedom I wish.

The greatest aspect of this freedom now becomes the most harmless, for I omit introducing or presenting modern theology to my readers. I do so in the conviction that they know as well as I with whom we should have to deal in such a ceremony. No one needs to hear from me who and what it is, nor the claims made for it, nor do I need to make any excuses for not recognizing them. I have never "participated" in its successes nor do I have the least doubt that my contemporaries will agree with this statement. It is not my name they have to remember but the fact that they do not find it in their memories of the theology that presently calls itself modern. If they remember this, they will not judge me severely for not exactly forcing myself into a position of mediation between them and modern theology. They are also asked to recognize that I have no natural calling to be this theology's historical master of ceremonies. And yet with this book I have ceremoniously pressed into my readers' hands another claim to hear something from me about modern theology. I have spoken of the duration of time during which I "watched" the birth and growth of modern theology: a whole human generation! Where the measure is the lifetime of a human individual, this is, in my case certainly, a long time. But how can I speak of modern theology so flippantly? My readers could well ask this question, and not only those who turn away from me in real distrust, who doubt that I learned anything at all from such a long observation of this spectacle. On the other hand, I can allow my credulous readers to remind me that I have already begun to explain why I speak as I do. I certainly do not do it in order to braid a wreath for my book at the cost of the honor due to modern theology, to belittle this theology and reduce it to nothing. To defend myself against this suspicion I brought in the discussion about the merits of modern theology, where I said at least as much about these merits as obligation required. Yet I have something else to say in my defense.

In the situation I now find myself in pursuit of my openly stated purpose, which is to lengthen the life of my book, I know nothing better to do than to limit myself, to keep within the boundaries of my purpose and to submit to its consequences. This means I should avoid giving the impression that I can dispatch modern theology with a few incidental remarks. I have not begun to dig out the rich material I have stored away for a real criticism of this theology. That is not only because of the lack of space for such a purpose here, but also because I well know what an undertaking it would be to "dispatch" a magnitude like modern theology, and I renounce every pretension of delivering any sort of serious argument with it here. In the few words I still have to say about it, no one is obliged to hear anything more than the confessions of an odd fellow. If they insist on dispensation, the admirers of modern theology will free themselves of any higher valuation.

I turn now to the question about what I think of the claim of modern theology, as representative of the theological present, to a special Christian character. I hope I can use, without falling to the charge of intolerable presumption, a characteristic confession of modern theology to itself. This may be taken as a simple consequence of my own insight into the confessional character of my further explanations about modern theology. If I gave these merely as my own subjective confessions, I would at least have to address them toward a defined object. But I have avoided going into the question about who and what this theology is, and neither for the reader nor for me does the general notion of modern theology that I have heretofore used, suffice to supply a really defined object. But a confession of this theology to itself can serve me very well, providing that I really believe I can hear the voice of modern theology speaking in its words.

I have found such a confession in a very recent publication whose author is well known for his membership in the school of this theology's most famous master. He expresses his gratitude to Harnack for not waiting for the person who would have been entirely able to write a book with the title, "The Essence of Christianity," and he continues: "Whomever God thrusts into the struggle between the old faith and modern culture, *whoever cannot and does not want to live*, if he is not allowed to be a whole Christian and a modern person *at the same time*, will thank Harnack for not waiting on this hero. He will thank Harnack for doing his part."[133] I assume there will be no formal objection to this confession and its quotation here. It presents itself as an oracle of a modern prophet, and none will doubt that it genuinely originates from the heart of modern theology or that the spirit of modern theology moves in its words. I did not in the strict sense choose it from a "cloud of witnesses," to use an expression from the Letter to the Hebrews (which was written by an early Christian married couple, that is, according to a myth recently manufactured by modern theology). For making such a choice I lack the necessary acquaintance with the clouds in the firmament of today's modern-theological literature. But I take comfort in the knowledge that the quotation is not an individual extravagance. I do think I am acquainted with enough of this literature in order to hear, if not all, then, modestly said, many, very many modern theologians speaking in its words. In the quotation what draws my attention materially is not its praise for Harnack, nor the broad scope of its whole content, as worthy of attention as that is. What I find interesting is that it challenges the reader to investigate both the modernity and the Christianity of modern theology. Even if one did this, there would still remain remarkable things to be heard in the oracle. However the interest I must dedicate to it here is limited by the boundaries I myself have drawn. I permitted myself to italicize several words in Rolffs' confession. I did so for the purpose of leading into my own confession, which I oppose to Rolffs'. I adjoin here only a very brief discussion of modern theology. It has the purpose of stating and closing my argument in advocacy of my book and mainly of its opinion concerning the Christianity of theology.

How unambiguously do Rolffs' words tear the veil from the situation into which Christianity has been brought among us today by the theology that calls itself "modern!" Christianity has no choice but to tolerate these theologians speaking to it in tones of an ultimatum: they are ready to "live" with it only under a certain condition. There was a time when Christianity had the right to possess its theologians. When one remembers this, how much more striking than the readiness to "live" with Christianity is that other readiness: to "live" with and from modern culture. There was a time when Christianity's confessors did all they could to assure Christianity of their readiness to die for it. Today Christianity has to put up with hearing that one is ready to live in and with something else. What Rolffs' words reveal with such astounding naivete is nothing other than what modern theology proclaims to the world with a thousand tongues. It may be true that this theology named itself "modern" not without hesitation. We can note that six years ago the current high priest of this theology spoke of its modernity as "so-called."[134] But generally speaking the ruling theology hardly seems in doubt about forever having made secure both itself and Christianity by wrapping itself in the royal robes of modernity. Under this robe theology has found so much courage and confidence in its calling that it believes all is in order with its Christianity when it confesses not only Christianity but also modern culture, clothes itself in the uniform of a moment of time and places itself beneath the flag of a religion that once called us into the struggle against all "temporality" [Zeitlichkeit].

I do not share this confidence. As the author of my book I cannot, because from the book's perspective the just mentioned situation is "nothing new." One of its basic theses is that theology has always been modern and for this reason it has always been the natural betrayer of Christianity. Hence the situation in modern theology is only the manifestation of an ancient relationship. So I can say I had the insight thirty years ago that could have enabled another to call a prophetic warning to the modern theologians of today: "You theologians have always been modern, and this has always been your weakest side. Guard yourselves against deriving your lost right to majesty from modernity!" I have already said and would like in conclusion to say again: this insight did not prompt me to utter such a warning. I kept myself within the boundaries of personal difficulties and, in so doing, saw nothing of the eve of things to come. To a certain extent I had to become a student of modern theology before I could understand it. And so I have to say that thirty years ago I wrote only a weak book. It is strong enough however to convince me that I have no reason to think differently about the Christianity of theology than I did then. The most recent event in the victorious course of this "modern theology" hardly leads me to think I have been mistaken: Harnack's secular book, which proves to me far more impressively the "non-essentiality" of Christianity than the "essence" of Christianity.

NOTES

Preface to the 1st Edition

1. {It has been repeatedly reprinted since, lastly by the author in his *Deutsche Schriften. Gesammtausgabe letzter Hand*, 2nd ed. (Göttingen, 1891).}
Editor's note: In the following my additions are in [brackets]. Overbeck's few additions to the text in the 2nd edition of 1903 are in {curved brackets}, which corresponds to his use of brackets in the 2nd edition.
2. {The words "a writing for conflict and for peace" stood on the title page of the first edition.}

Introduction

3. [The "Tübinger" that Overbeck mentions: Hilgenfeld (1823-1907) was professor in Jena; Volkmar (1809-1893) was professor in Zürich; Holsten (1825-1897) was at the time professor in Bern; Ritschl (1822-1889), professor in Göttingen.]
4. [Adolf Ritschl, *Entstehung der altkatholischen Kirche* (2nd ed. Bonn, 1857). With this work Ritschl had made a definitive break with Baur.]
5. [W.M.L. de Wette, *Kurze Erklärung der Apostelgeschichte*, 4. Auflage, bearbeitet und stark erweitert von F. Overbeck, (Leipzig, 1870).] I was able to write the preface of the book in Jena. It is dated at the beginning of April, 1870. On the Wednesday following Easter, which fell on April 20, I was in Basel.
6. [*Die christliche Kirche vom Anfang des vierten bis zum Ende des sechsten Jahrhunderts in den Hauptmomenten ihrer Entwicklung* (Tübingen, 1859).]
7 [*Kirchengeschichte des 19. Jahrhunderts* (Tübingen, 1863).]
8. I wrote a short review of the last-mentioned book for the *Literarisches Zentralblatt für Deutschland* 1863, No. 8. One can take from it what I thought of Baur at the time. [In 1863 Overbeck had not yet completed his habilitation at Jena. In the review he says he does not share Baur's "Grundgedanken und Voraussetzungen" (basic thoughts and presuppositions), and the book does not have the quality of his other works. Baur executes strict judgment on "restauration" theology and "toilsome theology of mediation," and of all "halfness" and "sophistry" in theology. But Baur's history places the reader before a "dilemma,"

by which Overbeck evidently means the alienation of criticism and church that I discuss in the first part of my introduction.]

9. [Christian K. J. Bunsen, *Hippolytus and his Age* (London, 1852). Baur's responses are published in issues of the *Theologische Jahrbücher* in the early 1850's. The difference of opinion was about the authorship of a newly discovered and published manuscript, the "Philosophumena" or "Refutation of All Heresies." While Bunsen attributed it to Hippolytus, Baur judged it the work of the Roman presbyter Cajus.]

10. [*Quaestionum Hippolytearum Specimen* summe venerabilis Theologorum ordinis Jenensis consensu et auctoritate pro gradu licentiati et docendi potestate rite obtinendis die IV. M. Augusti A. KDCCCLXIV in publico defendet Franciscus Camillus Overbeck Dr. Philos. cand. Theol. Jenae (Jena, 1864). Apparently the only extant copy of this work is in the Overbeck-Nachlass in Basel [A337]. It demonstrates that the "Treatise on Christ and AntiChrist" is correctly attributed to Hippolytus, a contemporary of Clement of Alexandria. The treatise is an instruction in Christianity and offers, especially through Overbeck's discussion, an interesting parallel to Clement's work. It contains an image of revelation—God's weaving together the Word with the flesh not only of Christ but also of human language—that may be important for Overbeck's understanding of revelation. Already in this work Overbeck speaks disparagingly of apologetics.]

11. Here I ask permission to refer incidentally to the interesting "honorable confession" of a man of the world, which has just come to my attention. He writes that he has "never found correct the basic assumption of Baur's school, which is that theology, as any other science, subjects its historical documents to the same rules of criticism that apply to all historical documents." A. von Mohl's *Lebenserinnerungen* (Stuttgart und Leipzig, 1902), I, 211. Considering Mohl's particular relations to the world of the university he is no homo saecularis in the strict medieval sense of the word. Otherwise, however, he most certainly is and in any case in the way he views religion and theology. As I add this further weakness of Baur's authority as a theologian, what is most interesting is a certain connection. On the one hand is the impartiality of Mohl's lay judgment, a judgment with which I, with unlimited respect for Baur as a scholar and as a person, have always agreed. This is connected with Mohl's unlimited respect for Baur, and Mohl's respect has a far more original basis than mine, as Mohl was from Baur's region, his colleague and brother-in-law. See Mohl's book, I, 191 f.

12. The two documents I here cite are dated the 8th and 10th of January, 1870.

13. [Daniel Schenkel, ea., *Bibellexikon, Real-Wörterbuch zum Handgebrauch für Geistliche und Gemeindeglieder* (Leipzig, 1869-1875).]

14. One memory causes me to be especially thankful for the way I was kept ignorant of these things. l refer to a conversation I had, in preparation for my move to Basel, in the Christmas vacation of 1869 in Frankfurt a.M. My partner in this conversation was the excellent man who at that time led the Curatel of the University of Basel. [He was Wilhelm Vischer, former professor of Greek language and literature.]

15. *Reform: Zeitstimmen aus der schweizer Kirche* 1873, 432.

16. [On Overbeck and pietism see Overbeck's comment on Robert Kübel in the 2nd part of the Afterword below.]

17. I have no more exact date for Nietzsche's publication than the one generally known from Nietzsche's *Werke*, Teil 1, Band I (Leipzig, 1895), VIII, of the "Nachbericht." [F. Nietzsche, *Thoughts Out of Season, Part 1: David Strauss the Confessor and the Writer*, translated by A.M. Ludovici (NY: Russel & Russel, 1964).]

18. Elisabeth Foerster-Nietzsche, *Das Leben Friedrich Nietzsche's*, Bd. l (Leipzig, 1895), 127f.

19. I wish to assure the reader completely about the relation of the following text to the text of 1873.

1) The changes I have made in the new text will be entirely acceptable to the reader and belong to the grain of salt with which every explanation about the differences would be read. I have corrected all the formal offences that I noticed in the old text, whether these had to do with printing errors in the narrow sense or with errors of style, especially imperfections in the punctuation, or with things I simply overlooked in the first manuscript.

2) Just as little worthy of serious consideration are the few changes in the format, which have been made merely for the greater comfort of the reader, e.g., the printing of the chapter titles at the head of each chapter. These stood originally only in the table of contents, which was found at the end of the book.

3) The real additions, which are not entirely lacking, hardly stand in the way of the text being called "unrevised." They are all taken from the marginal notes in my copy of the first book, where they gradually and only incidentally accumulated. They are without any inner significance that could mean a renewal or revision of the text of 1873. They consist of short notes that serve to illustrate individual points in the text and do not introduce anything new. They have to do with material I became aware of incidentally in my reading. There are only a few of these additions, not even a dozen. And I have made them very easy to recognize by putting them, without exception, in {curved} brackets. l could have made all of this much more "simple" and in any case shorter, had I stated on the title page that this second edition is "essentially" unchanged. This word always has the appearance of being used by authors to increase both the vexation of the reader and their own comfort.

Chapter 1

The Relationship of Theology to Christianity Generally

20. [On Hellenistic culture as a dying culture at the time of the rise of Christianity, see Ernst von Lasaulx, *Der Untergang des Hellenismus* (Munich, 1854), and Jakob Burckhardt, *Die Zeit des Constantins des Grossen* (Basel, 1855). The enlarged 2nd edition (1880) of Burckhardt's work is in translation: *The Age of Constantine the Great*, trans. by Mases Hadas (London: Routledge & Kegan Paul LTD, 1949), see esp. Chap. VII: "Senescence of Ancient Life and its Culture." Such interpetation of Hellenistic culture was hardly unusual; one finds it also in the standard church history of the time, Karl Hase's *Lehrbuch der Kirchengeschiche* and especially in Hase's published lectures: *Kirchengeschichte auf der Grundlage akademischer Vorlesungen*, Vol. 1 (Leipzig, 1890), 89. In the philosophy of F.W.J. Schelling and Overbeck's friend Nietzsche one finds an interpretation of pre-Christian mythology as an organic development from birth to death that peaked in classical Greece and thereafter degenerated: Schelling, *Philosophie der Mythologie, Philosophie der Offenbarung* (4 Vols., Stuttgart and Augsburg, 1856-1861). Nietzsche's *Birth of Tragedy*, e.g., speaks of a descent of Greek classical culture into later Socratic and Alexandrian culture: translated by Wm. A. Haussmann (NY: Russel & Russel, 1964), §10, 84f; §14ff, pp. 107ff. Texts from Schelling and Nietzsche are collected and compared in: J.E. Wilson, *Schelling und Nietzsche* (Berlin: W. de Gruyter, 1996), 96ff, 119ff, 170ff.]

21. Hermann Schultz, *Zu den kirchlichen Fragen der Gegenwart* (Frankfurt, 1869), 9. {Schultz gives an answer to my criticism in the *Jahrbücher für deutsche Theologie* 1879, 44. I cannot share the idealism he develops in the article.} [Schultz (1836-1903), at the time this book was written, was professor in Strassburg. He is grouped among the Ritschlians. He is quoted in connection with Ritschl in *Christentum und Kultur*, 51.]

22 [In Overbeck's 1873/1874 lectures on the Letter to the Hebrews (A99, p. 110) one finds the following: "In biblical language, namely in the New Testament, once the concept of time is removed, 'aeon' means world as the total [Inbegriff] of realities that fill time." In an earlier place (106): "...between [the death of Christ] and the near Parousia there is only a kind of transition time in which the things hover [schweben] so to speak between present and future world-time (Weltzeit); as the author says in Heb. 6:5, the future is tasted, but not yet owned."]

23. [The story is told in: E. v. Lasaulx, *Der Untergang des Hellenismus* (Munich, 1854), 105. The source is Rufinus' church history, II, §23.]

24 E.g., Origen, *Contra Celsum*, 11, §49, §52 [translated with an Introduction & Notes by Henry Chadwick (Cambridge: Cambridge U. Press, 1965). Concerning miracles, compare the following notes from Overbeck's Kirchenlexikon, under the title "Wunder (neueste Apologetik) Vermischtes," §11: "Too often and with too good grounds we have been warned by trustworthy wise men and thinkers not to overvalue logical principles nor to consider them the limits of the possible ...The causes of the loss of belief in [the miracles of the Gospels] lie rather in their distance from us ...The miracles of Jesus are either experienced by us ourselves and defend themselves through this their presence or they cannot be helped." Under another title, "Wunder (Vermischtes)," §9, one reads: "The Bible has the healthy faith in the miraculous, that is, the faith in it that begins where our science [Wissen] ceases. But the theologians do not want to recognize that since the Bible was written the limits of our science have changed, and they defend precisely what is the most transient in biblical belief in miracle, its historical part."]

25 Cf. H. Reuter, *Geschichte der religiösen Aufklärung im Mittelalter* (Berlin, 1875), 1, 165f.

26. E.g., Minucius Felix, *Octavius*, §20:4; §21:11; §26:6 [*The Ante-Nicene Fathers*. Vol. 4. Revised and chronologically arranged with brief prefaces and occasional notes, by Cleveland Cox. American Reprint of the Edinburgh Edition (Grand Rapids, Mich.: Eerdmans, 1976.)].

27. [In Overbeck's Kirchenlexikon under the title, "Mission (Allgemeines)," §2, one reads: "Christian missionaries preach Christianity, but before this they destroy the old faith of their proselytes. No great founder of a religion ever did that, neither Christ nor Buddha nor Mohammed. They all presuppose faith in religion among those they teach; none is missionary among believers in a religion foreign to him."]

28. [Kirchenlexikon, "Theologie (moderne) Urchistentum": "Genuine Christianity has never been anything other than the perception [Empfindung] of the nearness of the expected eternal life and the forgetting of the fact that world history steps between eternal life and temporal life."]

29. *Apology*, §21 [*The Ante-Nicene Fathers*. Edited by Alexander Roberts and James Donaldson. Vol.III: Latin Christianity: Its Founder, Tertullian. (American Ed. Buffalo, NY: Christian Literature Publishing Co., 1885), 36].

30. [In his lecture on the Gospel of John from the year 1877 (A92, p. 201), Overbeck briefly characterizes Gnosticism as a powerful direction of thought that, "based on certain metaphysical presuppositions, completely separates Christianity from its historical conditions and appearance, cancels it as religion and transforms it into a system of metaphysical world-explanation." In *Studien zur Geschichte der alten Kirche* Overbeck characterizes Gnosticism as "in acute form the secularisation [Verweltlichung] of the church generally and in all areas of

human endeavor." The church of the 2nd century "opposed it with re-
lentless energy and rejected it with such success that secularlisation at
least was now reduced to a creeping malady" (184). Cf. Adolf Harnack,
History of Dogma, translated by Neil Buchanan from the 3rd German
edition (New York: Dover, 1961), I, 241: "The thesis that Gnosticism is
identical with the acute secularising of Christianity in the widest sense
of the word is confirmed by the study of its own literature."]

31. [Overbeck alludes to the development of an orthodoxy that
only imitates the early church, i.e., it does not not have the creative
"driving forces" that early Christianity had.]

32. [Origen, *Contra Celsum*, translated by Chadwick, 6, cf. 432,
437; see also 27, 162, 178, 179. Origen, *On First Principles*, translated
with an Introduction and Notes by G.W. Butterworth (London: SPCK,
1936; NY: Harper Torchbook, 1966), IV: 2, 6. Origen, *Commentary on
the Gospel according to John*, Books 1-10. Translated by Ronald
Heine. Fathers of the Church, a New Translation, Vol. 80 (Washington,
D.C.: University Press of America, 1989), 286f. Franz Kletter quotes a
number of similar passages from untranslated works: *Der ur-
sprüngliche Sinn der Dogmatik des Origenes* (Berlin: Alfred Toppel-
mann, 1966), 48-51.]

33. *Against the Heathen*, Chap. I [Athanasius, *Contra Gentes*. Introduction, Translation and Commentary by E.P. Meijering (Leiden:
E.J. Brill, 1984), 8ff.].

34. Works, IX, 665B., ed. Montfaucon [see: "Discourse on
Blessed Babylas against the Greeks," and "Demonstration against the
Pagans that Christ is God," in: *St. John Chrysostom, Apologist*. Fathers
of the Church, a New Translation, Vol. 76. Translated by Margaret A.
Schatkin and Paul W. Harkins (Washington, D.C.: Catholic U. Press of
America Press, 1985)].

35. [Jerome's difficult personality and his often whimsical literary
style make him a most unusual saint and father of the church. See especially David S. Wiesen, *St. Jerome as a Satirist. A Study in Christian
Thought and Letters* (Ithaca, NY: Cornell University Press, 1964). A
later article by Overbeck in the *Historische Zeitschrift* (Vol. 42, 1879,
222-259), "Aus dem Briefwechsel des Augustin mit Hieronymus"
(From Augustine's Exchange of Letters with Jerome), focuses on the
character and behavior of each theologian emerging in the letters. See
the end of Chapter 5 below where I quote from Overbeck's article.
Wiesen discusses the exchange of letters 235-240.]

36. [Cf. the following note from Overbeck's Kirchenlexikon under the title "Glaube und Wissen (Vermischtes)": "The fundamental
confusion that underlies all theological attempts to lift faith to science,
to support faith through science" comes through apologetics, that is,
"the absurd need to prove through demonstration a faith that one asserts
has its certainty in itself where this faith (and therefore this certainty) is
not acknowledged." The date of the note is no earlier than the mid-

not acknowledged." The date of the note is no earlier than the mid-1870s.]

37.{Very instructive for the hindrances science encountered again and again as it tried to push its way into the church in this period, is Augustine's prologue to his treatise *De Doctrina Christiana*. (I translate this title "On Christian Science." On this translation see my work *Zur Geschichte des Kanons* (Chemnitz, 1880), 47.) Augustine has to excuse himself for writing a scientific guide for the interpretation of Scripture and for not leaving the understanding of it to the inspiration of every person by God.}

38. [Friedrich Schleiermacher is known for having given this as a reason for historical theology: see §84 in his *Brief Outline of the Study of Theology*, translations by Terrence Tice (Richmond, Va: John Knox Press, 1966) and by William Farrer (Edinburgh: T. & T. Clark, 1850). In a later note in his Kirchenlexikon, perhaps from the 1880's, under the title "Schriftstellerei (Kirchliche) Exegetische," Overbeck writes: "The historical form of the treatment of an object, as a [literary] form, makes the object subject to the form, pliable and changeable, in spite of [the opinion that] this form is necessary in order to preserve the object's original integrity."]

39. [Cf. Nietzsche, *Birth of Tragedy*, trans. by Wm. A. Hausmann (NY: Russel & Russel, 1964), §10, p. 84: "For it is the fate of every myth to insinuate itself into the narrow limits of some alleged historical reality, and to be treated by some later generation as a solitary fact with historical claims...For this is the manner in which religions are wont to die out: when of course under the stern, intelligent eyes of an orthodox dogmatism, the mythical presuppostions of a religion are systematised as completed sum of historical events, and when one begins apprehensively to defend the credibility of the myth, while at the same time opposing all continuation of their natural vitality and luxuriance; when accordingly, the feeling for myth dies out, and its place is taken by the claim of religion to historical foundations."]

40. O. Henne am Rhyn, *Kulturgeschichte der neueren Zeit* (Leipzig, 1872), III, 548f.

41. Willibald Beyschlag, *Ein antiker Spiegel für den "neuen Glauben" von D.F Strauss* (Berlin 1873). I, 30f. [Beyschlag (1823-1900) was professor in Halle. He belonged generally to the moderate-conservative Schleiermacher tradition in theology and worked for a union of faith and "culture" in the sense of a unification of religion, humanities, and the sciences.]

42. Beyschlag, 31.

43. Beyschlag, 35.

Chapter 2

The Apologetic Theology of the Present

44. [The order of the *Pensées* that Overbeck is apparently using is the same as or similar to the English translation by W.F. Trotter (New York: Dutton & Co, 1958). On the will and belief, see §99; §284. Pascal's discussion of the two infinities is in §72.]

45. Christian E. Luthardt, *Apologetische Vorträge über die Grundwahrheiten des Christentums* (3rd ed. Leipzig, 1864), from the preface.

46. Luthardt, 63f

47. [Cf. Augustine, *City of God*, XXI.9-13.]

48. *Commentar zum Brief an die Hebräer* (Leipzig, 1857), 231. [Delitzsch's remark is made in the context of his defense of Hebrews 6:4-6, to which he compares Isaiah 8:21f. There is no grace for the lost souls of Heb. 6:4-6, even if they seek it. "...as punishment for their vile denial [of Christ] God has forever excluded them from it.... For the pain of repentance and the seeking of grace are not completely excluded from the condition of the irredeemably lost.... [But] the door of repentance is closed and those seemingly better effusions are without value ... and soon overwhelmed again. Wailing and blasphemy are uttered in confusion. For here too there is not only gnashing of teeth but also weeping" (my translation). Cf. Matth. 8:12. Delitzsch (1813-1890) was a conservative Lutheran professor in Erlangen and later in Leipzig who published with great influence primarily in the area of Old Testament.]

49. {Qui enim loci sui necessitate exigitur summa dicere hac eadem necessitate compellitur summa monstrare. From Gregory the Great's Pastoral Rule 11:3.} ["For one who by the exigency of his position must propose the highest, is bound by that same exigency to give a demonstration of the highest." Gregory the Great, *Pastoral Care. Regula Pastoralis*, translated and annotated by Henry Davis, S.J. Ancient Christian Writers, the Works of the Fathers in Translation, No. 11 (NY: Newman Press, 1950), 48. Gregory is here speaking not of miracles but of the need for consistency between the words and the example of the leader.]

50. *Beweise des Glaubens* (Gütersloh, 1866), 11, 78f. {Parallel texts from J. G. Fichte's *Versuch einer Kritik aller Offenbarung* (Königsberg, 1793) are instructive: see §8 and especially §9 [English: *Attempt at a Critique of all Revelation*. Translated with an Introduction by Garrett Green (Cambridge: Cambridge U. Press, 1978), 100ff, 118ff.} [Otto Zöckler (1833-1906) was a moderate confessional Lutheran known for his apologetic work in the area of the natural sciences, e.g., against Darwinism and materialism.]

51. ["What lamentation can match these woes? What springs of tears are sufficient for them?" The words are those of Basil of Caesarea

in lamenting the state of the church in his time: *St. Basil, Letters and Select Works, in: Nicene and Post-Nicene Fathers of the Christian Church*. Second Series. Vol. VIII (Grand Rapids, Mich.: Wm. B. Eerdmans Publishing Co., 1955), 178. The letters contain frequent commentaries on the bad state of the church: see further 48-50, 132ff, 163, 189, 190, 242, 268. 280, 282. See also Basil's "The Judgment of God," in: *The Ascetic Works of Saint Basil*, translated by W.K.L. Clarke (London: SPCK, 1925), especially the beginning, 77ff. On Basil's criticism of the church and its connection with his advocacy of monasticism, see Klaus Koschorke, *Spuren der alten Liebe. Studien zum Kirchenbegriff des Basilius von Caesarea* (Freiburg, Switzerland: Universitätsverlag, 1991).]

52. Beyschlag, 7.

53. Ludwig Conrady, *Cultur und Christentum* (Wiesbaden, 1868), 35f. [For Conrady, a member of the clergy in Wiesbaden, Christianity and culture need one another, although modern culture is anti-Christian. He envisions a future reconciliation in the world supremacy of Christianity as the unity of "Percival and Faust."]

54. [traditionally ascribed to Thomas á Kempis (1380-1471), associated with the Bretheren of the Common Life, a lay monastic order of the late medieval period.]

55. Wilhelm Hoffmann, *Deutschland einst und jetzt im Lichte des Reiches Gottes* (Berlin, 1868), 493f. ["Ansicht" literally means a "view" of something; in common usage it often means an opinion, which is the way Hoffman has used it here. Hoffmann (1806-1873) had been called to Berlin in 1852 from an academic position at Tübingen by the Prussian king, Friedrich Wilhelm IV., where he became the king's confidant, rose to high church office and continued in that position after the king's death. Overbeck's patron in Jena, Karl Hase, published two polemical pieces against Hoffmann in the late 1860's: *Gesammelte Werke* (Leipzig, 1890), Vol. VIII/2, 23ff, where Hase writes it is generally known that the *Neue Evangelische Kirchenzeitung* stands under Hoffmann's pietist-orthodox tutelage. A series of sermons preached by Hoffmann at the Berlin "Dome" Church were published in English: *The Prophecies of Our Lord and His Apostles* (London, 1869).]

56. [For Hoffmann, the "view of life" is the shell, the dogmas are the kernel. For Overbeck these are reversed.]

57. [The Franco-Prussian War had ended in 1871.]

58. Hoffmann, 529.

59. [In Overbeck's Kirchenlexikon one finds long discussions of nationalism that date generally from the 1890's (see, e.g., *Christentum und Kultur*, 255-259). Under the title "Christentum und Nationalität" Overbeck writes: (§6) "A Christianity that is nationalistic today proves that it suffers from old age to the point of childishness." (§7) "Presently, when nationalism in Europe has become a plague, it is entirely in order that a Christianity for whom it is important to preserve itself, na-

tionalizes itself as much as possible...." (§11) "The opponents of nationalism in the present—which is probably the worst pestilence threatening our European culture—should almost expect to find among the representatives of Christianity [the theologians] something like leaders of it." In the same place Overbeck names anti-Semitic racism "a naked return to paganism." At the end of the section he writes: "Will today a well placed representative of Christianity at all risk preaching from his pulpit that in Christ there are neither French nor English nor Germans?!"]

60. [Hermann Lüdemann, *Die Anthropologie des Paulus und ihre Stellung innerhalb seiner Heilslehre* (Kiel, 1872). Lüdemann was professor in Kiel, later in Bern. Albert Schweitzer gives him prominent mention in *Paul and His Interpreters. A Critical History* (NY: Schocken, 1964) esp. 28ff. Adolf Hausrath, *Neutestamentliche Zeitgeschichte* (4 vols., Heidelberg, 1868ff.). (Cf. *Neue Evangelische Kirchenzeitung*, 1872, 142f., 537f.) Hausrath's work, which eventually consisted of 6 volumes, was translated into English: *A History of New Testament Times*, Part 1: *The Time of Jesus* (2 vols., London, 1878-1880); Part II: *The Time of the Apostles* (4 vols., London, 1895). Hausrath was professor of New Testament Exegesis and Church History at Heidelberg and a prominent member of the Protestant League.]

61. [Otto Zöckler, *Hieronymus: sein Leben und Wirken aus seinen Schriften dargestellt* (Gotha, 1865).]

62. ["Tendenz" was an important term in the theology of the mid- and late-19th century. F.C. Baur brought it into use in describing the points of view and interests with which, e.g., the author of a gospel wrote his work.]

63. [Theodor Keim, *Geschichte Jesu von Nazara* (Zürich, 1866).]

64. [Konstantin Tischendorf (1815-1874), Professor at Leipzig, was famous for his publications on ancient versions of biblical texts and especially for his discovery of the Codex Sinaiticus of the New Testament. He published two apologetic writings in defense of the traditional view of the New Testament, both of which appeared in English: *Wann wurden unsere Evangelien verfasst?* (Leipzig, 1865), English: *Origin of the Four Gospels* (Boston: American Tract Society, 1867); *Haben wir den echten Schrifttext der Evangelisten und Apostel?* (Leipzig, 1873).]

65. Philipp Schaff, *Geschichte der alten Kirche* (Leipzig, 1867), 725. [Schaff (1819-1893) was professor of theology at Mercersburg in Pennsylvania, later at Union Theological Seminary in New York. The historical issue to which Schaff speaks is the Donatist insistence on the moral purity of bishops and priests.]

Chapter 3

The Liberal Theology of the Present

66. [*Lessing's Theological Writings.* Selections in Translation with an Introduction by Henry Chadwick (Stanford, Calif.: Stanford U. Press, 1957), 106. Lessing's "Religion of Christ" is very brief.]

67. [See the discussion of this statement in the last part of my introduction. The disjunction between a life of Jesus and Christianity arises through the intent to go behind the Gospel's account of Jesus and to reconstruct a life apart from the form of their belief in him.]

68. [Strauss, *Das Leben Jesu für das deutsche Volk bearbeitet* (2nd Ed. Leipzig, 1864), 5 (my translation). English: A New Life of Jesus (London & Edinburgh, 1865), I, 3.]

69. Theodor Keim, *Die Geschichte Jesu von Nazara*, Bd. 1 (Zürich, 1867), 6. [On Keim's life of Jesus see Albert Schweitzer, *The Quest of the Historical Jesus* (NY: Macmillan, 1961). Keim (1825-1878) was professor of New Testament in Zürich and later in Giessen.]

70. Keim, *Der geschichtliche Christus* (Zürich, 1866), esp. 202f. [Overbeck reviewed Keim's work in *Literarisches Zentralblatt für Deutschland* 1866, 841-845. There he brings the problem of Keim's "rhetoric" in connection with a confused methodology: Keim mixes dogmatics (or faith) and history.]

71. Heinrich Spörri, *Der alte und der neue Glaube* (Hamburg, 1873), 12. [Sporri (1838-1904) was a Swiss liberal who had studied under A.E. Biedermann and Alexander Schweitzer in Zürich and became a university lecturer. In 1868 he became pastor of the reformed congregation in Hamburg, where he developed considerable influence.]

72. [See Hans von Campenhausen, *Ecclesiastical Authority and Spiritual Power in the Church of the First Three Centuries*, translated by J.A. Baker (London: Adam & Charles Black, 1969), 254, where the author quotes from Origen's commentaries comparisons of believers within the martyr church with those in a period of nonpersecution.]

73. [This phrase is perhaps taken from Paul Lagarde, *Über das Verhältniss des deutschen Staats zur Theologie, Kirche und Religion*, 18-20. Cf. Overbeck, *Über Entstehung und Recht einer rein historischen Betrachtung der neutestamentlichen Schriften in der Theologie* (Basel, 1871), 15ff. Lagarde's point is that the forms of Protestantism are set by the Reformation and that the following period of Protestant Orthodoxy and all other truly Protestant theologies repeat them. The Enlightenment is scientific, not religious.]

74. R. A. Lipsius, "Die Zeit des Irenaeus von Lyon und die Entstehung der altkatholischen Kirche," *Historische Zeitschrift* Vol. 28, 1872, 253.

75. [Compare the following note from Overbeck's Kirchenlexicon under the title "Christentum (asketischer Charakter)," §4. (In the previ-

ous section §3, the same words of R.A. Lipsius, from the *Historische Zeitschrift* of 1872, are quoted that are quoted above.) Overbeck writes: "One is not simply of the opinion that original Christianity (the Christianity of Christ) was world-denying but also that, while it referred beyond the world to something better, it did so with the reservation of returning to the world. Such an opinion is based on an optical illusion: the transference of the later history of the church immediately back into the standpoint of original Christianity and Christ. One takes from Christianity its entire energy, when one allows it to express its inmost essence [innerstes Wesen] only with reservation. Christianity refuses science [Wissen], it leaves the state alone, not in order—once it has grasped persons in their inmost being [im Innersten gefasst hat]—to refer them again to science and state. Rather, it is content with the inmost being [dem Innersten] and will have nothing to do with science and state either with or without reservation. And therein consists its entire power ."]

76. ["Judaistic hopes": Overbeck is probably referring to the chiliastic beliefs of the early church.]

77. Spörri, 36

78. W. Brückner, *Die Entstehung der christlichen Kirche in der Zeit der Apostel* (Karlsruhe, 1873), 53.

79. [Strauss, *Der alte und der neue Glaube,* 65; English translation I, 74 (Blind's translation of the words Overbeck quotes is not literal). Strauss mentions this in a series: Jesus gives a model neither for the virtues of conducting war, nor for patriotism, nor for bourgeois virtues, nor for the family.]

80. Spörri, 9.

81. [Augustine, "The Good Marriage," *Nicene and Post-Nicene Fathers of the Christian Church.* Edited by Philip Schaff. Vol. III (Grand Rapids, Mich.: Eerdmans, 1956), 397-413.]

82. [Cf. above: the discussion on Keim's life of Jesus. The German words I translate here as "thinking observation," "denkende Betrachtung," can be found in F.C. Baur as an expression of the work of scientific thought: *Kirchengeschichte der ersten drei Jahrhunderte* (3rd ed., Tübingen, 1863), 13. Overbeck also used the expression to describe patristic theology's reflection on Jesus in his lectures on the doctrine of the Trinity and Christology (A 108, p. 204).]

83. "The Chaplet, or De Corona," chap. 10 [*The Ante-Nicene Fathers.* Edited by A. Roberts and J. Donaldson. Vol. III. Latin Christianity: Its Founder, Tertullian (American Edition Buffalo, NY: Christian Literature Publishing Co, 1885), 99]. {That does not prevent Tertullian from evaluating the ritual laws of the Old Testament as the religious consecration of all the business of daily life: "Against Marcion," Book II, chap. 19 [*Ibid,* 312].}

84. E. von Lasaulx, *Der Untergang des Hellenismus und die Ein*

ziehung seiner Tempelgüter durch die christlichen Kaiser (Munich, 1854), 115.

85. [Cf. the following quotation of Clement from Alexandria in Overbeck's *Studien zur Geschichte der alten Kirche* (I give here a literal translation of Overbeck's German): Clement says of the highest of the holy that "among the elect there are the especially elect that are this all the more the less they distinguish themselves, while they bring their ship out of the world-sea into the harbor and themselves into safety, do not want to appear as holy and are ashamed when someone calls them this, conceal deeply within their thoughts the unspeakable mysteries and are too proud to let their nobility be seen in the world. The Logos calls them the light of the world and the salt of the earth..." The quotation is in §36 of "The Rich Man's Salvation." *Clement of Alexandria,* translated by G.W. Butterworth (London: W. Heinemann, NY: G.P. Putnam's Sons, 1919), 345.]

86. Quotations from Spörri, 11.

87. ["Jesuitism" in 19th century Protestantism represented a theology in conformity with church dogma, to which science also was made to conform.]

88.[*Sammlung gemeinverständlicher wissenschaftlicher Vorträge,* edited by R. Virchov and F. von Holtzendorf. *Protestantische Vorträge* 1870ff; see also *Protestantische Kirchenzeitung,* 1854ff.]

89. [*Protestanten-Bibel Neuen Testaments,* ed. by P.W. Schmidt and F. von Holtzendorf (Leipzig, 1872). The book gives Luther's translation of the New Testament with commentaries written by some of the most outstanding liberal theologians of the time.]

90. [Franz von Holtzendorf was a famous professor of law. His chief concerns included the abolition of the death penalty and the reform of penal systems and procedure. His interests were broad; he was co-editor of the collection of popular scientific lectures mentioned above.]

91. [I have translated Overbeck's word "Geist" as "spirit" or "Spirit," according to the context. The distinction is warranted by the distinction between fides humana and fides divina in his inaugural lecture: *Über Entstehung und Recht einer rein historischen Betrachtung der neutestamentlichen Schriften in der Theologie* (Basel, 1871). His demonstrative work on the "spirit" of an individual book is his revision of de Wette's *Kurze Erklärung der Apostelgeschichte* (Leipzig, 1870). See my introduction.]

Chapter 4

Critical Theology and Its Positive Relationship to Christianity in the Present

Strauss' Confession

92. [D.F. Strauss, *Der alte und der neue Glaube: ein Bekenntnis* (Leipzig, 1872). References in the following text are from the 4th German ed. of 1873, and from the English translation by Mathilde Blind: *The Old Faith and the New* (2 Volumes). Blind is designated in text references by the letter B. Her translations are in some cases not literal.]

93. Plutarch, "The Oracles at Delphi," §28, cf. §23 [in: Plutarch, *Moralia*, Vol. V. Loeb Classical Library (London: Wm. Heinemann; Cambridge, Mass.: Harvard U. Press, 1936), 337f, 321f.]. Tacitus, "Dialogue on Oratory," [in: Tacitus *Dialogus, Agricola, Germania*. Loeb Classical Library (London: Wm. Heinemann; Cambridge, Mass.: Harvard U. Press, 1963), 123ff.]

94. [*Nathan the Wise* is a play by Lessing; Hermann and Dorothea is an idyllic poem by Goethe.]

95. [Strauss' ethics is based on the "Gattung," humanity in general, and recommends to each person a profession in which one may find the greatest satisfaction in serving the whole community.]

96. [This sentence not only contradicts Strauss, but also Albrecht Ritschl's assertion that Christianity makes for "victors" in the struggle for the domination of nature (see my introduction). Cf. the "need" of a parish in the following chapter. Cf. Baur, above p. 8.]

97. [Strauss, e.g., 299; B, II, 119f.: "...we are members of the most varied professions, and by no means exclusively consist of scholars and artists, but of military men and civil employees, of merchants and landed proprietors..."]

98. [Since Overbeck speaks of no other protector against misunderstanding, the "also" (auch) in this sentence seems to have no meaning. Perhaps he means to refer to the Gospel itself.]

Chapter 5

The Possibility of a Critical Theology in Our Protestant Churches

99. [*Über das Verhältnis des deutschen Staates zu Theologie, Kirche und Religion. Ein Versuch Nicht-Theologen zu Orientieren* (Göttingen, 1873).]

100. [Karl Hase discusses the origin of the vows (subscription to the Lutheran Symbolic Books) and the use of force in establishing them in: *Evangelisch-Protestantische Dogmatik* (5th ed. Leipzig, 1860), 478f. He also discusses the contemporary problem of the vows (482f.). He finds them highly problematic because of subsequent theological developments and the issue of the cleric's conscience. However, the contemporary church cannot formulate new vows because of the disunity in contemporary theology, and to do without vows altogether would expose the church to danger both from Catholicism and from unchristian teachings. Continuing subscription to the symbols of the church is therefore the best alternative. While the clerics should treat them "with piety and not directly attack them with churchly authority," they cannot be obligated to conform their preaching to everything in the Symbolic Books "but only to what they hold as true, scriptural and helpful for their parish." Hase also discusses the vows, with the same conclusions, in *Hutterus Redivivus* (11th ed. Leipzig, 1868), §50-§51, pp. 97-101.]

101. E.g., Eduard Zeller, *Theologische Jahrbücher* 1849, 143ff. [Zeller did become a member of a philosophical faculty. The point made by Overbeck (see also the following sentence) is especially important, insofar as it has to do with his own behavior: he never left the theological faculty. If he had truly been a non-Christian scientific critic of Christianity, and indeed since the publication of the first edition of the *Christianity of Theology* (see the 4th part of my introduction), then by his own statement he would have had to leave the theological faculty.]

102. [See the second part of my introduction.]

103. *Religionseid und Bekenntnisverpflichtung*, (Heidelberg, 1869). [Krenkel was associated with the Tübingen School.]

104. J. Seebens, *Das Recht der religiösen Überzeugung in der evangelischen Kirche* (Berlin, 1871).

105. [Overbeck's reference to the ancient church is especially to Origen's distinction between "simple believers" and the theologian (see chap. 1), which intends the distinction between the (exoteric) authoritative tradition of the church, which Origen accepts, and (esoteric) higher theological learning and speculation. See R.P.C. Hanson, *Origen's Doctrine of Tradition* (London: S.P.C.K., 1954); Owen Chadwick, *Early Christian Thought and the Classical Tradition* (NY: Oxford U. Pr., 1966), 75ff; Hans von Campenhausen, *Ecclesiastical Authority and Spiritual Power in the Church of the First Three Centuries* (London: Adam & Charles Black, 1969), 192-264.]

106. [In the *Christianity of Theology* religion and faith [Glaube] are interchangeable terms that refer specifically to the Christ of Christian tradition. As was seen in the exchange of letters with Biedermann (see the beginning of my introduction), Overbeck rejected abstract conceptions or definitions of religion. The immediate impression of the term "religion in itself" is abstract and, insofar as it is not defined, enig-

matic and probably concealing. In considering what such a personal representation of "religion in itself" means, one may compare the following. In his lectures on the Pastoral Letters from the year 1864/65 [A96] (one finds much later dates in the lecture, e.g., 1875, 1880), Overbeck writes that both in Paul's letters and in 1 Timothy, church office arises from the gifts of the Spirit given in different ways to the whole community. In the section on gifts 1 Cor. 12, Paul addresses the whole community, not just its leaders. Timothy is recognized as having specific gifts that qualify him for a specific function, symbolized by the laying on of hands [370, 380f.].—This is reminiscent of Luther's interpretation of church office. Among Overbeck's manuscripts [A9] one finds excerpts from G.F. Puchta's work on church office and secular law, *Einleitung in das Recht der Kirche* (Leipzig, 1840). Puchta's understanding of the relationship between gifts and office in the apostolic church is the same as Overbeck's; both emphasize the importance of the expectation of the return of Christ for the first church as a spiritual, not "worldly" community. For Puchta, in the contemporary church "the spiritual church is the basis and the soul of the outward [institutional] church.... Church institutions require the existence of the church in the world, in which the church must fight [for its faith]; the Kingdom of God is in conflict with the world" [72]. (Theologically Puchta is associated with the later Schelling.)—In another place in the lecture on the Pastoral Letters [395f.] Overbeck interprets the "mystery of godliness" or "religiousness" in 1 Tim. 3:16 as "the content of Christian piety concealed from the world." Similarly in another place: the "Spirit" of the church was "turned away from all worldliness" [314]. Overbeck compares 2 Tim. 2:3-4 with 1 Cor. 9:24f: "A good combatant for Christ ... should have nothing to do with the world. Therefore the conclusion is, do not hesitate to break with the world...."]

107. [Overbeck speaks of this forgetting of self in a later article in the *Historische Zeitschrift* (Vol. 42, 1879, 222-259), "Aus dem Briefwechsel des Augustin mit Hieronymus" (From Augustine's Exchange of Letters with Jerome), 255. Jerome is hardly an admirable figure in the discussions of points of disagreement, but Augustine, who has the better arguments and comports himself with far greater "moral character," is faulted by Overbeck for not entirely overcoming his superiority and therefore behaving toward Jerome with "a certain overly dignified stiffness." Overbeck finds Augustine "not completely at the high point of that highest 'Liebenswürdigkeit' (literally: being worthy of love) where he would have completely forgotten the advantage he had in this case in being himself." "While such a strict requirement of the 'Liebenswürdigkeit' of self-forgetting is only very seldom justified, it may well be applied to Augustine, who truly seems to be one who could furfill it and who will always belong among the most admirable figures that have made the ideal of holiness a law of their lives." Overbeck also faults Augustine (254) for attributing to the God of history moral quali-

ties and motives [esp. jealousy] that he, almost in the same breath, rejects as unworthy of human rulers and certainly also for his own personal behavior (*City of God*, 5:25, cf. 24). One purpose of Overbeck's article is the demonstration of how the work of the "theological apologist" (254) exposes his character.]

108. [In a note in Overbeck's Kirchenlexikon entitled "Theologie (Gegenwart) Vermischtes" that probably dates from the time of the *Christianity of Theology*, Overbeck writes: "Today every practical theologian [pastor] is in the sad situation of thinking out for himself what he is to preach to the people. But precisely in this practical work it is of inestimable value to be able to join with the given forms of the tradition. For there is something in each person that resists the attempt to express openly his personal, deepest, religious and generally metaphysical convictions. One expects only from a few, and from these only at exceptional times, that they will forget the world so much that they speak as if none heard them. Protestantism has no room for the idea of the priest who completely denies himself, which belongs to the highest mysticism of the Catholic Church."

AFTERWORD

109. [The sense of "Grundgedanken" is that these are the thoughts or concepts on which all else is based. A related expression used by Overbeck in the same way is "Grundanschauungen," essential perceptions. Overbeck will reiterate this point several times in the Afterword.]

The Public Criticism of My Book

110. Only the wish for precision forces me to confess a very unclear memory of an article in one issue of the Berner *Reformblatt* that is not mentioned in my list. It says that my book is an attempt to keep my professorship and its emoluments. I am sorry to say I forgot to write down all the necessary information on the article, which is the coarsest, most improper thing I have encountered with my book in our public adventure. It seemed to me unnecessary to spend the time to find the article merely for the purpose of completing my list, for I could not possibly give attention to this unicum in these pages, neither immediately after the list nor later.

111. [The fifth entry on the list is definitely sympathetic, the seventh, not at all. Perhaps Overbeck meant the sixth entry, the lecture by Dickson. Hilgenfeld, No. 12, concludes his review by saying: "A theology can be practically fruitful only if it neither takes its point of departure from the irreconcilable antagonism of Glauben and Wissen nor ends in an irredeemable contradiction of theory and practice." Hart

mann's appraisal of the book (No. 24) is included in the discussion of his book in my introduction.]

112. I do wish to lift one detail from the book for purposes of clarification. The book is based on a view of theology that sees theology standing in problematic relation to both spheres of mental life between which it works, i.e., both to science and to Christianity (or religion). In the book I delivered proofs for the damage theology does to Christianity, but I did not go into proving that theology is not a science but only a parasite at the table of science. Yet when I wrote the book, 1 was even more certain of this second point than I was of the first, so certain, in fact, that I could suppose myself lifted almost above every need to give proofs.

113. I have certainly found no reason to do so in the presently ruling form of theology, which distinguishes itself with the name "modern." Ernst Rolffs openly betrays the secret of one of modern theology's schools in his book, *Harnacks Wesen des Christentums* (Leipzig, 1902), 10f. The betrayed secret is significant because Harnack is so highly respected in modern theology. Perhaps more instructive is seeing even such a strict systematic theologian of modern theology as Ernst Troeltsch weaken and concede that "in practice and above all in the dogmatic instruction of theologians wishing to serve churches standing under definite historical authorities, *a carefully sparing and softly reforming accommodation* is necessary." The significance of this admission is not lessened when Troeltsch adds the requirement of "great style" to an accommodation recommended on the presupposition of treading softly. E. Troeltsch, *Die Absolutheit des Christentums und die Religionsgeschichte* (Tübingen and Leipzig, 1902), ix. The emphasis in the text quoted from Troeltsch is, naturally, mine. [Ernst Rolffs was one of Harnack's popularizers. The pages Overbeck cites in his book contain the following: The hearers of Harnack's lectures (published as *Das Wesen des Christentums*) "were modern persons living in an age when one thinks one can know everything and unhesitatingly excludes what does not fit with the laws of reason. Therefore Harnack only satisfied a requirement of pedagogical tact when he left out elements that were essential to original Christianity, e.g., eschatology...."]

The Consequences of My Book for Me

114. [All of Overbeck's contributions to this journal are brief book reviews having to do with patristic themes.]

115. ["Von Haus aus" (from house out) is not a rare expression of the time—one finds it, e.g., in D.F. Strauss. Overbeck employs it in important contexts to denote origin. He will use it later in the Afterword to speak of theologians who are "von Haus aus" critics. It is perhaps not irrelevant that he comments on the use of this word in his early lec-

ture on the Pastoral Epistles [A96], namely in 2 Tim. 2:20 "house" means the Christian community, "the true Christians."]

116. After 1873 the only product of contemporary theology that I read with any sympathy is the [pietist] book *Christliche Bedenken über modernes christliches Wesen, von einem Sorgenvollen* [Christian Doubts about Modern Christianity, by One Concerned] (revised and enlarged 2nd ed., Gütersloh, 1889). But no more than a shimmer of edification could grow for me from this sympathy, since I had too clear an awareness of not sharing the "concerns" of the author. As is known, the book was written by Robert Kübel, professor of theology in Tübingen who died in 1894. [Kübel represents the "positive" or pietist conservative biblicist side of the theological debate and also made contributions to contemporary apologetics. While he affirms the need for historical-critical work, he limits it in conformity with his pietist-conservative theology. At Tübingen Kübel replaced and carried on the heritage of Tobias Beck, who was F.C. Baur's biblicist counterpart at that university. Both the work Overbeck mentions and especially an earlier work of Kübel's, *Über den Unterschied zwischen der positiven und der liberalen Richtung in der modernen Theologie* (On the Difference between the Positive and the Liberal Direction in Modern Theology) (Nordlingen, 1881), Kübel asserts (as had Beck) that Christianity, in contrast to the theology and also church of his time, is world-denying. In a note in his Kirchenlexikon entitled "Christliche Bedenken...von einem Sorgenvollen," Overbeck wrote: "A basic conviction of the author is that Christianity is 'not of this world,' that is, that in this world it has nothing to do with power [Macht].... The little book represents Christianity in the only way that can give it respect again." In another note, entitled "Theologie (moderene) Vermischtes," Overbeck writes: "By far the most interesting appearances among the contemporary representatives of so-called 'modern theology' are certain Swabian desperados á la Kierkegaard, such as the 'one concerned'..." Overbeck's mild criticism of Kierkegaard is given in *Christentum und Kultur*, 279: he faults the "presumption of his office as defender" of Christianity when he pretends to attack it.—The reason why Overbeck does not share Kübel's "concerns" is that he realizes there is no purpose in it; the "proof" or lack of it for Christianity belongs to Christ (fides divina).]

117. I may here disregard two incidental interruptions of this cycle in the summer of 1875 and in the winter of 1891-1892, when I was ill. These interruptions had no consequences that further disturbed the designated system as announced on the seminar blackboard and in the printed schedule of courses.

118. [In his published work of 1882, *Über die Anfänge der patristischen Literatur* (reprint Darmstadt: Wissenschaftliche Buchgesellschaft, 1963), 62f, cf. 40f., Overbeck speaks of this same problem as a characteristic of world literature and as one of the problems that Clement of Alexandria wrestled with in making the transition to a Christian

world literature (see the third part of my introduction). The form of all world literature designates the work as written for anyone in the culture who reads it. No personal relationship is involved or presupposed.]

119. [It is notable that the "theologian" was missing, especially for the questions of "young theologians." Irony is also at work here. Overbeck's students seemed to have been thankful for him as a teacher. I cite one example: According to a funeral oration by the Dean of the theological faculty of the University of Bern, Overbeck was "always named with thanks and joy [Dank und Freude]" by Professor Wilhelm Hadorn, a major leader of the Swiss church. *Prof: D. Wilhelm Hadorn—Ansprachen gehalten an der öffentlichen Trauerfeier im Berner Münster am 20. November 1929*, p. 14 (Staatsarchiv Bern). This is especially notable given the fact that Hadorn was a leader not only of the church, but also of its pietist wing. He is the author of *Geschichte des Pietismus in den Schweizerischen Reformierten Kirchen* (1901).]

120 [The words, "something that sounded like the influence of belief in the object, for here it was missing" are, in the original German: "etwas vom Mitwirken eines Glaubens an die Sache, der nun eimnal hier fehlte." The sentence is the clearest evidence in the Afterword of the late Overbeck's intention to indicate his unbelief, but the reference is ambiguous, as are other such statements. The "Sache" (object) may be and probably is the history that he presented his students objectively, as stated above. What he actually meant can only be seen in the lectures themselves.]

121. *Zur Geschichte des Kanons* [On the History of the Canon] (Schloss-Chemnitz, 1880). The little book was written for a specific occasion in a double sense. It was intended as a tribute to Karl Hase on the fiftieth anniversary of his teaching, and it was to supply the solemn form of thanks for the University of Jena's award to me in 1870 of a doctorate in theology. 1 assumed that Hase especially was responsible for the award. [In his tribute to Hase in the preface Overbeck says that his decision to habilitate in Jena was motivated by "the friendly acceptance you had for my scruples and your encouraging goodness."]

122. [Two important works in the *Historische Zeitschrift*: "Aus dem Briefwechsel des Augustin mit Hieronymus," 1879; "Über die Anfänge der patristischen Literatur," 1882. The publications in the *Göttinger gelehrte Anzeigen* are all book reviews in the area of New Testament and patristic literature.]

123. I gladly take this opportunity to express the gratitude due the editors of the two named journals for their offer to have me as co-worker. 1 ask them to take from what I have said here what value their offer had for me and why I made such non-industrious use of it.

124. [*Über die Auffassung des Streits des Paulus mit Petrus in Antiochien (Gal. 2, 11ff.) bei den Kirchenvätern (1877). Über die Anfänge der Kirchengeschichtsschreibung (1892). Die Bischofslisten und die apostolischen Nachfolge in der Kirchengeschichte des Eusebi-*

us (1898).—The *Programme* were published in Basel in limited editions on the occasion of a yearly academic celebration.]

125. Adolf Harnack, *Dogmengeschichte*, 3rd Ed. (Tübingen, 1897), III, in the preface.

126. [Bernoulli's book, "The Scientific and Churchly Method in Theology, an Encyclopedic Attempt," is based essentially on Schleiermacher's theology of religion as an aspect of human mind that is in unity with God (perfectly in Christ, imperfectly in the church); science is another aspect and disengaged from this unity. He divides the work of the theological faculty into purely scientific disciplines, Bible and Church History, and churchly disciplines, Dogmatics and Practical Theology. Churchly theology serves the church as theology of mediation, which understands both the difference between and the relationship of religion and culture. In scientific theology, Bernoulli takes "religion is history" from Bernard Duhm, professor of Old Testament at Basel. From Overbeck he takes "the purely historical concept of the church" [VII]. Benoulli interprets the *Christianity of Theology* along these same lines: churchly theology's task is practical, its theology is a combination of science and focus on the practical needs of the church. The practice of the cleric means being "priest" for the people on the basis of a traditional dogmatics. Pure science must rule the historical disciplines in theology. While the two theologies remain in conversation (which represents the unity of the theological faculty), conflicts are freely decided by theologians within their respective areas, scientific or practical.—Overbeck's concept of the relationship between science and faith does have connections with Schleiermacher, and Schleiermacher's understanding of religion no doubt helped form his first theology. But in his mature work faith and science are based not on aspects of mind, but on the realities with which they interact. For science it is the whole world of culture, including all philosophy, whereas Bernoulli places philosophy of religion in churchly theology.—Late in life Bernoulli, who died in 1937, affirmed the positions he had taken in this book, both in his introduction to Overbeck's translation of Clement of Alexandria's *Stromata*, and in a journal article, "Franz Overbeck," *Neue Schweizer Rundschau*, January, 1931, 53-62.]

The Modern Theology of Contemporary Protestantism and What Has Resulted from It for Me as the Author of My Book

127. [The following attack on Harnack was not taken lightly in the theological world. Harnack chose to ignore it. Overbeck had already criticized Harnack in a publication of 1892, *Über die Anfänge der Kirchengeschichtschreibung*. In the *History of Dogma*, translated by Niel Buchanan from the 3rd German edition of 1900 (recently re-

printed by Dover Press), I, 39, and in other works Harnack mentions only Overbeck's *Über die Anfänge der patristischen Literatur* as an important contribution to church history. Overbeck's daughter, Agnes v. Zahn-Harnack, in her biography, *Adolf v. Harnack* (Berlin: W. de Gruyter, 1951), writes about her father's understandably bitter reaction to Overbeck's criticism (60-63, cf. 91, 107, 401).]

128. [Adolf Harnack, *Das Wesen des Christentums* (Leipzig, 1900). English: *What is Christianity?* (NY: Harper & Brothers, 1957). The translation by T.B. Saunders has been reprinted several times since the first edition of 1901 and the revised edition of 1903 (NY: G.B. Putnam's Sons). The literal English title of Harnack's book is "The Essence of Christianity."]

129. Paul Rohrbach, *Die Bagdadbahn* [The Bagdad Railroad] (Berlin, 1902). [Cf. the following note in Overbeck's Kirchenlexikon under the title "Theologie (moderne) Mission": "When one hears modern theologians speak about mission, it will always be good advice to take a close look at whether or not they mean 'spreading the Gospel' or the founding of a colonial empire. We live in a time when 'Christian travels to Palestine,' the travels of a Christian pilgrim in the near east, are connected with those of an agent for the Bagdad Railroad."]

130. [On "profane church history" see Overbeck's Introduction above. The provocative title is probably intended to offend "modern" theology, but its sense is the method of "purely scientific" history that Overbeck advocated in his earliest historical work (see my introduction). In the Kirchenlexikon under the title "Kirchengeschichte (profane)" Overbeck defines it as a history that is "not limited and 'penned in' by theology." (See Walter Nigg, *F. Overbeck*, 125.) On Hippolytus see my note in Overbeck's Introduction.]

131. [In Saunder's translation, *What is Christianity?*, 190f. In the place cited Harnack writes that Christianity in history developed "new forms, and new forms also meant limitation and encumbrance." The forms of original Christianity are not to be regarded "as possessing a classical and permanent character." "As Christianity rises above the Here and the Beyond, life and death, work and the shunning of the world ... it can also exist under the most diverse conditions."]

132. Harnack, 121. [translation by Saunders, 194: "As every individual has the right to be judged ... by what he has done, so the great edifices of history, the States and the Churches, must be estimated first and foremost, we may perhaps say, exclusively, by what they have achieved. It is the work done that forms the decisive test." Harnack is known for this understanding of history. Overbeck criticized it in an earlier publication, *Zur Geschichte des Kanons* (Chemnitz, 1880), 74ff., 104: In an article in the *Zeitschrift für Kirchengeschichte*, Vol. 3, 358ff., Harnack had said that the church "produced" the canon from a developing concept of canonicity. Overbeck argues that the canon recognized only writings the church believed apostolic as authoritative.

Had it produced them from such a concept, it would have done what the Gnostics and Montanists were doing, which the apostolic canon was meant to oppose (79).]

133. Ernst Rolffs, *Harnacks Wesen des Christentums* (Leipzig, 1902), 48.

134. Adolf Harnack, "Zur gegenwärtigen Lage des Protestantismus," *Hefte zur Christlichen Welt* 1896, No. 25, 10.